An Intellectual History of School Leadership Practice and Research

ALSO AVAILABLE:

An Intellectual History of School Leadership Practice and Research

HELEN M. GUNTER

Bloomsbury Academic
An imprint of Bloomsbury Publishing Plc

B L O O M S B U R Y
LONDON · OXFORD · NEW YORK · NEW DELHI · SYDNEY

Bloomsbury Academic

An imprint of Bloomsbury Publishing Plc

50 Bedford Square	1385 Broadway
London	New York
WC1B 3DP	NY 10018
UK	USA

www.bloomsbury.com

BLOOMSBURY and the Diana logo are trademarks of Bloomsbury Publishing Plc

First published 2016

© Helen M. Gunter, 2016

Helen M. Gunter has asserted her right under the Copyright, Designs and Patents Act, 1988, to be identified as Author of this work.

British Library Cataloguing-in-Publication Data

A catalogue record for this book is available from the British Library.

ISBN: HB: 978-1-4725-7898-3
PB: 978-1-4725-7897-6
ePDF: 978-1-4725-7900-3
ePub: 978-1-4725-7899-0

Library of Congress Cataloguing-in-Publication Data

A catalog record for this book is available from the Library of Congress.

Typeset by Deanta Global Publishing Services, Chennai, India
Printed and bound in India

Contents

Abbreviations

ARK	*Absolute Return for Kids*
BERA	*British Educational Research Association*
BELMAS	*British Educational Leadership Management and Administration Society*
CASEA	*Canadian Association for Studies in Educational Administration*
CTC	*City Technology College*
CCEAM	*Commonwealth Council for Educational Administration and Management*
CKPE	*Consultancy and Knowledge Production in Education Project*
ESRC	*Economic and Social Research Council*
EAQ	*Educational Administration Quarterly*
EMAL	*Educational Management Administration and Leadership*
EFEA	*European Forum on Educational Administration*
IQEA	*Improving the Quality of Education for All*
ICSEI	*International Congress for School Effectiveness and Improvement*
KPEL	*Knowledge Production for Educational Leadership Project*
LPSH	*Leadership Programme for Serving Headteachers*
LA	*Local Authority*
LEA	*Local Education Authority*
LMS	*Local Management of Schools*
NCSL	*National College for School Leadership*

NPQH   *National Professional Qualification for Headship*

NLPR   *New Labour Performance Regime*

NZEALS   *New Zealand Educational Administration and Leadership Society*

NCLB   *No Child Left Behind*

OECD   *Organisation for Economic Co-operation and Development*

OfSTED   *Office for Standards in Education*

PRR   *Policy Research Regime*

PISA   *Programme for International Student Assessment*

PwC   *PricewaterhouseCoopers*

SESI   *School Effectiveness, School Improvement*

SLR   *School Leadership Regime*

SPSO   *Distributed Leadership and the Social Practices of School
                      Organisation in England Project*

TIMSS   *Trends in International Mathematics and Science Study*

UCEA   *University Council for Educational Administration*

Introduction: Towards an Intellectual History

Overview

Embarking on this book as a single author could be read as an authoritative fixing and settling of the field, but I am mindful of Steadman's (2001) observation that 'at the centre of the written history ... lies a recognition of temporariness and impermanence' (p. 148). So what is about to be written has already been unwritten several times by myself and will continue to be so through reader engagement and organic historiography. In this sense I am locating with Blount's (2008) call for 'a well-developed historical consciousness' (p. 18) within and about the field, because such thinking 'can show us with unparalleled depth and fullness how our social relations have come to exist as they do, to understand more deeply our social conditions, and to enhance our ability to ask the kinds of questions that might provoke social justice work in the future' (p. 19). Therefore this book requires reading as thinking, as a form of enactment and co-construction, with simultaneous confirmation and refutation: I have produced 'a' history and not 'the' history of a field. As such, it is a history that is sociological – it is about *Knowledge Production* within the interplay between agency and structure regarding interests, agendas and choices; and it is political – it is about how *Knowledge Production* within and for the promotion of education services and the resolution of conflicts is located within and external to the polity (civil society, public and private institutions at national and supranational levels). It is a history that is located within a power process (my authoring) and is about power (how those within and for education author practice for the self and others).

Knowledge, or what is known and is worth knowing, does not exist outside of practice, and this is no more important than in the way teaching and learning is organized and conducted within schools, colleges and higher education. Such practice is social, economic, political and cultural, and how it has been labelled through professionalism (e.g. teacher, head of subject, principal) and through the recognition of power processes (e.g. administration, entrepreneurialism, management, performance, leadership) is a core concern. I engage with the remodelling of professional roles and titles through the current demand for leaders, leading and leadership by presenting an account of the *knowledges* that underpin and are developed through the practice of leaders, leading and leadership, not least by drawing on thirty years of research into those who generate, popularize and use those *knowledges*. Importantly, the book will report on events, policies, research accounts and theories of leadership from published sources. In addition, I have access to transcripts of over 300 people both from the UK and internationally regarding their contribution to the field as policymakers, consultants, professionals and researchers. At the same time, I am mindful that much of what is thought about, used and discarded, in regard to the interplay between ideas and action, is not in the public domain; it is embodied, it is fleeting, it is in confidential minutes of meetings and in remembered and forgotten memories. Hence studying research and practice is inevitably based on what has been encoded and is available for scrutiny which in the end are just fragments from and about social and political dynamics.

Towards an intellectual history

My starting point is to present an approach to *Knowledge Production* within which the development of an intellectual history is located. This enables the power dimensions of the interplay between ideas, thinking and action within an intellectual history to be foregrounded: the production of ideas and how they relate to action, and undertaking of action and how this relates to ideas, are about what is known, what is worth knowing, how it is known and who claims to know. So I am concerned with the *knowledges* or canon of the field, the ways of *knowing* or methodologies within the field and the *knowers* or those who are regarded as being 'in the know' or *knowledgeable*.

My use of the term 'field' is important because I begin on the basis that I am engaging with a field and not a discipline: it is a metaphor of a terrain that is inhabited by a range of *knowers* as *knowledge actors* (parents, children, professionals, ministers, civil servants, consultants, philanthropists), who draw on a range of *knowledges* and experiences to develop understandings and explanations about, for and within educational services. The field is therefore a plurality of people and interests, where disciplinary knowledge from the social sciences is a resource opportunity, rather than a set of agreed disciplinary methodologies and foundational claims. This is evident within biographies, experiences and formal learning, and so I am able to examine the mobilization of knowledge: the flows and silences involved in border drawings and crossings. I give significant attention to the claims that are made and how knowledge is exchanged.

I have shown a commitment to the utility and complexity of using theory to describe, explain and understand in my *fieldwork* (Gunter 1999, 2012a, 2014), and in this particular project I again engage with the social sciences for a number of reasons, particularly the self-evident conceptualization that 'history is inevitably ... theoretical' (Silver 1990, p. 7). Perhaps, more pertinent to the job in hand, I would have associated with Mills' (1959) contention that historical investigations should be more than identifying trends and discontinuities: we should not ask, 'has something persisted from the past', but instead 'why has it persisted?' (p. 171). While I draw on a range of thinkers, the main conceptual framing of the intellectual history is located in Bourdieu's (2000) thinking tools, where the dimensions of *field, habitus, capitals, doxa* and *misrecognition* enable explanations as a social and political practice. This makes sense because he argues: 'There is no doubt a theory in my work, or, better, a set of *thinking tools* visible through the results they yield, but it is not built as such. ... It is a *temporary construct which takes shape for and by empirical work*' (Wacquant 1989, p. 50, emphasis in original). Bourdieu is concerned with social relations, with a central aim to remove dichotomies between the individual and society, and between subjectivism and objectivism.

How such theorizing is located in the relationship between the state, public policy and knowledge is developed through an analysis of the claims and exchanges between *knowledge actors* in public policymaking. I examine various approaches to politics and networks, and in particular the endurance of hierarchy within a *knowledgeable polity*. Here I give recognition to how knowledge creation, use and decay is related to how borders create places (e.g. public institutions) and crosses borders that create spaces (e.g. markets). Governments rely upon, sustain and generate *Knowledge Production* within public institutions such as their own departments and agencies, but also call upon and invite those who produce knowledge for sale within the marketplace that can be global, and those who live their lives and sustain their interests within society. The explication of this approach is a necessary anchor for the study, and the *Knowledge Production* framework provides the underpinning dimensions for how ideas and actions at a moment in time are located in a complex strategizing for agency interplayed with the structures that enable and limit.

There are many challenges involved in doing this, and such challenges are not new. How I as an individual and as a member of the field go about doing the task I have set myself has to be made explicit, not least because there is a dual process taking place. I am presenting an account of how those who are located in the field do *Knowledge Production* in different territorial and temporal contexts, and at the same time I am doing an intellectual history based on a conceptualization and methodology that I will outline as a form of *Knowledge Production*. Therefore I present an account of *Knowledge Production* that is itself a form of *Knowledge Production*, and so I communicate my approach and my account as part of the same project. At least one irony is evident here. As Schwandt (2007) has shown, a 'book ... depends for its success on precisely the fact that the publishers are able to promote it as a knowledge commodity to a particular segment of the academic market' (p. 4), and so while I am presenting a book that is critical and problematizes *Knowledge Production*, I am aware that in order to do this, my work has been economized through the publishing business.

Once I have 'dropped' the anchor of *Knowledge Production*, I go on to present a framework for an intellectual history. This has five dimensions: first, I begin with **traditions** where I focus on ideas, ways of thinking and doing within five main theory traditions within the field: *experiential, positivist, behaviourist, values* and *critical*. These traditions are the intellectual resources that structure the field, and are available for field actors to access and shape practice. Second, I move onto **purposes** in which I identify the 'what', 'how' and 'why' those traditions are accessed: *situational, functional, realist* and *activist*. Here I am concerned with examining intentions, the rationales provided, the narratives used to articulate and the outcomes of and by field members to justify the exercise of agency in accessing and using resources. Third, I present four main **domains** as field position outcomes from the interplay between traditions and purposes: *philosophical, humanistic, instrumental* and *critical*. Each domain is a field position regarding ideas and actions, and how change is conceptualized and engaged with. Hence the understanding of change is located in *philosophical* matters; living change is *humanistic*, delivering change is *instrumental* and *working for change* is *critical*. Fourth, the relationship between ideas, purposes and positions takes place within **contexts**, and so I focus on the political, economic, social and cultural situation in which ideas and actions interplay in regard to the structuring of the knowledge domains, and so I present four main contextualizing structures: *Civic Welfarism, Neoliberalism, Neoconservativism* and *Elitism*. These impact on positions and positioning through determining, shaping, making possible and burying ideas and actions, and are located in the activity of elite groups and their engagement/disengagement with professionals, researchers and wider civil society. Fifth, I focus on the agency of *knowledge actors* as individuals and groups, and their scoping and agenda setting regarding traditions, purposes and domains to position taken within structuring contexts, and so I present four main **networks**: *educational administration* (EA), *educational effectiveness and improvement research* (EEIR), *entrepreneurs and popularizers* (EP), and *critical education policy and leadership studies* (CEPaLS). These networks are the ones that those within them may recognize through their own labelling (e.g. EEIR), and are labels that I am using in order to codify similar activity (e.g. EP).

I therefore present a framework of five dimensions for understanding *Knowledge Production* within, for and about, the field, and in so doing I show the importance and contribution of intellectual histories. In order to provide an illuminating and grounded example, I take *Transformational Leadership* as the model of leadership that has dominated education policy, business and professional practice for over thirty years. I use this model (and its hybrids, e.g. distributed, instructional, system) as the site by which I explicate the approach to the production of an intellectual history in this project, and how I develop the analysis through the subsequent chapters. Such an approach not only enables the discussion of terminology (e.g. administration, management, leadership, culture, organization) but also the ideas underpinning the labelling and relabelling of professional practice (e.g. vision, strategy, performance, moral purpose).

Let me now outline the site of all of this activity, the leadership field and in particular the identification of *Transformational Leadership* as integral to the construction of this intellectual history.

The leadership era?

Leaders or those appointed to a role, leading or the activity that leaders undertake and leadership or the relational power processes, within educational services and organizations, have grown rapidly as a field of practice and study in the last thirty years. This can be evidenced through increased adoption of the labels of 'leader', 'leading' and 'leadership' for educational professional practice, whereby professional titles such as principal, headteacher and president are used interchangeably with, and increasingly subsumed by, the leadership lexicon. The acceptance that role incumbents within a division of labour hierarchy are leaders, who do leading and who exercise leadership is normal and normalizing, to the extent that much is expected of those who inhabit what O'Reilly and Reed (2010) call 'leaderism' (p. 960). For New York Mayor Giuliani (with Kurson 2002), it is about how his business experiences enabled his response to 9/11:

Every single principle that follows was summoned within hours of the attack on the World Trade Center. Surround yourself with great people. Have beliefs and communicate them. See things for yourself. Set an example. Stand up to bullies. Deal with first things first. Loyalty is the vital virtue. Prepare relentlessly. Underpromise and overdeliver. Don't assume a damn thing. And, of course, the importance of funerals. It was ironic, prophetic, and very useful that all these principles had been discussed and analysed so recently. (p. x)

Leadership is therefore a symbolically rhetorically powerful power process, whereby the leader doing leading in an appointed or elected post with a title, separate remuneration, reward structure and job description is given authority and legitimacy to variously direct and influence others. Much can be mundane, but events, some of them truly terrible, can reveal this through the observation and articulation of practice.

The 9/11 events also generated other forms of leadership, and for Professor Michael Apple (2011), it is about how his commitment to equity and social justice enabled his response to 9/11 as an activist and teacher:

> I wanted my students to fully appreciate the fact that the US-led embargo of Iraq had caused the death of thousands upon thousands of children each year that it had been in place. I wanted them to understand how US policies in the Middle East and in Afghanistan itself had helped create truly murderous consequences. However, unless their feelings and understandings were voiced and taken seriously, the result could be exactly the opposite of what any teacher wants. ... None of us are perfect teachers, and I am certain that I made more than a few wrong moves in my attempts to structure the discussions in my classes so that they were open and critical at the same time. But I was impressed with the willingness of the vast majority of students to re-examine their anger, to put themselves in the place of the oppressed, to take their more critical and nuanced understandings and put them into action. (pp. 294–5).

In this sense leadership is not the property of one person who is functionally effective and emotionally resilient, but is a resource that is shared and used to generate learning opportunities. There are functional issues in Apple's account, he has a class to teach within an organization, with a curriculum and assessment frameworks, but there is something about how power is within the pedagogic relationship, and how the focus of the learning is about power within international relations.

This short flurry into stories of practice suggests that there are personal accounts of what leader, leading and leadership means, how it is experienced and what people feel about doing it and the results. Any search on the internet brings with it millions of hits with claims and counter claims, and as such I could fill volume after volume with narrations and claims about meanings and experiences of craft knowledge. What I would like to do is to give recognition that many of us live in a leader-centric world, where much has been and continues to be invested in the single individual at the top of an organizational pyramid, and much of our language and debates begins and ends with this, and much of our culture through film, art and music reflects our appreciation and acceptance of the leader. Within education this is a major issue, with much inscribed upon and expected of vice-chancellors, college principals and school headteachers, and much has been invested in leaders, leading and leadership in educational settings around the world as *Transformational Leaders*.

Transformational Leadership has a number of features: first, there is an identified set of factors – *idealized influence* through visioning and charisma, *inspirational motivation* through emotional connections to necessities and aspirations, *intellectual stimulation* to challenge and be challenged to be innovative and *individualized consideration* through coaching, mentoring and aligning individual beliefs with the vision (Northouse 2010); second, through these four 'I's there is recognition of the leader *in relation to* those who are followers, but the divide is overcome through the importance given to satisfying and integrating follower needs with the productive influence of the leader, doing leading and exercising leadership; third, the relationship between leaders, leading and leadership with change is embedded in the notion of 'transformation' where something major as distinct from incremental is to take place, and this is scripted against both transactional exchanges based on deals and rewards, and laissez-faire approaches where there is an absence of leadership through a failure to exercise responsibility and accountability; and, fourth, in response to the limitations of previously advocated models, this 'new' approach fits current times where there is a need for security, but at the same time it generates risk-taking.

While this form of *Transformational Leadership* has been developed outside of public services education (e.g. Bass 1985; Bennis and Nanus 1985; Burns 1978), it has been used to enable radical modernization projects through the introduction of business models and professional identity formation, training and performance audit (Gunter 2012a). While there have been hybrids such as *Distributed Leadership* (Gunter et al. 2013), and empirical work continues to raise questions about the causal relationship with student outcomes (Leithwood and Sleegers 2006), *Transformational Leadership* is the accepted orthodoxy. Test bed projects are happening on a global basis around the world (e.g. Balyer 2012; Geijsel et al. 2003; Nguni et al. 2006; Yu et al. 2002), and this has fixed the canon regarding what is known and worth knowing, and any developments or 'new' models are scripted in relation to it and in its image (see Hallinger 2003).

Much of what is presented as best practice in western-style democracies is increasingly disconnected from the intellectual traditions in which it is located, and is disengaged from traditions in other states, not least the impact of decolonization on *Knowledge Production*. However, models of best practice have become a globalized phenomenon as nation states have been exhorted to adopt particular leadership language, behaviours and accountability in order to bring about particular types of change in publicly funded schools, colleges and universities. This is in the form of a 'Transnational Leadership Package' (Thomson et al. 2014) that eschews context and history but is presented as necessary for problem resolution regarding educational standards in a globalizing economy. For example, researchers, consultants, politicians and philanthropists emphasize on how schools can and should generate data to demonstrate effectiveness, efficiency and excellence through prescribed curriculum packages combined with testing and league table competitiveness. The problematics of such forms of *Transformational Leadership* have been identified with a recognition that the field of leadership studies is in difficulty in regard to the failure to adopt democratizing forms of what Shields (2010) identifies as *Transformative Leadership* (e.g. Foster 1986), the impact on educational matters in regard to children, staff and the curriculum (e.g. Shields 2004; Smyth 1989a), matters of equity (e.g. Blackmore 1999), the realities of professional practice (e.g. Lingard et al. 2003) and the relationship with capitalist forms of production (e.g. Ball 2012).

An important thread within these concerns is not only about the current and emerging conceptualizations, branding and developments of *Transformational Leadership*, but what such practice is actually called. Historically the label of educational administration has been used to capture *Knowledge Production*, and this remains a feature of the field internationally with conferences, journals and practices described in this way. The rebranding of this label as toxic happened in a range of Anglophone countries from the 1970s onwards, as educational management, based on the notion of 'managing directors of companies', became the new label for strategic change, and administration was relegated as clerical work. From the 1980s onwards, school leadership knocked management into a lower delivery and implementation position, and took over the claims for transformation and reprofessionalization on a par with private business (Gunter 2004). It seems that 'transformational' is interchanged with 'educational', but often the use of 'educational' is problematic as much of what is discussed and promoted at various times is disconnected from pedagogy, where the focus is on the organization rather than teaching and learning within the organization.

For this book, I have adopted 'school leadership' as the descriptor, as it is generally accepted, but it is not automatically the most appropriate one. What I mean by school leadership is the focus on the school as an organization that under forms of decentralization and autonomy must be efficient, effective and excellent, and how successive governments have created the conditions in which schools as 'independent' businesses can operate through corporate standards and data-determined balance sheets. This enables me to primarily focus on the main developments over the past thirty years, but with recognition that labelling and relabelling, with the popularity of adjectival leadership (e.g. teacher leadership and student leadership), is ongoing and central to the political and economic setting in which *Knowledge Production* is taking place. It also enables me to demonstrate how other forms of leaders, leading and leadership are evident within field history, and so ask questions about the dominance of particular forms of school leadership as *Transformational Leadership* and the alternative trajectory located as *Transformative Leadership*.

In addition to this, I have tried to avoid the generic use of 'school leaders' as the descriptive term for educational professionals who have a role within the school as an organization. I do this because it seems sometimes as if everyone is addressed as a 'leader', but scrutiny suggests that the authors seem to be talking about those with position, power and authority. Hence I intend to use formal professional titles such as 'headteacher' and 'principal', and as this book has an international audience I will primarily use the most popular title of 'principal' unless I am talking specifically about England where 'headteacher' remains the most common professional role title (though 'principal' is gaining in popularity).

Authoring an intellectual history

I am inspired by Dimitriadis (2012) to reveal 'critical dispositions' in how I approach this project, and so I would want to align with researchers and colleagues who not only work for social justice within and through *Knowledge Production* but also seek to deploy activist methodologies (e.g. Apple 2013; Griffiths 1998). These are matters that resonate within the social sciences (see Parker and Thomas 2011), and as my colleagues at the University of Manchester have shown, this is not easy work, but it is productive and necessary (Gunter et al. 2014).

In taking up a critical position I am locating within an established but not an establishment way of thinking and doing in the field. I began with a review of the literatures (Gunter 1997, 2001) and have continued to be concerned to map the field (Gunter et al. 2013; Gunter et al. 2014b), to develop professional biographies of field members and their positioning within the field (Gunter 1999, 2012a,c), as well as working with and on behalf of professionals and children in understanding change and developing learning (Gunter 2005a; Thomson and Gunter 2006). As such I associate with colleagues, projects and texts that are concerned with revealing educational opportunities and restoring education to educational relationships within and outside of schools.

I am clearly in good company as researchers have examined the problematics of school leadership from a range of positions (e.g. Marshall and Oliva 2006a; Hoyle and Wallace 2005), but only a few have examined *Knowledge Production* issues as a historical project (e.g. Ribbins 2006a). Indeed, there are many challenges involved, where Samier (2006) identifies how in writing histories we are located within history, not least 'the conceptual frameworks through which we perceive and interpret the world' (p. 136). Consequently, and following Bourdieu (1988), I know that this project continues to be dangerous, 'it is bound to be read differently by readers who are part of this world as opposed to those who are outsiders' (p. xv). I align here with Greenfield who, in challenging the underlying ontology and epistemology of field knowledge claims in the 1970s, experienced personal attacks instead of valuable intellectual debates (Greenfield and Ribbins 1993). Nevertheless, the project ahead is an important one where in spite of scholarly intentions and robust methodologies my authorial practice (not least citations) will no doubt reveal dispositions that have different degrees of familiarity for readers. Furthermore, there are potential issues regarding what it means to enter a field and locate employment in higher education, in which work, research and theory have been identified as being socially unjust (Cole and Gunter 2010; Mertz 2009).

Since becoming a student, and then a researcher and teacher, I have developed a sense of being within a field of study, and how I see my position and how others seek to position my work. This may appear, with hindsight, to be neat and tidy. Data collection for a range of projects (e.g. Gunter 1999, 2012a) has enabled me to both seek and be given access to the professional, and sometimes personal, lived experiences of field members, both past and present. In doing this, my understanding of the complexity and richness of networks has increased, and has facilitated my reflection on how I have both sought entrance and been co-opted into the field. My membership of a range of seminar series, for example, *Redefining Education Management* (Bush et al. 1999; EMA 1999) has enabled me to engage in debates about theory and research, and how field members are reviewing their position. I inhabit border territory where I do and do not belong within the field, (see Deem 1996). While much of my practice is the same as other field members in HEIs, my research interests have focused away from immediate problem-solving agendas towards the historical setting and development of how such problems are constructed and promoted as relevant to teaching and learning. The creativity of being on the margins is evident in my aim to chronicle and analyse the growth of the field, but I have also experienced the drawing of boundaries that aim to exclude this type of thinking. Following Bourdieu (1988) I would agree that any attempt to try to be neutral or to hide behind method 'is doomed in advance to failure' (p. 25), but at the same time attempts to categorize and position my work in particular ways also has to be confronted (e.g. Caldwell and Spinks 1998; Thrupp and Willmott 2003). Like Greenfield, I see my research and writing as representing 'a groping towards understanding, not a uniform and logical line of extrapolation' (Greenfield and Ribbins 1993, p. 269).

Resources and contribution

This book has been long in the planning and thinking, but could only be written in the current format once I had developed a set of resources. Underpinning this book are the following resources:

Primary: a database of over five hundred policy texts;

Empirical: data sets of over three hundred interviews;

Secondary: a library of over a thousand published accounts; and

Conceptual: thinking tools based on Bourdieu's sociology, and Arendt's political analysis.

Within this book I intend drawing primarily on four main projects: first, my doctoral studies entitled: *An Intellectual History of the Field of Education Management from 1960*; second, the *Knowledge Production and Educational Leadership* (KPEL) project funded by the ESRC (RES-000-23-1192); third, the *Distributed Leadership and the Social Practices of School Organisation in England* (SPSO) project (led by David Hall) funded by the ESRC (RES-000-22-3610); and fourth, the *Consultancy and Knowledge Production in Education* (CKPE) project funded by the British Academy and Leverhulme (SG121698).

The contribution to the field and to the wider social sciences reported in this book is located in three main areas: first, I begin by scoping through developing an approach to *Knowledge Production* before going on to present a position regarding the construction of intellectual histories; second, I then present a framing of intellectual histories through five interrelated dimensions of *knowledge traditions, purposes, domains, contexts* and *networks*; and, third, I then go onto deploy this framing to write intellectual histories of particular networks of *knowledge actors*. I conclude the book by examining the possibilities for the approach I have taken regarding the intellectual histories that might be developed and used within and for the field.

PART ONE

Scoping Intellectual Histories

1

Knowledge Production

Introduction

The design and development of an intellectual history requires conceptual locating and anchoring, and I intend doing this by explicating and taking a position in relation to, within, about and for *Knowledge Production*. The case for doing this is based on a need to examine *knowledges*, *knowings*, *knowers* and *knowledgeabilities* as a means through which the research and practice for an intellectual history can be examined, understood and explained. I begin the chapter by examining what I mean by the knowledge or canon in the field, the ways of knowing, the recognition of *knowers* and the deployment of knowledgeability. I then take a particular focus about *Knowledge Production* by asking questions about the relationships between the state, public policy, politics, networks and *knowledges*. I investigate this through the presentation of *knowledgeable polities* as a conceptual framework based on four main positions: *knowledgeable state*, *knowledgeable politics*, *knowledgeable networks* and *knowledgeable theorizing*. I do this because the generation and relationship between research and practice as historically located *Knowledge Production* requires an understanding of the public policy process: the identification, use and legitimization of policy as knowledge and knowing through the political, economic, social and cultural practices of *knowers* and knowledgeability. The final analytical layer is by deploying Bourdieu's thinking tools of *habitus, field* and *capitals* where I engage with the power processes about what is known, what is worth knowing and in whose interests that knowing is promoted.

Knowledge production

In the opening section of *The Eighteenth Brumaire of Louis Bonaparte*, Marx (2009) states, 'Man [*sic*] makes his own history, but he does not make it out of the whole cloth; he does not make it out of conditions chosen by himself, but out of such as he finds close at hand. The tradition of all past generations weighs like an alp upon the brain of the living' (p. 9). Hence research as a social practice is located within a historical context, it 'is both a "constructed" and a "constructing" activity' (Usher 2001, p. 54). Consequently, I am related to *Knowledge Production*, located *within Knowledge Production*, at the same time I am writing *about Knowledge Production*, and I am making a contribution *for Knowledge Production*. But it is more than this. I am exercising agency through my authorial voice in setting the agenda for this project, but I am also located in complex structures regarding my own history, work context and wider political, economic and cultural discourses and events that shape intellectual work and its location in the academy (Gunter 2010), but as Skeggs (1997) argues, 'there is no straightforward correspondence between our circumstances and how we think: we are positioned in but not determined by our locations' (p. 18).

While I recognize the structuring push and pull of history within *Knowledge Production*, I am also concerned with the interplay with agency, and how a person learns in time and over time a dialogic sense of self in the stories that are being written. The emplotting of histories, the living in the present and the imaginings about the future are contemporary and are concerned with the inheritance from the dead with possible conflicting urges to raise and bury the dead. So my approach to *Knowledge Production* is historical in the sense of how the present is read and understood through and in spite of the past, but it is also sociological and political. If history is a construction about the past for the present, and usually written by and for elites, then it is enriched by sociological analysis of the social and cultural location of knowledge, and it is political through an examination of options and how choices are made, how conflicts are resolved and the institutions and networks where it takes place.

I approach *Knowledge Production* by taking inspiration from Bates (1980, 2013) through a consideration of what is known, how it is organized, where it is known, what is worth knowing about, how it is known and who knows it. This is just a starting point that opens up the opportunity to consider *knowledges*, *knowings*, *knowers* and *knowledgeabilities*:

> *Knowledges:* the canon or set of key theories, ideas, data, experiences and arguments as a resource. This can be made visible through what is said and done, usually inscribed, for example, within books, in building architecture and in a curriculum vitae. Importantly this includes the underpinning ontology and epistemology, together with the debates and historiography of the canon.

Knowings: the methodologies and methods that generate *knowledges*. This is concerned with sources and where they originate, this can be through life experiences of doing a job and/or through formal research design with findings and recommendations.

Knowers: the *knowledge actors* who deem something knowable through creating, sustaining and challenging *knowledges* and *knowings*. This can be espoused and/or accredited experts through to the diverse publics who constitute civil society.

Knowledgeabilities: the accessing, owning, deploying and exhibiting of *knowledges* and *knowings* by *knowers* in ways that illustrate insight, expertise and 'in the know'. This is concerned with recognition and selection/editing, as well as emphasis given to and the production of claims through arguments and evidence.

My approach here is to use the four 'K's in the plural, and this is because *Knowledge Production* in regard to school leadership demonstrates plurality within and external to the canon, the methodologies being used, the range of people in different organizational as well as geographical locations who know, and the approaches to *knowledgeabilities*. The creation of a knowledge base from the four 'K's is through the including and excluding of knowledge, actors, methodologies and claims. These do include ontological and epistemological matters about realities and truths, but they do not sit outside of the people that create, access and use them. Indeed Bogotch (2012) and Waite (2012) ask: Who controls our knowledge? Such a question embraces matters such as the nature of intellectual labour, through to how quality is determined through citations, audits and indexes, and how the publishing industry impacts on *Knowledge Production* as big business (Biesta 2012). Therefore the approach to *Knowledge Production* as a political and sociological project is not directly concerned with the *philosophical* debates and claims about ontology and epistemology, but instead I approach it as a power process where notions and strategies about purposes, rationales, narratives and outcomes matter when framing an intellectual history.

Following Freeman and Sturdy (2014a) *knowers* know about, for and within knowledge that is 'embodied' or tacit within the person and is made public through activity (p. 9), 'inscribed' or codified through artefacts such as photographs, buildings, published texts and minutes of meetings (p. 10), and 'enacted' through what is said and done, or remains silent (p. 12). However, as Freeman and Sturdy (2014a) admit, their phased 'schema' does not tell the full story, because there is a need to draw on political and sociological resources in order to examine the what, how and why of 'how knowledge can be organized, both intellectually and socially, or about how different groups acquire control of certain bodies of knowledge, or about why some bodies or forms of knowledge may become more prominent in the policy process than others' (pp. 16–17). Consequently, I would like to align with Blackler (1995), who shifts the researcher's gaze away from knowledge 'in bodies, routines, brains, dialogue or symbols' (p. 1022) by making the case that knowledge is *'mediated, situated, provisional, pragmatic* and *contested'* (p. 1021, emphasis in original).

So, *Knowledge Production* is a social and political process involving matters of legitimacy and authority, where, following Blackler (1995), 'mediation' suggests dynamic interactions within exchange relationships and the claims being made; where 'situatedness' generates the importance of interpretation; where 'provisionality' suggests the temporal and developing nature of accessing and utilizing knowledge; where 'pragmatism' suggests a focus on outcome delivery that can be in tension with values and processes; and where 'contestation' suggests the interpersonal and micro-political engagements in which people frame problems and seek solutions. Indeed there is a need to consider physical and mental health issues regarding how people experience their work, and the levels of anxiety that can impact (pp. 1041–2), particularly when people think and do things they do not agree with. These are matters that have been debated over centuries, and while it is out of the scope of this particular account to give a full historiography of *Knowledge Production*, the standpoint taken within my account needs to be clear. Specifically I have a commitment to expose elite, and increasingly corporate elite, control of *Knowledge Production* and to open up opportunities to work for participatory democracy.

Elite approaches to *Knowledge Production* focus on the discipline as a formal set of data and methodologies that are agreed and controlled by an epistemic community, usually located in particular universities and learned societies. The canon is sacred, methodologies agreed and where *knowers* are out of reach. Knowledgeability is through accreditation (and from particular high-status universities), projects (particularly esteemed funding such as research councils) and acclaim through outputs and media. Following Kuhn's (1975) analysis of 'paradigm shifts' change takes place when a knowledge community gives recognition to different evidence and methodological innovation. Hence knowledge is located in the library and seminar rooms, knowing is strictly controlled and *knowers* are recognized through formal titles such as doctor, reader, fellow and professor. This is the usual benchmark against which other forms of *Knowledge Production* are scoped and assessed, hence Becher (1989) differentiates the status attributed to disciplines where 'hard' 'pure' maths is deemed to outrank 'softer' 'impure' education.

Changes and challenges to knowledge have been mapped by Gibbons et al. (1994), who have formulated disciplinary knowledge as Mode 1, where 'its cognitive and social norms determine what shall count as significant problems, who shall be allowed to practice science and what constitutes good science' (p. 3) as the starting point for scripting Mode 2 knowledge in relation to it. Gibbons et al. (1994) make the case that Mode 2 is 'new' and is distinctive through its 'interdisciplinary' approach, where '*Knowledge Production* is increasingly a socially distributed process ... the expansion of the number of sites where recognizably competent research can be undertaken has implications for the management of the *Knowledge Production* process and for the maintenance of quality control within it' (p. 156). It seems that the widening of the pool of elite people and institutions (e.g. businesses, think tanks) that are recognized as legitimate sites for 'competent research' enables the relationship between producers and users, and purposes and funding to be examined.

Like Grundmann and Stehr (2012) I am concerned with knowledge, truth and power, where the three are combined in Mode 1 terms, but this does not 'answer the question of *why* knowledge can be powerful, or for whom knowledge may be powerful' (p. 3, emphasis in original). Mode 2 extends the sites where this question might be asked but does not resolve it. I would suggest that this is because the framing of newness around an emerging 'socially distributed process' is not interrelated with a democratizing agenda, particularly since challenges to elite *Knowledge Production* in Modes 1 and 2 would need to give inclusive recognition to *knowledges, knowings, knowers* and *knowledgeabilities* that are currently 'othered' and 'silenced' in the acknowledgement and legitimation of what counts: first, feminist approaches (e.g. Stanley and Wise 2002); second, post-colonial approaches (e.g. Connell 2007); and third, student, family and community voice approaches (e.g. Paechter 2001).

The approach I intend taking in this book is to ensure that elite control of *Knowledge Production* is made evident, not least by giving recognition to the plurality within the canon, and how as a field rather than a discipline, the emphasis is on purposes of *Knowledge Production* rather than its conservation (Mode 1) and increasingly its marketization (Mode 2). Ways of knowing through methodology and methods will again be examined, where belief systems are recognized as powerful forms of knowledge alongside and often trumping robust data sets. *Knowers* are also opened up to scrutiny where I follow Baron (1969) that the field 'viewed in the widest sense, as all that makes possible the educative process, the administration of education embraces the activities of Parliament at one end of the scale and the activities of any home with children or students at the other' (p. 6). Therefore children and families are as much a part of *Knowledge Production* as are professors, where there are both shared and different forms of knowledgeability.

What I am interested in revealing as integral to intellectual histories are the *claims* and *exchanges* taking place regarding the rendering of practice knowable and worth knowing: what is said and why this matters, and how this draws boundaries that silence and exclude; and how what is said is engaged with, used, replied to, and importantly, traded through formal and informal contractual processes. Contact between people, whether this is through a team giving a pitch for a commissioned project, or through chatting at a conference, enables *knowledge mobilizations* as 'flows' and 'uses' to be given recognition, and in ways that are local, national and global (Saint-Martin 2001; Moss 2013). Hence *Knowledge Production* is not a neutral process or practice, it is replete with standpoints. Harvey (2007) encapsulates this by describing how neoliberal ideas on the economizing of everyday life have become normalized, through how ideas speak 'to our institutions and instincts, to our values and our desires, as well as to the possibilities inherent in the social world we inhabit' (p. 5). This can be witnessed and experienced in a range of places and spaces where what Thrift (2005) calls the '"cultural circuit" of capitalism' is evident in 'business schools, management consultants, management gurus and the media' (p. 6), and so is integral to professional training and organizational culture. People in receipt of *knowledges* and *knowings* are not passive recipients, but exercise agency through how their world interplays with what is read and heard. What is interesting is how people ascribe the right to know and be known about to themselves and others, not least how activity is accepted as legitimate and relevant, or rejected as threatening, or 'not for people like me'. Importantly, this is connected to place and space, where geographies of *Knowledge Production* enable matters of the local and the global to be taken into account, and how uses and flows across boundaries, and within local, national and supranational organizations, enable links to and dislocations from territory and borders to be examined.

Knowledgeable polities

My task is to develop a way through the complexity of *knowledges, knowings, knowers* and *knowledgeabilities* by generating perspectives that can enable description, meaning and explanation of knowledge exchanges and claims. The interplay between agency and structure within and for the self, the family, the community and formal organizations such as schools requires thinking about, not least the interrelationships between the state, public policy, politics, networks and *Knowledge Production*. I therefore intend drawing on political science and sociology in order to use selected conceptual tools within an overarching framework that I call *knowledgeable polities*.

I am using *polity* as a way of framing *Knowledge Production* by giving due attention to people organizations and the spaces that they inherit, inhabit and create. There are questions to be addressed regarding the relationship between public institutions, politics and the state both nationally and globally, where *knowledges, knowings, knowers* and *knowledgeabilities* are located within the wider publics who constitute a polity, and are usually visible through elections to public office and appointments to specific public services based on approved and transparent expertise and accreditation. By *knowledgeable polity* I mean how *Knowledge Production* is defined and engaged with, not as an objectified or unit of analysis, but in a place and as a dynamic space where boundaries may be fixed but also challenged and stretched (or demolished, rebuilt, decayed). I now present this through four interconnected sites for examining and understanding *Knowledge Production*, where I draw on selected research and thinking from the political sciences and sociology: first, the *knowledgeable state*: the focus is on the relationship between public institutions, policy and knowledge; second, *knowledgeable politics*: the focus is on the relationship between publics and organizations, including but not exclusively the state; third, *knowledgeable networks*: the focus is on the formal and informal interconnections that generate groups and organizations with claims for expertise and delivery; and fourth, *knowledgeable theorizing:* the focus is on the use of Bourdieu's thinking tools to provide explanations of power processes.

Knowledgeable state

I intend deploying *knowledgeable state* as a site for *Knowledge Production* exchange and claims that gives prime attention to government institutions within the nation state, and interlinks to supranational organizations. In framing public policy, the government, as an institution of the state, presents itself as knowledgeable through the legitimacy of the mandate to govern. In doing so it draws on *knowledges, knowings* and *knowers*, and through such investment contributes to and structures *knowledges, knowings* and *knowers*. The state does more than set the legal requirements and tone through bureaucracy and hierarchical relationships, but can determine the ontology and epistemology required in the knowledge it needs to use to support and validate policymaking within such relationships. Certainly, while the state as an assumed unitary 'it' suggests objectivity and rationality, the engagement with *Knowledge Production* has complex features, where as Grundmann and Stehr (2012) note, it is more than functional utility and legitimacy, where 'knowledge can also operate at the level of influencing the construction and framing of policy problems ... without leading to specific policies' (p. 19).

Consequently, and following Pearton (1982), I would identify the *knowledgeable state* as 'researcher', 'producer' and 'user' (p. 254), where his analysis of warfare speaks to centralization. I would want to make a contribution by following Clarke and Newman (1997) who identify the state as 'manager', and Neave (1988) who focuses on the state as 'evaluator'.

Deploying this framework I would characterize the state as: first, *researcher*: confirming and developing theories and evidence to support and legitimize strategy and policies; second, *user*: knowledgeability by identifying and commissioning *knowledges* and *knowings* that can be handled, processed and represented within policies; third, *producer*: constructing strategies within policies that can be defended and acted upon through knowledge and *knowings*; fourth, *manager*: controlling and regulating external knowledge sources and production through contractual exchange relationships; and, fifth, *evaluator*: controlling outputs and *knowers* through performance audits of standards with judgements and feedback, particularly in regard to investment and disinvestment.

Giving such attention to the state, public institutions and the endurance of government as a feature of a *knowledgeable polity* can be illuminated through the empirical and conceptual work of Scott (1998), who through his analysis of large-scale reform and planning talks about 'seeing like a state'. Indeed, many gains in regard to civil rights, housing, transport, health, welfare and education, have been a product of such 'seeing' and 'doing' by the state. Scott (1998) identifies how reform happens through what he calls 'state simplifications' (p. 80) as a means of making reality legible. Such simplifications are based on particular approaches to *Knowledge Production*, where knowledge is about facts, where patterns matter and where distinctions and particularities can be ignored. The adoption by governments in a range of countries of *Transformational Leadership* as a form of legitimized knowledge and knowing based on approved of *knowers* is a good example of state simplification and how knowledgeability about its 'fit' with problem solving is demonstrated. It enables performance and privatization to be pursued by communicating logical and common-sense beliefs about what is wrong with schools and what needs to be done to put things right. For example, Barber's (2007) construction and enthusiasm for 'deliverology' in the UK government, and more recently through globalized consultancy (Barber et al. 2011) regarding the transfer of policy requirements from the minister to the child in a school. This illuminates what Scott (1998) calls 'simplification, abstraction, and standardization' (p. 81), whereby the causal importance and requirements of school leadership are codified and normalized as delivery. In addition, Scott (1998) argues that this seeks 'to create a terrain and a population with precisely those standardized characteristics that will be easiest to monitor, count, assess, and manage' (pp. 81–2), and if governments and other agencies (see OECD 2013) colonize professional practice and pedagogy, then this remodels the composition and identities of the workforce and students in ways that generate the very effectiveness activity that is subjected to simplification. An important way in which this is taking place is how schools, and other agencies, determine their approach as 'little states' whereby they are legally contracted to improve and audit data gathering with measures of effectiveness and improvement.

The relationship between the *knowledgeable state* and supra states is important, not least in the school leadership field, where Pont et al. (2008a) claim the following:

> School leadership has become a priority in education policy agendas internationally. It plays a key role in improving school outcomes by influencing the motivations and capacities of teachers, as well as the school climate and environment. Effective school leadership is essential to improve the efficiency and equity of schooling. (p. 2)

Such claims are lifted out of the national context but are consistent with national policies – and so appropriate attention needs to be given to globalizing knowledge flows and carrier knowledge workers – and with super-national sites of activity (e.g. European Union, OECD, see Moos 2009). For example, Lawn and Grek (2012) and Grek (2013) stake claims for an emerging European policy space by downplaying the place of the nation state and public institutions. However, research within Europe shows that the nation state remains the prime place, not least because much seemingly global knowledge has its origins and legitimacy in a national education system, and as *knowledge actors* carry ideas on and off planes they can be received and read in different places (see Gunter and Fitzgerald 2013a,b; Gunter et al. 2016a,b). Nevertheless, such challenges do put the spotlight on other sources of *Knowledge Production*, where my adoption and development of Pearton's analysis (1982) could be criticized as hegemonic in regard to education, because it is a conceptualization located in the state as defender and war machine, and so it is questionable whether 'its role as planner, banker and sole or dominant customer' (p. 250) is appropriate and accurate for educational services. For example, unitary states such as the United Kingdom and federal states such as the United States of America have never had a monopoly on the provision and funding of education in the way that they have in regard to defence and the military, not least the continued existence of private education but not private armies.

Other challenges to normalized state hegemony are located in Scott's (1998) presentation of examples of large-scale modernizing plans, and shows how they can fail the people they were meant to benefit: 'If I were asked to condense the reasons behind these failures into a single sentence, I would say that the progenitors of such plans regarded themselves as far smarter and farseeing than they really were and, at the same time, regarded their subjects as far more stupid and incompetent than *they* really were' (p. 343, original emphasis). When tensions and contradictions emerge within the simplification process, the state can and does exclude – sometimes in highly visible and dramatic ways (see Gunter 2014). There is considerable work on how and why children (Smyth 2006a) and teachers (Ball 2003) are positioned as ignorant and in need of the simplifications, along with work on how children and teachers (Fielding 2006, Wrigley et al. 2012) work in ways that challenge, reject and replace those simplifications. These are networks that are involved in exchange relationships that can also 'see like a state' such as research councils, university bureaucracies and institutions in civil society such as pressure groups, political parties and unions. At the same time, there is a need to examine activity that aims to work differently and develop education policy through individuals and networks that does not use the state (and its reform simplifications) to script their agenda against. So there is a need to undertake an analysis of *knowledges, knowings, knowers* and *knowledgeabilities* in ways that recognize alternative sites of exchange and claims. Whether, how and when this interacts with state policy processes is crucial to developing analysis about activity that is independent of and potentially resistant to official external policy.

Knowledgeable politics

I intend deploying *knowledgeable politics* as a site for *Knowledge Production* exchange and claims regarding choices and conflicts that gives prime attention to people in relation to each other in the public domain. People in their everyday lives present themselves as knowledgeable through comment (in letters to the editor, on social media, in a queue at the supermarket) and in doing so draw on and contribute to *knowledges, knowings, knowers* and *knowledgeabilities*. People may also claim to represent or be responsible for others and so know on their behalf, for example, parents and carers. Various contested terms such as 'civil society' and 'public(s)' are used to frame this, where both are regarded as fruitful regarding how they enable interdisciplinary perspectives to generate new insights about human activities (see Anheier 2005; Newman and Clarke 2009). In returning to Scott (1998), he argues that what 'seeing like a state' misses and often destroys are the *knowledges* (skills, know-how, having the knack) that are identified and learnt politically and sociologically within families and communities, not least how people know when and how to invoke and engage in *Knowledge Production* in relation to their locality. While there is plurality of positions and ways of rationalizing it, I would like to draw on Newman's (2007) notion of 'settlements' whereby there is an acceptance about what is and is not negotiable, and there are times when such settlements are disrupted, and indeed as researchers we need to be disruptors through how we give recognition to what is never settled.

One settlement is through the idea of what Marquand (2004) terms 'the public domain' where 'central to it are the values of citizenship, equity and service' (p. 27). Distinctive from, but connected to this, is the creation of public services variously known as the 'public sector' or 'welfare state' whereby concerns and issues held in common are politicized through public funding and public political design and regulation. Where the boundary is drawn between what is public and private, is a strong feature of political and social exchanges and claims, and has intensified in western-style democracies over the past fifty years. Politicization through the *knowledgeable state* has been critiqued, whereby there are demands for the state to shrink: for neoliberals this is about freedom within the economy and to take responsibility for the self and family, and for neoconservatives this is about how values and morality is a private matter not only through the self and family, but also through the development and sustaining of homogeneity. For the former, education is a private good to be traded through business, and for the latter, education is about essential truths to be communicated to the next generation through the home (e.g. sex education, behaviour) and through sites of learning that represent and educate approved of social norms (e.g. segregation based on fees, biological sex, faith). *Transformational Leadership* is located in this contradiction: principals are meant to be both entrepreneurial risk-taking and conservative risk averse.

Forms of depoliticization and repoliticization continue to be a feature of *knowledgeable politics* whereby what is seemingly settled continues to be open for challenge (see Flinders and Wood 2014). The state as knowledgeable continues to be tested through political processes that demand that the state enters or withdraws from economic, cultural and social matters, not least through the privatization of services and the entry into public services by private companies. The emerging 'settlement' from within this dynamic is one that is neoliberal in alliance with neoconservative angst about the state, where current analysis claims that ideas do not exist outside of the practice of those who speak, think and talk about them, and so depoliticization through *Neoliberalism* is less a set of coherent ideas and is more about what people say and do (Jessop 2014). Such practices are not homogenous, but there are struggles and debates within *Neoliberalism*, whereby we should not be fooled into thinking that the ideas and activity are agreed and of one form. Indeed, Wood and Flinders (2014) present 'discursive depoliticisation' (p. 153) regarding how what is normal and the norm can be typed and spoken into the truth: 'The promotion of an issue, *but* alongside a single interpretation and the *denial* of choice would, therefore create a form of *depoliticisation* from this discursive perspective' (p. 161). This is evident in the principal as *Transformational Leader* of the autonomous school as a business, where 'transformation' is about controlling or removing professional groups which are characterized as acting in their own interests.

While there is much conceptual work underway regarding the interrelationship between politicization, repoliticization and depoliticization, there are legitimate concerns regarding the characterization of 'friend/enemy distinction' (Hay 2014, p. 296). Hay (2014) argues that while political analysis needs to take note of divisions, he makes the case that politics is more than one interest winning and hence subjugating another. Connected with such arguments are the recognition of how forms of resistance operate, in ways that challenge traditional forms of politicization (e.g. feminist critiques of paternalism of welfare state services), and relocating politicization to localized alliances within 'little polities' (Vincent et al. 2000). Those who work within and support public services may seek out new sites for and forms of politics which could be framed as subversive (Barnes and Prior 2009). Such complexities lead me to consider how *knowledgeable politics* is not only interconnected to the *knowledgeable state* but requires recognition of how politics works through the establishment and challenges to boundaries, not least how social and political cleavages simultaneously divide and associate people through networked relationships.

Knowledgeable networks

I intend deploying *knowledgeable networks* as a site for *Knowledge Production* exchange and claims that gives prime attention to the interactions and relationships between people as self-promoted and/or recognized 'experts'. The development of governance as an approach within political science has given recognition to those who are organizationally located as 'experts' in public services (e.g. education, medical, legal professionals with accreditation, titles and recognition), in private business (e.g. consultants, philanthropists, business owners) and in civil society (e.g. parents and children). The importance of networks in explaining exchange relationships within political conduct, and the interconnections between governmental hierarchy and civil society, has grown rapidly (e.g. Ball 2008b; Davies 2011; Goodwin 2009; Grek 2013; Olmedo 2014; Ozga 2009; Spring 2012).

Ball (2008b) presents his forensic work on 'new policy communities' in education, where people bring ideas and influence, and 'through social relationships trust is established and views and discourses are legitimated' (p. 753). Hence when principals are being presented with *Transformational Leadership* as legitimated professional practice, there is a need to examine not only how people are in contact with each other to produce such a model but also how power works to give status and acclaim to particular *knowledge actors* (Ball 2009; Goodwin 2009).

Data and projects demonstrate that there is a need to give more attention to the role of hierarchy in simultaneously generating and anchoring networks, particularly since as Davies (2011) argues, 'there is a pronounced tendency for governance networks to re-enact the practices they are meant to complement or displace' (p. 55). Researchers continue to show the importance of the public institution (Béland 2005; Radaelli 1995), not least through how networks are constrained by history as well as stabilized through the necessary rule following required for public accountability. In my own work I have developed and deployed *institutionalized governance* as a conceptualized means to describe and explain how political, social and economic interests are crucial to understanding how knowledge exchanges and claims take place within government *regimes* that are institutionally located (Gunter 2012a). Networks in relation to policymaking do not exist outside of or independent from the *knowledgeable state*, where those who inhabit public institutions (ministers, civil servants, advisors) call in and contract outsiders who are networked. Indeed, as Scott (1998) argues, 'state simplifications can be considered part of an ongoing "project of legibility", a project that is never fully realised' (p. 80). So, networks of people with organizational locations (think tanks, businesses, universities) can operate as *little states* that embrace simplification as a means of generating new business with the state, and recognize how conducive it is to non-state business. When governments leave office, simplification as a process continues, and can include some of the same plans and actors who present themselves as neutral simplifiers.

Knowledgeable theorizing

The development and explication of a position in relation to, for, within and about *Knowledge Production* has generated at least two important contributions: first, that conceptualizations of *Knowledge Production* need to give due recognition of *knowledges*, *knowers*, *knowings* and *knowledgeabilities*; and, second, that *Knowledge Production* as a power process means there is a need to engage by developing and using vantage points that generate perspectives on, about and within complex interrelationships between the state, politics and networks within and external to a polity. There is a third important contribution to be made through how theory and theorizing is accessed and deployed, and in doing so I intend drawing on Bourdieu's thinking tools because they provide a language and conceptualization of, within and for *Knowledge Production*, and in ways that relate what might be regarded as everyday, and perhaps even unremarkable, encounters to wider social and political processes.

I intend beginning with *doxa* as a self-evident truth, whereby the *doxa* of school leadership is about providing certainty and prediction: the role incumbent must demonstrate confidence that what they do delivers outcomes, and they can base this on cause-and-effect calculations (Bourdieu 2000). This *doxa* underpins but is often masked by the vivacity surrounding *Transformational Leadership*, and the rebranding processes around hybrids such as 'distributed' and 'instructional'. The interplay between agency and structure is the location where the generative *codification* of *Transformational Leadership* is revealed, where the language of vision and mission is explicated, where the embodiment of charisma is displayed, and where followership by listening, talking, emoting and obedience is created and enacted. Bourdieu (2000) provides a series of interrelated thinking tools that enable the researcher to focus on the normality of day-to-day practice and how *Knowledge Production* within and for *Transformational Leadership* is itself regarded as normal.

In Bourdieu's (1990) terms, the game in play in western-style democracies is that of privatization through the entry of private markets into the provision of educational services based on financial and cultural exchange relationships, and through the managerialization of residual 'public' services regarding basic skill provision and behaviour control. This game is being played through a range of sub-games, such as school leadership, whereby the field of education has been breached by the fields of politics and the economy that shape and develop that game through *Knowledge Production* that meets their objective interests (Thomson 2005). The codification of the *Transformational Leadership doxa* enables educational professionals to engage in economic and economizing practices such as data management, performativity and bidding in order to access funding streams, in ways that are modernizing and generate equivalence 'with' and 'as' entrepreneurs, with an espoused value system that is orientated on producing children as a work-ready human resource.

Having a language and a set of tools that can describe, understand and explain such *Knowledge Production* requires a focus on practice. Through *habitus* Bourdieu (1990) presents a thinking tool that enables the regularities of practice to be recognized as *codification* without the determinism of rule-bound and abstracted codes. Within a *field* as an arena of struggles, *knowers* take up positions and so reveal the structured and structuring dispositions that make such positioning around *knowledges*, *knowings* and *knowledgeabilities* attractive. Hence the *doxa* underpinning *Transformational Leadership* is created, developed and strategized through position taking and how the breaching of education by the fields of the economy and politics have made the game where this form of leadership can be played attractive. Teachers, headteachers, parents, children, ministers, officials and researchers who locate within the *doxa* 'have a feel for the necessity and the logic of the game' (p. 64), and so they stake their interests, ideas and careers in the school leadership *game* through the regularities of a harmonized disposition. Hence playing is about how 'a set of people take part in rule-bound activity, an activity which, without necessarily being the product of obedience to rules, *obeys certain regularities*' (Bourdieu 1990, p. 64, emphasis in original).

Capitals (economic, social, cultural, symbolic) can be staked and increased by playing (those deemed to be successful *Transformational Leaders* receive acclaim and rewards). Such practice attracts and generates the revealing of shared dispositions, and while players may assume they are dominating the game, they *misrecognize* how the dominant fields of power and the economy dominate practices. Not playing is unthinkable. All principals in public services education are positioned as *Transformational Leaders*, and resistance to the logic leads to punitive exclusion, sometimes quietly through early retirement but mainly through show events such as sacking following a declaration failure through data, league tables and inspections.

Thinking about *hysteresis* enables recognition to be given to the relationship between *habitus* and *field*. *Habitus* is 'the system of dispositions to a certain practice' where 'the effect of the habitus is that agents who are equipped with it will behave in a certain way in certain circumstances', but this is not a predictive rule because '*habitus goes hand in glove with vagueness and indeterminacy* (emphasis in original)' (Bourdieu 1990, p. 77). What Bourdieu (1990) is saying is that there is a 'generative spontaneity which asserts itself in an improved confrontation with ever-renewed situations, it obeys a practical logic, that of vagueness, of the more-or-less, which defines one's ordinary relation to the world' (pp. 77–8). Hence the thinking about this as *illusio* is important, where playing the game through *Transformational Leadership* is related to 'a fundamental belief in the interest of the game and the value of the stakes which is inherent in that membership' (Bourdieu 2000, p. 11).

Shifts and changes in the logic of the field create generative practices, where *capital* investment is focused on the relationship between previous 'structuring structures' that have become 'structured structures', and the new emerging structuring interplays with agency (Bourdieu 1989). In other words, educational professionals who experience reworkings of the *doxa* (e.g. transformational, instructional, distributed and entrepreneurial) and how it relates to changes to the job (e.g. from using data to inform assessment to removing teachers) have to read and interpret and see how they are located. *Hysteresis* enables productive thinking about how the revealing of *habitus* within practice is related to context and time, and how positioning and repositioning does and does not take place. In Bourdieu's (2000) terms it seems that 'habitus has its "blips"' or 'critical moments when it misfires or is out of phase' and where there is no rule following, but instead there is interpretation as a form of '*practical reflection*' (p. 162, emphasis in original). Hence the educational professional can examine the relationship between their own positions and how they are positioned, and can make adjustments to their practice. For some, this is a 'blip' whereas for others it is a rupture with possible resistance, and/or with relocation within or outside of the field. This is where critical researchers make a contribution, not only by providing accounts of those who engage in *Transformative Leadership*, but also by helping to provide a counter *doxa* that lives within practice.

Summary

I have now anchored the project through a conceptualization of *Knowledge Production* located within a *knowledgeable polity*. Hence the canon, methodologies, actors and display of know-how as revealed in exchanges and claims need to be read and engaged with through understandings of the state, politics, networks and thinking tools. While much is written and said about school leadership that claims neutrality, and is a necessary break with the past, this is a fabrication. The historical location of current and future practice is at the core of an intellectual history, and I take this forward in Chapter 2 by providing and using a framework for undertaking this stage of the project.

2

Intellectual Histories

Introduction

In this chapter I identify a range of different but often interconnected approaches to the design and delivery of intellectual histories for school leadership. I move from the tradition of focusing on the abstraction and explication of ideas over time to the contribution made by intellectuals, and then the relationship of ideas with practice as intellectual work. All have their merits, and within this book the approach I intend to take is that an intellectual history is a form of *Knowledge Production* and is located within *Knowledge Production*. Therefore an intellectual history makes demands on *Knowledge Production*, and in explicating the critical standpoint I intend to take, I outline how I will draw on and use what is known, how it is known, who knows and how such knowing is demonstrated.

Ideas

A focus on ideas as an approach to intellectual histories is located in the conceptualization of *Knowledge Production* as a 'history of ideas', or to use the vernacular, it is about narrating 'one idea after another' as a form of descent from then to now with both continuities and breaches. Kelley (2002) states that this is 'the habit of tracing ideas in terms on an inner dynamic, or familiar logic, similar to what the eighteenth century called "reasoned" or "conjectural" history' (p. 2). The focus is cerebral where 'the center of this intellectual space locates the intellectual subject (conscious, intentional, or even unconscious) or perhaps a single act of discovery, creation, or conceptualisation – a pure spiritual or phenomenological moment that becomes a target of historical inquiry' (p. 3). What such an approach enables is the identification of an idea – its origins, its ontological and epistemological location, its methodological integrity, its utility and its trajectory – through a study of generation, development and extinction. This assumes forward tracking from idea to impact with judgements about progress and evolution. Integral to this are processes of codification, often through the citation of key texts, with the composition of historiographies including accounts of the formation of disciplines. This form of inheritance might best be described as the canon, or the main claims about what is known and how it is worth knowing because of the methodological rigour in its production.

If I was to write such an intellectual history then the questions that I would need to ask are:

What are the key ideas in the field?
What projects are taking place?
What methodological developments have there been?
What accumulation of evidence is there, and where are the gaps?
What further projects are necessary?

The resources that I could draw on to write such a history would be the field outputs such as books, journals, conference agendas and papers, and project reports.

In studying these outputs it is clear that there are contributions to such an undertaking, but there is no definitive text, and indeed such an all-encompassing and definitive text may be impossible. What is evident are accounts that seek to examine and draw together what might be called the 'knowledge base' for a range of purposes but which demonstrate outputs as sites that sort, catalogue and often seek to settle knowledge claims: first, there are texts that examine *Knowledge Production* and claims (e.g. Clarke and Wildy 2009b; Evers and Lakomski 1991, 1996, 2012; Greenfield 1988; Gronn 2010; Oplatka 2009, 2010, 2012; Willower and Forsyth 1999), sometimes with particular contributions as the focus (e.g. Greenfield and Ribbins 1993; Gunter, 2013a; Hyung Park 1999; Mulford 2012; Stewart 2006); second, there are texts that examine the possibilities of a knowledge base by representing a range of positions and positioning (e.g. Baron and Taylor 1969; Culbertson 1988; Donmoyer 1999; Donmoyer et al.1995; English 2006a; Lane 1996); third, there are handbooks/ edited collections/journal special issues that include a range of work within the field (e.g. Davies and West-Burnham 2003; English 2011; Young et al. 2009), some with historical analysis (e.g. Mitchell 2006; Ribbins 2006a) and some focusing on the journal as a site of production (e.g. Gunter and Fitzgerald 2008; Fitzgerald and Gunter 2008; Ross Thomas 2012; Oplatka 2009, 2012); and fourth, there are meta-analyses that seek to provide an overview or targeted review of what is known (e.g. Eacott 2011a; Hallinger 2013; Leithwood and Duke 1999; Robinson 2007). In addition there are state-of-the-field reviews in special issues of journals (e.g. Blackmore 2010; Clarke and Wildy 2009a; Eacott 2013; Leithwood and Sleegers 2006; Reynolds 2014; Rousmaniere 2009a) and with some reviews in books and journals that focus on the nation state or geographical region as the unit of analysis for the field (e.g. Bush 2007; Bush et al. 1999; EMAL 1999; Gunter and Fitzgerald 2014; Hallinger and Chen 2015; Lumby et al. 2005; Møller 2009; Pounder 2000a,b; Sapre 2000). In regard to the development and popularization of *Transformational Leadership*, there is a range of work that has been undertaken to codify meaning and applicability for education (e.g. Bush 2011; Hoy and Miskel 2013; Leithwood et al. 1999), and the contribution of this approach is by examining what it is, and as such the technical analysis, methodological security, the accumulation of evidence can be laid out and examined. In many ways this is what a literature review in support of a project is meant to be about: the evidence base for the issue that is under investigation.

Understanding and explaining research is more than the collected and curated volume, it is about developing understandings of the people and context, and following Steadman (2001) 'we have to be less concerned with History as *stuff* (we must put to one side the content of any particular piece of historical writing, and the historical information it imparts) than as *process*, as ideation, imagining and remembering' (p. 67, original emphasis). On its own an abstracted intellectual history can only go so far, it can categorize and create historical eras, and so describe the state of knowledge as an object, and it can synthesize what is known in order to bring control and understanding, but it cannot say much about the relationship to and between *knowings, knowers* and knowledgeability. What is needed is an approach that recognizes that 'stuff' only matters because it is illuminative of *doxa* production, where ideas and authors have been given recognition that Bourdieu (2000) describes as 'ritual embalming' where the 'scholastic disposition' constructs fallacies of acclaim and denunciation (pp. 48–9). This is evident not just in terms of report research and arguments made, but also who is included and excluded as an author and as a citation. This is where work that interrupts by opening up the plurality within the field, and by providing alternative histories of ideas, particularly in regard to post-colonialism and social justice debates (e.g. Blackmore 1999; Foster 1986; Smyth 1989a), requires recognition. There is a need to associate with Kelley's (2002) second form of intellectual history, away from ideas as the prime unit of analysis and towards setting 'ideas in the context of their own particular time, place, and environment, without assuming any spiritual continuities over time' (p. 3). The emphasis is not so much on the product of knowledge in the form of a fact or a theory, as the embedded process of where the analysis of ideas is 'brought down to a human level' (Kelley 2002, p. 3), and therefore I now turn to an analysis of *knowledge actors* as intellectuals.

Intellectuals

Attempts to define the *knowledge actor* as 'intellectual' is difficult particularly as Furedi (2004) argues there is a 'creative tension' (p. 32) between autonomy and accountability. Such tensions are replete within what is thought, said and done, and how such activity is to be paid for.

The term 'intellectual' can be dated to the time of the Dreyfus affair when artists and writers were labelled by the right-wing, but whether intellectuals have a political as well as a thinking role is a matter of dispute (Maclean et al. 1990). On the one hand, the intellectual can be conceptualized as someone who devotes their life to cerebral activity; 'by "an intellectual" I mean here to refer to anyone who takes a committed interest in the validity and truth of ideas for their own sake' (Montefiore 1990, p. 201). However, the conceptualization of a knowledge worker as an 'alienated' thinker has been challenged (Lemert 1991; Molnar 1961; Pels 1995), where how a *knowledge actor* understands and acts out their role has increasingly become a focus of analysis (Maclean et al. 1990; Martindale 1987). Therefore the 'public intellectual' assumes a political role (Fuller 2005), and while an intellectual focuses on autonomous thinking and within practice reveals a scholarly *habitus*, a public intellectual 'is thus someone who applies intellectual activities for a whole community, or nation, in a way that is open and accessible to the members of that community or nation, however defined' (Lyon 2009, p. 70).

Public intellectuals may engage with ideas in ways that distinguish them as an elite 'intelligentsia' with privileged access to knowledge and ways of knowing. Such access may be through the deployment of what Bourdieu (2000) identifies as forms of capital that may be combined: *economic* through the funding of *Knowledge Production*; *cultural* through the identification of how certain types of people are more important because they know; *social* through how networks of *knowledge actors* maintain and enhance recognition of position, not least through how entry and exit is managed; and *symbolic* through how titles, credentials and acclaim are awarded. Giving recognition to this problematizes knowledge rather than accepts it as a given, and it sees *Knowledge Production* as connected to structural factors such as class, and to construction factors such as pedagogic processes. The purpose of knowledge is to regulate what is known and when it is to be known, and the rewards for knowing are limited to an elite.

If I was to write such an intellectual history then the questions that I would need to ask are:

Who are the intellectuals within the field?
What epistemic groups are located in the leadership field?
Who are the people who form these groups, where do they come from and how are they socialized?
What knowledge claims do they make, what debates do they have and how are disputes resolved?

In addressing such questions I would not only examine field outputs but also the biographies of those who locate within the field through their practices. In doing so I could give recognition to those who acknowledge their intellectual resources (e.g. Starratt 2003), where an important focus can be on particular people, with autobiographical contributions (e.g. Mulford 2012), and biographical accounts, for example, Samier (2003) and colleagues' Festschfrit in honour of the work of Hodgkinson; Hyung Park's (1999) analysis of Bates' contribution; and my own review of Ball's contribution through not researching school leadership (Gunter 2013a). Greenfield's contribution regarding the interruption of the Theory Movement is widely recognized as significant, where he raised questions about knowledge claims by arguing for values to be integral to how organizations are studied (Greenfield and Ribbins 1993). This relationship between ideas and the intellectual work of an individual is helpful, not least through how formal and informal networks develop as sites where ideas are debated within the context of personal careers and wider policy discourses. Core to this is how projects get funded, and how funders can control *Knowledge Production* by scripting outcomes. Therefore how intellectuals associate is important (see Burlingame and Harris 1998), and internationally there are examples of formal networks such as the UCEA in the United States of America, and BELMAS in the United Kingdom, and where historical accounts enable ideas, people and relational exchange encounters to be examined (e.g. Culbertson 1995; Gunter 2012b, 2013b).

Typologies of intellectuals have been developed and Martin (1987) argues that a criterion to distinguish one intellectual from another is whether their role is to legitimize the status quo or to critique it. This is particularly important in regard to the development and promotion of *Transformational Leadership*, whereby field intellectuals have invested their careers into the translation, development and evidence base within and for education, and have impacted in regard to policy trajectories (e.g. Leithwood et al. 2006; Leithwood and Levin 2005). Such knowledge workers have been identified as 'textual apologists' (Thrupp and Willmott 2003, p. 5), with serious concerns raised about the conceptualization and promotion of this model (e.g. Allix 2000; Smyth 1989).

However, while the participation of intellectuals in public life is acknowledged as essential by Lyon (2009), how that is read and viewed is not necessarily informed, 'when push comes to shove, the "people" will choose among themselves those they will listen to, and it may not be those with the wisest or most informed judgement' (p. 71). What is interesting are questions about in whose interests does an intellectual work, and where do they come from? (Gramsci 1971). In this sense, the contextual setting in which intellectuals are located assumes importance, where technology increasingly means that intellectuals no longer have control over ideas, and Maclean (1990) talks about the growth in 'theatocracy', and Bourdieu (see Gunter 2012c) characterizes *Le Fast Talkers*, where the sound bite and superficiality combine in modern modes of communication.

The professionalization of *Knowledge Production* in higher education with performance audits, combined with marketization through demands for grant capture with impact evidence, means that the 'media guru', 'expert', or the 'consultant' has emerged as a more modernized *knowledge actor* (see Gunter 2012c; Gunter and Mills 2016). The identification and commodification of expertise enables knowledge to be packaged in ways that are identifiable as 'relevant' and 'making a difference', and so knowledge exchange with clients provides 'recommendations towards public policies and avoid what intellectuals regularly do, namely criticizing a given social, political or even cultural condition' (Fleck et al. 2009, p. 7). In this sense, an elite form of *Knowledge Production* remains, but in ways that are marketable rather than overtly political, where Furedi's (2004) use of 'portion control' as a metaphor means that 'the knowledge that is peddled by the merchants of the *Knowledge Economy* is in fact a mundane caricature of itself' (p. 7). Consequently, there is a need not only to examine the social, political and economic location of the intellectual, but also to trouble this by shifting attention away from the person to the issue of practice.

Practices

So far the argument has been that the relationship between *knowledges*, power and practice cannot be fully explained or evidenced as a rational set of ideas abstracted from those who produce and use it, and that those who do the production and use it display the trappings of *Elitism* but face challenges from consumerism. Such arguments are deeply rooted (see Kurzman and Owens 2002), whereby Mannheim (1954 [1936]) examines the social context in which ideas are generated, and makes the case for a critical analysis of intellectual activity because without such an approach 'a large part of thinking and knowing cannot be correctly understood, as long as its connection with existence or with the social implications of human life are not taken into account' (p. 241). Consequently, I intend examining arguments that *Knowledge Production* is not only located in the library and/or the especial work of an elite caste, but is an intellectual activity open to all.

Bourdieu (1988) argues for the need to examine *Knowledge Production* through objective relations within an intellectual field rather than focus on intellectuals *per se*, but he is also very concerned about what this means for *activism* (see Bourdieu 1995). I would want to argue that the writing of an intellectual history is a form of scholarly *activism*, whereby the relations of production within a field are exposed. By mapping a plurality of *knowledges, knowings, knowers and knowledgeabilities* within and for *Knowledge Production*, there are opportunities for exposing and taking action for democratic approaches to and within *Knowledge Production*. This is based on a fundamental challenge to the certainty of progress and the dominance of rational method and scientific logic. Feminist critiques have confronted modernity and the binary nature of knowledge, for example, rational/irrational, subject/object and nature/culture. In the dichotomies presented, the male is associated with what is seen as superior and is privileged as being rational, while the female is located at the antithesis and is subordinated (Stanley and Wise 2002). Post-colonial critiques have also questioned the dominance of imperial-like methodologies (Smith 2012), combined with 'metropolitan' knowledge from the north (Connell 2007, p. 44), and as such the critiques have not only challenged but also put 'other' ways of thinking and theorizing onto the agenda.

Connell (1983) argues that there is a need to stand outside of the traditional power structures that have created and sustained intellectualism as an elite activity and see it instead as a labour process. In this sense, intellectual work undertaken by those in society who are not structurally or socially regarded as intellectuals is made visible (Gramsci 1971). This approach to democratizing *Knowledge Production* is socially and politically critical in that it highlights the exclusivities within who can speak and with what authority, and identifies how those traditionally positioned as listeners and accepters might be originators of new ideas and strategies (see Moore 2007). Therefore knowledge about and for education can be generated by children, parents and communities with political alliances and partnerships that support the process (see Apple 2013). This is important because as Connell (2007) has stated, 'social science has a broad anti-democratic heritage' (p. 230), particularly through how it is linked to imperialism and the development of corporate interests. Importantly, intellectual work can be implicated in totalitarianism, where Arendt (2009) has raised questions about the failure of social science to develop and use methodologies that recognize and give attention to inhumane catastrophes such as the holocaust, and how intellectuals did important ideas work for fascism.

If I was to write such an intellectual history, then the questions that I would need to ask are:

What intellectual activity is involved in leaders, leading and leadership?
How is this activity interrelated with practice?
How is this activity interrelated with change?
Why is this taking place, in whose interests is it happening and how may alternatives be developed?

In addition to the texts and the biographies of those who produced them, I would also want to examine the ideas, lives and contributions of those who may be othered within intellectual histories. Therefore an intellectual history of school leadership needs to give recognition to a range of important contributions: first, the challenges to narrow elite approaches to *Knowledge Production*, particularly by giving recognition to a plurality of knowledge claims, where there are different forms of 'transformation' in the understandings and practices of *Transformative Leadership* (see Smyth 1989); second, the revealing of teacher and student transformations within practice (e.g. Crowther 1997; Mitra 2008; Smyth 2006a); and third, the adoption of scholarly activist approaches in partnerships with children, teachers and wider communities where transformation connects with social justice, and leadership is a communal and shared resource (e.g. Gandin and Apple 2003; Shields 1999). Integral to this are commitments to the democratization of *Knowledge Production* through critical post-colonial and feminist approaches to the knowledge base (e.g. Blackmore 2003), and through the development of inclusive methodologies (e.g. Thomson and Gunter 2011). This approach to intellectual histories as practice means that there is a shift away from the normality of forward tracking from and to designated points of reference in time, to a focus on the current with backward tracking to examine in the intellectual resources, and purposes located within networks and contexts, which have produced and reproduced, and are producing and reproducing, *knowledges, knowings, knowers* and *knowledgeabilities*.

Dimensions of intellectual histories

The economizing of intellectual work combined with field disputes over purposes and knowledge claims means that there are important debates that continue to take place about such constructions (see McMahon and Moyn

2014). It is out of the scope of this book to engage with such debates in full, suffice to say that what my analysis has so far generated is a position that the construction and narration of an intellectual history requires consideration of both the abstraction and embeddedness of ideas, the activities of *knowledge actors* and how they are recognized and located by themselves and by others. This enables such historical accounts to be socially and politically located through a *knowledgeable polity*, where the endurance and promotion of ideas, the acclaim given to certain thinkers (and talkers) and access to intellectual work within civil society are related to the state, politics and networks. Processes of codification within *doxa* production take place within objective relations within the field, where *habitus* generates a feel for the game. The volume of projects and writings for *Transformational Leadership* do not exist because they are 'a' or even 'the' truth, but because power structures create and recreate the legitimacy of this model to enable the school leadership *doxa* of certainty and prediction to endure.

Kelley (2002) argues that intellectual histories may be located, but they are in the end dependent on texts as sources and as a means of communication, where interpretation of traces and trends is contingent, 'there are human wills behind texts, but also texts – *ad infinitum* – behind wills' (p. 311, emphasis in original). So it is vital that the creation and use of texts by field members is central to this intellectual history, but in doing so there is one significant difference. I do locate with Kelley (2002) on the limitations for our work, because some *knowledge actors* are sadly dead, and I too recognize that 'we carry on "dialogues with the dead," but the responses to our questions come mainly through texts which we can only interpret in our own words' (p. 313). However, in the intellectual history that I am developing within and through the project reported in this book I do dialogue with field members who are sadly gone, but the contemporary nature of this intellectual history means that I have been able to collect the biographies and narratives from field members who have shaped and informed knowledge claims. Hence I will draw on published texts, but also the narratives of field members, and the wider public context that makes up a *knowledgeable polity* in which *Knowledge Production* is located.

In doing so I am mindful of my own location, not least that my work depends on powerful interests, including the state, to fund it, and so I am located within and positioned in relation to this. Bourdieu (1996) is helpful in at least two main ways: first, his arguments about whose problems we address as researchers, and how in framing our own (rather than the states') research questions we need to do so 'within a scientific frame' (Bourdieu 1996, p. 239), and how we open up our projects to reflexive analysis 'in order to watch themselves when practising science' (p. 240); and second, his confrontation about position taking as a researcher, where my position like other researchers is 'to provide political action with new ends – the demolition of the dominant beliefs – and new means – technical weapons – based on research and a command of scientific knowledge, and symbolic weapons, capable of undermining common beliefs by putting research findings into an accessible form' (Bourdieu 2003, p. 36). Hence in outlining ideas, people and practices I am presenting an intellectual history as a contribution to field members in homes, schools and higher education who are working against the neoliberal *doxa* and for the reconstruction of educational leadership. In this sense, I am alongside the movement to create the 'collective intellectual' (Bourdieu 1996, p. 246) whereby interventions can be made based on scientific competence, and more importantly respectful reflexivity (see Apple 2013; Smyth et al. 2014).

In undertaking this I am aware of the vast array of material, where it is unlikely I will be able to give due attention to everything and everyone, and so examples are illustrations rather than axiomatically totemic. As an intellectual project this has been thought through over time (e.g. Gunter 1997, 1999, 2001, 2005b, 2012a), where I draw on this to present a framework for an intellectual history: *traditions, purposes, domains, contexts* and *networks*. This framework will now be deployed through Part 2 where there is a chapter on each of the five dimensions, and where the layering is developed. Following the case already made that intellectual histories are located in the practice of those who do and study school leadership, I will focus in Part 3 on four networked groupings regarding how they access and produce knowledge, use and develop *knowings*, recognize and give acclaim to *knowers*, and position and shape their *knowledgeabilities*.

PART TWO

Framing Intellectual Histories

3

Knowledge Traditions

Introduction

This chapter is focused on IDEAS. Specifically I begin with the intellectual resources that the field has developed in regard to ontological and epistemological claims made within and for knowledge exchanges. By field I mean an arena of practices where *knowledges, knowings* and *knowledgeabilities*, with cited and incited *knowers*, are drawn on, used and ignored. These ideas are written about and considered in the histories of field knowledge claims, and so the available knowledge for and developed within the field is best described as 'plural', with claims that are positivist and objective through to interpretive and subjective. Reading across the field reveals this, but attempts to settle and focus the field regarding a knowledge base is a strong feature, where particular traditions dominate.

I present five *knowledge traditions* that are resources for and within the field: *positivist scientific, behaviourist science, values, experiential* and *critical science*. Each of these will be examined, and how they are evident in this intellectual history of the field will be demonstrated through examples, not least the use of *Transformational Leadership* as a model that can illustrate the visibility of these traditions.

Experiential traditions

The doing of school leadership is as old as the various roles within formal educational organizations that have been established, and talked and written about. As Rousmaniere (2009b) states, the reality of the school principal is recent, where the shift from teacher as classroom manager to being managed by a principal is significant: 'Power relations, the delivery of educational programmes, and the texture of school culture immediately changed with the appointment of a principal' (p. 215). Within the field there are numerous examples of professionals – usually principals – voicing their experiences. This is evident in a number of ways, first, *autobiographies*: professionals write their own accounts of their working lives (Clark 1998; Evans 1999); second, *narrative interviews*: researchers invite professionals to give accounts of their working lives, (Hoffman 2009); and third, *ethnographies:* researchers work with professionals to create accounts of working lives (Southworth 1995; Wollcott 1973).

What such studies do is to put emphasis on the agency of the person to give an account and/or allow researchers to enter their working lives and examine how the organization is created (Wilkinson and Kemmis 2014). This is particularly important because research shows how principals learn the job by working with others, not least learning how not to do it, where reading and accessing research can be way down the agenda but is accelerated when professionals do their own research and then connect with research outputs (Anderson and Jones 2000).

An example of principals talking about their work is Mary Gray, a headteacher in England, in conversation with Agnes McMahon (Gray and McMahon 1997) who talks about her approach to school leadership focused on encouraging staff to contribute. A central issue for examining *Knowledge Production* is how this is learnt and accepted as a way of working with other professional colleagues. Gray gives a glimpse of this: 'Having worked for a variety of heads, I think I was astute enough and interested enough to see how other people worked and identify what approaches appeared to be successful and unsuccessful. I felt that with that experience I could succeed' (Gray and McMahon 1997, p. 25). This is the sort of *Knowledge Production* that is not normally visible, where through a narrative account the complexities within the learning process can be made visible. This is particularly important when issues of context such as type of school, location of the school and the wider policy context is engaged with (see Riley 2013). Hence Gray talks about how fourteen years on from her first appointment her role has shifted through major reforms: 'Basically I'm a managing director now. I am the curriculum leader, but I'm the curriculum leader who identifies and delegates and that is only one part of the strands of my role as head' (p. 26).

This interplay between agency and structure is historically located (Brooks and Miles 2008; Grace 1995) where the location of the school and the bigger picture of reform and policy intervention have impacted on experiential knowledge. For example, principals speak about how they are making policy work in ways that demonstrate support (e.g. Goddard 2014), while others engage with the realities in ways that trouble policy (e.g. Evans 1999; Winkley

2002). While the language of *Transformational Leadership* has entered the lexicon of school leadership, the interplay of vision with realities is central to professional accounts. For example, Bates (1999) describes the vision she developed for Lilian Baylis school in Lambeth South London following the public identification of it as 'one of the worst schools in the country' (p. 86). She recognizes the challenges of the transformation that is needed when she gives an account of going into the community and meeting people: 'I introduced myself cheerfully as the new headteacher ... several looked horrified, others looked doubtful, one looked sad, took my hand and said pityingly, "You poor cow"' (p. 87). She is able to give an account that shows improvements were made with celebrations and onward visioning.

What this story shows is that *Transformational Leadership* can enable the crisis to be engaged with, and other principals give similar stories (e.g. Clark 1998), but the majority of schools are not in such a crisis where such dramatic visioning may not be appropriate. Indeed, research with principals shows that there are different positions over time, where principals learn from experience how to build professional relationships in support of teaching and learning (e.g. Gunter and Forrester 2009; Grace 1995). Research also shows that principals tend to be multilingual (Gronn 1996) and hence may speak to the orthodoxy of *Transformational Leadership* to those who want to hear it, and can speak in other ways to different audiences. The word vision may be used, but it can be used differently according to circumstances. What the Bates (1999) account does is to show how *Transformational Leadership* is complicit with the need to identify and generate crises for change, and where it has become integrated into the learning of principals through how the normalization of crises is proactively avoided and/or responded to.

What this short analysis does is to reinforce how there is more we do not know about the experiential learning with, for and about leaders, leading and leadership than we do know, where Sugrue (2009) makes the case for more work to reveal practices. But what we do have are versions of working lives that suggest there is learning, and that it is over time and within context, and that accounts of such learning can be risky and personally challenging (see Ribbins and Sherratt 1999). While principals talk about personal commitments to transformation as a form of ongoing change and their contribution to that, the intervention of a particular form of *Transformational Leadership* is a tool for enabling their work, a language for describing their work and an approach that conforms in a public space. Both Gray and Bates talk about the tensions between educational and professional loyalties and the shifts in identity that require them to work in ways that have been developed outside of education. Gray talks about forms of professional learning as transformation, and talks about changes to business management that foretell the position that Bates is in, where transformation is meeting external demands.

The research partnership between the professional and the professor is helpful, because as Anderson and Jones (2000) argue 'raw practitioner narratives and anecdotes too often contain … unsystematic observations, and personal prejudice' (p. 430). Therefore collaborations between researching professionals who are within practice and professional researchers who are within the university mean that knowledge generation is underpinned by research methodology, and challenges the limited model of knowledge transfer from the library to the school. However, what the history of the field shows is that such partnerships are important (e.g. Gunter 1999), but in other nation states, the emphasis has been on how others outside of schools seem to know better. In this sense, the formal introduction of *Transformational Leadership* as the approved of model of leadership for change in ways that are global illuminates the trend to intervene within and fit or change accepted identities and dispositions to work in particular ways. The fracturing of personal learning is what positivist and *behaviourist* science has been designed to do, particularly by shifting from 'muddling through' to a form of certain and predictable practice, and this is where I move to next. Following this I examine how there has been a return to the experiential world through a connection with values, and how social justice agendas take a different approach through *critical science* within the leadership process.

Positivist scientific traditions

The emphasis within and for school leadership about the efficient and effective school is located in positivist methodologies. The drive to move away from common sense and learning on the job as a form of 'craft' and 'tacit' knowledge towards a model of predictable and predictive practice is evident in the adoption of a positivist ontology and epistemology regarding the organization and delivery of work outputs.

The demand for a scientific approach to the emerging field of educational administration led to the adoption of the work of F. W. Taylor where in his 1911 book, *The Principles of Scientific Management*, he outlined the importance of separating the control of work from the production of outcomes. Taylorism is about the organization as a machine where workers and managers deliver outputs according to directed, measured and ergonomic best practice. Importantly, the management decides and the workers deliver, production is divided into particular tasks and labour skills, the worker is motivated by pay, and so the speed of production increased. Scientific management had a major impact on private sector business, not least through Fordism with its emphasis on systems and control, specialization and the assembly line, and fast food restaurants with its emphasis on a production line, standardization and delivery.

This 'science' of management puts emphasis on neutral processes that determines behaviour, and as such it is transferrable across national and organizational boundaries. Within education the emphasis has been on organizational effectiveness, and how work and workers can be effectively designed and deployed. Indeed inspections such as those undertaken by Ofsted in England from 1992 are illustrative of the Taylorist time and motion studies, whereby watching a lesson enables data to be constructed, and a grade to be given that measures effectiveness. This approach to the school as an organization operates in a range of ways: first, the strengthening of hierarchy with a clear division of labour between leaders and managers, and followers as the managed; second, the organization of activity as work that can be broken down into clearly defined and measurable tasks, where everyone knows their task in the division of labour; and, third, the use of planning tools, for example, management by objectives, strategic planning and target setting.

This idea of modernized production is evident in the work of Peters and Waterman (1982), who identified the characteristics of the successful company and promoted the idea of 'excellence' through bite-sized phrases such as 'a bias for action' and 'stick to the knitting' (p. vii). This has been influential in education, where the field has produced intellectual resources to support scientific practice: the school is conceptualized as a unitary organization, and this is evident in the promotion of the effective 'self-managing' (Caldwell and Spinks 1988) or 'intelligent' school (MacGilchrist et al. 1997). The structure can be effective, for example, departments (Sammons et al. 1997), teachers and teaching can be effective (Muijs et al. 2014) and processes can be effective, for example, leadership (Harris et al. 2003). The knowledge claims are Taylorist in the sense of the production of objective characteristics that can be identified, observed, measured and improved, and this can be illuminated by the adoption of adapted forms of 'adjective' leadership (e.g. distributed, instructional, transformational) as a means through which leaders, leading and leadership can be even more effective. There is an acceptance of hierarchy; for example, distribution is about leadership being 'handed out' from the principal to others, in the sense that the delegation of tasks is based on securing efficiencies (see Gunter et al. 2013).

Behaviourist science traditions

The school leader who is trained in and adopts the right type of behaviours (or attributes) and who creates the conditions in which 'followers' can be committed to the vision outlined by the leader is located in organizational psychology. The Hawthorne studies (1924–33) was a series of experiments based on scientific management (see Mayo 1933), with findings that showed that the manipulation of the variables on a production line affecting output (e.g. lighting) were not as important as group membership and norms. This has two main legacies: first, the development of formal and informal group membership, and second, the emotional interconnection between people and their work. Both are linked to positivist approaches through the causal importance of the supervisor as the close-to-practice overseer and 'friendly face' of management.

This human relations approach to organizations impacted on education through the promotion of teams as a productive way to operate within schools, where the link with non-educational processes dominated through the adoption of team building by Belbin (1996) in business (see Everard and Morris 1985). The emphasis on knowing your own preferred way of working and how this might be corrected was helpful to efficient production, but the legacy of Hawthorne in regard to micro-politics remained a key feature for the field (see Hoyle 1982, 1999). The Hawthorne studies had shown that power worked in ways that had not been given recognition: 'Not only did the workmen control the work that they physically produced, but individual members were found to be giving incorrect reports to management on the output achieved' in order to prevent job losses, and so 'the group members agreed between themselves what was a fair day's output (neither too high nor too low)' (Buchanan and Huczynski 1997, pp. 185–6). Hence micro-politics could interrupt production, and when combined with trade unionism (e.g. lines of demarcation regarding who does what job) then production and profit could be threatened.

Behavioural science continues to dominate particularly through the influence of Barnard (1938) and Simon (1945), and is evident in key texts in educational administration (e.g. Hoy and Miskel 2013). However, the power relations within leader–follower relations remains a troubling issue, with solutions in the form of different approaches to leadership as trait (e.g. Stogdill 1974), style (e.g. Blake and Mouton 1964) and contingency (e.g. Fiedler et al. 1977). Importantly, the focus on the person through attributes and characteristics known as 'traits' has a strong legacy, particular in approaches that put emphasis on articulating standards that performance can be measured against (Gunter 2012a). Recognition for appropriately structured interactions with followers by using 'style' as a correct balance between a concern for the task and people, through to locating this within the context of a need for a more flexible 'contingent' approach, continues to be based on behaviour definition and control (See Gunter 2001).

The more recent promotion of emotional intelligence (Goleman 1996) in school leadership is a development of this, particularly through how it has enabled the assumed disruption of worker control to be reworked from manager responsibility for motivation (e.g. Herzberg 1992) and participation (e.g. Likert and Likert 1976) towards self-control. Hence schools should not only be effective in the Taylorist tradition but also humane in the sense of enabling people to feel positive about the followership demands of delivery and performance. This is particularly evident in the work on *Distributed Leadership*, whereby school improvement researchers have handled the lack of definitive cause-and-effect evidence about distribution and outputs by taking normative standpoints regarding how such a model is an imperative for change (e.g. Harris 2008). Hence functionality remains, but it has been glossed over by arguments that are the legacy of the human relations movement, where the use of emotions has enabled people to feel good about radical shifts in identity, work and values (Hartley 2010).

Values traditions

The school leader who is concerned with values that underpin professional priorities and practices is located in the thinking of Hodgkinson (1978, 1983, 1991), and in particular Greenfield's (Greenfield and Ribbins 1993) ontological and epistemological counter *doxa* to the Theory Movement in North America. The Theory Movement worked on developing a scientific approach to administration, drawing on the Taylorist and *behaviourist* ontology and epistemology in which facts and values are separated (Griffiths 1958, 1964, 1969; Halpin 1958, 1966).

The aim of the Theory Movement was to move away from what Evers and Lakomski (1996) call 'folk wisdom' (p. 2) and develop claims to support practice: 'It was expected ultimately to deliver true generalisations about schools, bureaucracies, teaching, leadership, and organisational design, and to locate these truths within justified claims on more general matters such as the behaviour of social systems' (p. 2). In addition, a second aim was to make an impact: 'The knowledge thus provided would be in a form that could readily be applied' (p. 2). Hence decision-making could be handled through a reasoning process that is concerned with 'the most efficient option' (p. 3), where Evers and Lakomski (1996) confirm how *Knowledge Production* with current school effectiveness operates within this tradition.

The Theory Movement was challenged in a range of ways, not least by the emphasis on values in educational organizations, where, as Greenfield (1988) argues, 'administrators know administration; scientists don't' (p. 137).

Here the work of Hodgkinson (1978) challenges notions of administration as a factual science and argues that it is a values-based activity, (see Greenfield 1991). What is core to these debates is the issue of decision-making, and how administrative procedures as a science fail to connect with *philosophical* considerations regarding values. This focus has remained a feature within field debates and practice (e.g. Begley and Leonard 1999; Evans 1999; Willower 1998), and here I intend focusing on Greenfield, who, in 1974, at a conference in Bristol, raised serious questions about the value-free management of Simon (1945), and he went on to question the legitimacy of the Theory Movement based on the objectivity and unity of the school as an organization.

Greenfield's (Greenfield and Ribbins 1993) thesis is that organizations exist in the subjective phenomenology of the individual and are invented social reality. Greenfield was concerned about the technicist approach of management science within North America and its impact on the preparation of administrators, and he argues that such an approach failed to enable the professional to engage with issues to do with power, moral responsibility and legitimacy. For Greenfield the power of the arts provides both a spiritual and humane engagement with issues that have dominated human thinking and activity for centuries: 'I think the most valuable form of training begins in a setting of practice, where one has to balance values against constraints – in which one has to take action within a political context' (Greenfield and Ribbins 1993, p. 257). Greenfield's challenge has been characterized as intellectual turmoil (Griffiths 1979), with personal attacks on Greenfield (Greenfield and Ribbins 1993). By the late 1960s, Griffiths (1969) argued that 'the search for one encompassing theory (if anyone is searching) should be abandoned', not least because 'we have learned that a modest approach to theory pays off. Theorizing in terms of basic understanding of administration is proving more fruitful than did the highly abstract and formal theories of a decade ago' (pp. 166–7).

The recognition of values in educational administration means that the field has approached *Transformational Leadership* with two main trajectories. The first retains the positivist and *behaviourist* science approach of causal location with the single leader, but seeks to humanize this. For example, Sergiovanni (2001) identifies the 'moral questions' involved in asymmetrical power relationships, and so 'leadership involves an offer to control. The follower accepts this offer on the assumption that control will not be exploited' (p. 14). This approach to values is particularly evident in writers who wish to humanize change management through the promotion of 'moral purpose' as key to the rationales and narratives within and for transformation (e.g. Fullan 2001). Such an approach tends to be located in what has been learnt through the *experiential knowledge tradition* through how people talk about what matters to them, and based on this there is a trend to exhort people to embrace particular types of thinking, because it is located in notions of professional values.

A second comes at this from a different direction, particularly in regard to engaging with the realities of the job. Researchers such as Gronn (2000) are less concerned with exhorting people to do or think this or that, and is more focused on how work gets done. Hence the idea of distribution is not just about delegation based on a formal division of labour, but are about recognizing that not all activity is causally linked to a leader or a manager. People can and do show initiative and make decisions, and in ways that enable the organization to be successful. Ultimately this leads Gronn (2009) to argue for a 'hybrid' approach based not only on recognizing structure and hierarchy, but also on the reality of practice within professional habits and relationships. Importantly, the relationship with science is undergoing development through the gains made in neuroscience as a resource for the field (Evers 2003), where Allix and Gronn (2005) examine the contribution to be made from leadership researchers examining the relationship between the 'human knowledge, mind and cognition' and how this relates to 'distribution socially within other knowers' and within context (p. 193).

Critical science traditions

Critical social science opens up the *positivist, behaviourist* and *values traditions* to scrutiny (see Brooks and Miles 2008). An important starting point is to examine methodologies and methods, and how projects are framed in relation to knowledge claims. Accounts tend to regard the underlying knowledge claims as narrow, whereby Watkins (1989) concludes that the literatures are 'simplistic, ahistorical, static and lacking in a sense of human agency' (p. 30). In other words, models of leadership that begin with the leader present a limited form of agency for that leader, and the emphasis on followership renders everyone else as 'others' who are regarded as 'empty' and 'barren' (Gronn 1996). The 'science' of the organization is challenged in regard to its assumed ontology and epistemology, whereby the causal relationship between the leader and the led is challenged, and an underlying goal of control is exposed. Such challenges have examined the Taylorist and Behavioural resources that the field draws on, with arguments that examine how the focus is on how the person does and could fit the organization (and fit better). Hence principals have to fit with the requirements of the school to perform, and teachers have to integrate with the principal's requirement to demonstrate the right type of performance (Ball 1994; Thomson 2009).

This is examined in a range of ways, where Blackmore (1999) argues that non-fit is engaged with as the normalized problem of the individual where external issues (e.g. family) and power structures (e.g. gender, race, class) are not recognized. This 'disciplinary technology' (Blackmore 1999, p. 49) within knowledge claims has been uncovered in a range of ways: first, a study of the intellectual underpinnings of the field, such as Acker's (1992) examination of the gendered approach to the design and conduct of the Hawthorne studies, with critiques of a range of theories that were popular in education, not least motivation and the popularity of emotional intelligence (Blackmore 2011). Second, there are challenges to current theories and models of 'good practice', not least problematizing science and *Knowledge Production*, and the interplay between the person, professionalism and values (Blackmore 1999; Gunter 2012a; Smyth 1989). Third, there are examinations of the way oppression works in regard to the intersectionality of class, gender, race and sexuality, and how identities are central to educational processes (see Blackmore 2010; Normore 2008). This latter point is significant, whereby Smyth (1993b) argues that the promotion of the school as a business through the 'self-managing' school is a scientific construction that is 'an unreal world that is remote from social relations of inequality, cultural hegemony, sexism, racism or any of the social and educational disadvantage and conflicts that surround and pervade schooling' (p. 22).

In drawing on the social and political sciences those who take up a *critical* position are concerned to both reveal and develop alternatives through a range of studies, particularly projects that are about the communication of socially just ways in which education can be organized and developed. As Bates (2006) argues 'social justice is central to the pursuit of education and therefore should also be central to the practice of educational administration' (p. 184). For example, there are large-scale studies that examine the work of teachers and children in ways that challenge accepted hierarchies and confront major social and political concerns (e.g. Apple and Beane 1999; Gandin and Apple 2003). In addition, individuals talk about their experiences of school leadership (e.g. Addison 2009; Thomson and Blackmore 2006), and provide accounts of *activism* (e.g. Jean-Marie and Normore 2008; Marshall and Oliva 2006a), where accounts are given about how and why principals are 'astute activists, ready with strategies and the sense of responsibility to intervene to make schools equitable' (Marshall and Oliva 2006b, p. 1). The argument is made that leaders are public intellectuals who must think deeply and commit to taking action regarding social justice, and do that by working for and developing 'solutions for issues that generate and reproduce societal inequities' (Dantley and Tillman 2006, p. 17).

What such analyses do is remove leadership from the property of an elite leader who does leading, and instead conceptualize professionals, parents and children as a community who can draw on and share leadership as a process for making a difference. This is illustrated by, for example, Allix (2000) who critiques functional forms of *Transformational Leadership* as a form of domination, where Foster (1986) shows that to be transformational the leadership has to be activist and shared, and so needs to be *transformative*. In this sense, social and political *activism* is integral to identity and practice for students (Smyth 2006a), for teachers (Crowther 1997), and for principals (Shields 2010). Consequently, conceptualizations of *Distributed Leadership* are concerned with practices of and opportunities for inclusion and participation (e.g. Hatcher 2005), and where anarchic theories have relevance for how power is conceptualized and practised (Gunter et al. 2013).

Methodologically this means that people's experiences and stories have validity, where alliances and associations are made public regarding projects that work for change (see Normore 2008). Hence there are accounts of partnerships between higher education and schools regarding the curriculum, pedagogy and leadership (e.g. Czerniawski and Kidd 2011; Thomson and Gunter 2006; Wrigley et al. 2012). The approach to change is through respect for *experiential knowledges* that are outside of the professional biographies and accounts of elite leaders, particularly those of children (e.g. Smyth 2006), and by working for social justice there is a commitment to emancipation through change that meets the interests of a wider group than elite interests (Foster 1986).

Integral to this work is the recognition that exchange relationships between professionals are located in micro-politics, and so power needs to be a starting point for any investigation into school leadership, and for examining the ways in which it might develop (Blase and Anderson 1995). Accessing and deploying of theories of power is therefore integral to *critical science* research, whereby the work of particular individuals is identified and used (e.g. Bourdieu, Butler, Foucault, Fraser, Freire) as a means of engaging with issues of oppression and generating a transformative agenda (e.g. Eacott 2013b; Gillies 2014; Niesche 2013, 2014; Rawolle et al. 2010; Thomson 2010a). There is a sense in which seeking to understand and explain what is going on in the reform of schools is site for legitimate and ongoing enquiry.

Dynamics of knowledge traditions

Leithwood et al. (1999) have selected and engaged with *Transformational Leadership* as a model where there was sufficient evidence to support their work on enabling school improvement and effectiveness. Based on the four 'I's of *idealized influence, inspirational motivation, intellectual stimulation* and *individualized consideration* (see Introduction), they examine this in ways that are primarily *behavioural* and *positivist*.

The *behavioural knowledge tradition* is evident in the focus on asking teachers about the principal's vision and the principal as the 'keeper of the vision' (Leithwood et al. 1999, p. 60). In studying the knowledge claims from the literatures and examining visioning in a school, Leithwood et al (1999) conclude that 'setting directions is an absolutely key task for leaders, and *Transformational Leaders* perform that task in ways that give special meaning to those directions for each member of the school' (p. 70). The account is about enabling, controlling and developing the right type of behaviours that enable the vision set by the leader to be received, interpreted, adapted and accepted. Much attention is given to what is said and done, the tone, the language and the process of extrinsic motivation that 'speaks to' someone's intrinsic motivation.

The *positivist knowledge tradition* is evident in a number of ways, not least the identification and explication of the key features of *Transformational Leadership*, through bullet points, and the use of positivist methods to identify professional acceptance of this model. In addition, the conceptualization of the school as a unitary organization where predictability is a necessity is important, and here Leithwood et al. (1999) join with school effectiveness in the endorsement of high-reliability organizations. What it means is that the school is equated with a machine, where goal utility and achievement is a key feature, because non-delivery is at best a 'breakdown' that can be fixed, but at worst is a disaster that should be equated with failures that the public would not accept if repeated over and over again (e.g. airplane crashes).

Values are located in this account, whereby the approach taken is about processes rather than the substantive focus of those processes. Hence, if a school is to be a learning organization then the pertinent values are openness, toleration, speculation and interconnectedness. The links with pedagogy are limited, whereby children are the objects upon which adults impact, and demonstrate compliance with the vision. Gold et al. (2003) present an examination of the situation in England, and make claims that values are integral to principal practice as leaders, particularly through their concern to develop participative cultures and processes within teams. However, Wright (2001, 2003) argues that these are second-order values, where more fundamental first-order values are about the purposes of education in regard to inclusion and exclusion (see Hodgkinson 1991). This is where there is a parting of the ways in regard to *knowledge traditions*.

While power is integral to the Leithwood et al. (1999) model of *Transformational Leadership*, the relationship between power processes and oppression are not featured, and so issues of compliance in general and specific structures such as gender, race and class are disconnected from transformation as a form of *activism*. In order to embrace this, the reader would have to leave Leithwood et al. (1999), and examine how power actually works in principal–teacher exchange relationships (Blase and Anderson 1995). And go further than this and engage with social justice accounts of *Transformational Leadership* as *Transformative Leadership*, where Shields (2010) argues that the job is not just about test results, but 'it is the essential work of the educational leader to create learning contexts or communities in which social, political, and cultural capital is enhanced in such a way as to provide equity of opportunity for students as they take their place as contributing members of society' (p. 572). Shields (2010) examines the shared links to advocacy and morality between *Transformation* and *Transformative*, and the confusions that can take place in the lexicon, but shows how the latter is more concerned with *activism* and rights than organizational structures and cultures. Leadership is not the property of a leader who 'must' and 'should' behave in relation to followers within the rationality of a unitary organization, but instead is a shared resource for all to engage in. Forms of democratic leadership are recognized as important for the field (e.g. Woods 2005), with some reported studies (e.g. Karagiorgi 2011; San Antonio 2008) but clearly a need to capture more examples (Blase and Anderson 1995). This approach to *Transformative Leadership* draws on *experiential, values* and *critical science knowledge traditions* that interconnect experiences of oppression with commitments to political and social change, which utilize the methodologies of *critical science* to both expose and intervene in educational practices (see Marshall and Oliva 2006a).

Summary

The *knowledge traditions* within the field show plurality, but the field is dominated by conceptualizations that are concerned to secure and convince about certainty and predictability. The problem of *experiential knowledges* is recognized as a site for interventions with *positivist* and *behaviourist* ontologies and epistemologies, where *Transformational Leadership* is rooted in the school as a unitary organization. While the Theory Movement is dead, the 'scientific' approach to theory continues to determine how *Knowledge Production* is about abstraction and so the idea of theorizing from other knowledge claims continues to face exclusion (see Willower 1980). Nevertheless, counter *doxas* are evident through the challenge from the *values tradition* of education as different, and from the *critical sciences tradition* of education needing to be different or *transformative*. How and why these *doxas* are produced and engaged with is a matter for how *Knowledge Production* is located within the *knowledgeable polity*, and that is a matter for discussion later in this book. For now, a examination of the *knowledge traditions*, and exposing the conceptualization of *Transformational* and *Transformative Leaderships* to these traditions, enables the first layer of this intellectual history to be constructed. On its own, the focus on ideas is limited, and what is now necessary is to consider the purposes behind the production and engagement with these traditions.

4

Knowledge Purposes

Introduction

This chapter focuses on ACTIONS. If the previous chapter was about the intellectual resources that the field has drawn on and developed, then this chapter is about the purposes of engagement with those resources – what do they offer, and why? Ideas on their own are interesting and could be epistemologically elegant, but how those ideas are accessed and impact on thinking and action within a context is significant. Ideas are various and often both useful and useless. I therefore present the need to understand the contribution of intellectual histories in illuminating and explaining *Knowledge Production* by relating the claims about ideas and practice to purposes, rationales, narratives and outcomes within the field. I will present four main purposes: *situational, functional, realist, activist*. Each of these will be examined, and again I will show how they are evident in this intellectual history of the field through the use of examples, not least the purposes of *Transformational Leadership*.

Purposes

I move this intellectual history forward by confronting the issue of intention or what *Knowledge Production* is concerned to do and achieve. Debates are evident in the literatures regarding such matters (Anderson and Jones 2000; Baron et al. 1969; Bolam 1999; Culbertson 1969), where there has often been a distinction made between different purposes. There are different positions about purposes, some are about the immediacy of 'making a difference' as the vernacular for doing, and some who are focused on linking the doing with *activism*, where making a difference is about wider political and social changes.

Fay's (1975) work is helpful in thinking this through, where he presents three approaches to the relationship between theory and practice:

Positivist social science and technological politics: the *positivist* and *behaviourist knowledge traditions* have produced *functional* dispositions about the world as it is and how they can be corrected by the removal of dysfunctions. In Fay's (1975) analysis the focus is on causation and variables where the 'ability to predict results that is the basis of the power which scientific knowledge gives' (p. 21). Such an approach hands over decisions to experts who know, and eliminates the need for debate because of what the evidence is saying, 'there is no other way that such knowledge can be useful in making practical decisions *except in an instrumental manner*' (p. 39, emphasis in original). Such instrumentalism is about how information (facts, procedures, behaviours) 'is the means by which, through certain technical operations, he [*sic*] can produce or prevent it, or in the case of systems over which he has not control, how he can prepare himself in order to mitigate its effects' (p. 39).

Interpretive Social Science: the *experiential* and *values knowledge traditions* have produced *situational* and *realist* dispositions about experiences and reflexive learning. For Fay (1975) the focus is on developing meanings of the world with 'attempts to uncover the sense of a given action, practice or constitutive meaning; it does this by discovering the intentions and desires of particular actors, by uncovering the set of rules which give point to these sets of rules or practices, and by elucidating the basic conceptual scheme which orders experience in ways that the practices, actions, and experiences which the social scientist observes are made intelligible, by seeing how they fit into a whole structure which defines the nature and purpose of human life' (p. 79). Such an approach locates decisions with people, and can facilitate partnerships with experts who seek to know about the realities of working lives through ethnographic approaches: 'It creates the conditions for mutual understanding' (p. 81) between people who do and who do not know each other: 'The aim of an interpretive social theory is to make possible a successful dialogue in speaking and acting between different social actors or within oneself' (pp. 81–2).

Critical Social Science: the *critical science knowledge traditions* have produced *activist* dispositions about the relationship between ideas and action. In Fay's (1975) analysis the focus is on changing the world in socially just ways, and as such it accepts interpretive approaches but goes further through a concern to understand and account for 'the sufferings and felt needs of the actors in a social group by seeing them as the result of certain structural conflicts in the social order, and its seeks to explain these conflicts' and in doing this 'tries to show that it is only by conceptualizing the social order in the way that it suggests that one can comprehend the dissatisfactions which the members of this order experience' (p. 96). Such an approach locates decisions with people, and can facilitate partnerships with experts who seek to know about the realities of working lives and to bring perspectives by connecting with theories of power: 'Theories must not simply explain the sources and nature of discontent experienced by social actors, but also must demonstrate how it is that such discontent can be eliminated by removing, in some specified way, the structural contradictions which underlie it' (p. 97).

Fay's (1975) contribution shows how particular approaches to the conceptualization of the human condition determine the type of questions to be addressed. The *knowledge traditions* cannot just be used willy-nilly, but shape what can be asked and why, and are shaped by such enquires. Therefore I now intend illuminating the four main intentional purposes that Fay's (1975) analysis has generated:

Situational: accounts of experiences and pragmatism;

Functional: improving structures, cultures, systems and people;

Realist: narrating the actualities of how people experience their work; and

Activist: working for social justice values and strategies.

I intend building on previous work (see Raffo and Gunter 2008) where rationales are about the reasons and justifications that people give for what they say and do. Rarely are there single and clear reasons given, but Raffo and Gunter (2008) identified three main rationales:

Delivery: doing what is required, usually by external and central government demands;

Localizing: interpreting, customizing and 'making things work here'; and

Democratizing: stimulating and recognizing opportunities for participation in options and decision-making.

How people talk about such rationales generates a need to examine the narratives being used. Again this is rarely clear-cut, but Raffo and Gunter (2008) have identified three main narratives:

Instrumental: how the values, ethos and organization of the school are focused on efficiency and effectiveness through targets, data, outcomes and performance. Hence school leadership is articulated through the characteristics of effective leadership.

Biographical: how the person's experience, situation and beliefs focus on what they know they can do and achieve outcomes within structures and relationships. Hence school leadership is articulated as the character of effective leaders doing leading.

Questioning: how the person's experience and values standpoint focus on questioning education policy and its likely impact, and developing alternative and more equitable approaches. Hence school leadership is articulated as challenges necessary to limit damage and work for social justice.

Rationales and *narratives* tend to have a focus on *outcomes* or what the 'end' situation is for the leader, their leading and the leadership processes. There seems to be at least three ways in which this is talked about:

Satisfaction: that an outcome has been achieved that is acceptable (or not with espoused dissatisfaction);

Measured: that an outcome has been achieved that has been performance managed through data;

Inclusive: that an outcome has been achieved through appropriate participation.

I present Figure 4.1 as a summary of the way of building an intellectual history regarding what people think they are doing and saying about the field:

	Situational	Functional	Realist	Activist
Intentions	Use of experience and pragmatism	Changes to structures, cultures, systems and people	Understanding the realities of how people experience their work	Taking action on social justice values and strategies
Rationales	Delivery focused, Localising	Delivery focused, Localising	Localising, Democratising	Localising, Democratising
Narratives	Instrumental, Biographical	Instrumental	Biographical, Questioning	Biographical, Questioning
Outcomes	Satisfaction	Measured	Inclusive	Satisfaction

FIGURE 4.1 *A summary of knowledge purposes.*

The argument that I am constructing is that a leader, doing leading and exercising leadership needs to be examined in relation to these *knowledge purposes*, and this is the focus of the next sections.

Situational

Situational purposes draw mainly on the *experiential tradition* with learning by doing and reflecting on doing, and can incorporate other traditions through formal and informal learning over time. These purposes focus on *Knowledge Production* within the realities of multifaceted circumstances that can be immediate and resolvable, and long term and challenging, and where it may not always be possible to read and assess clearly and accurately. In Fay's (1975) terms, *situational purposes* are about 'uncovering' what people have done/may do, and what this means. *Knowledge Production* may appear to be commonsensical, with not a little 'trial and error' or 'suck it and see' involved, and such approaches have a long history in the realities of human relational and exchange encounters. Indeed professional researchers have set out to make this visible through ethnographic work (e.g. Ribbins 1997a). It is possible that a person or team may not give recognition to the knowledge claims underpinning what is done, where forms of 'craft' and 'experiential' knowledge about what works is deployed, and might be enabled through particular language and motives. The embeddedness of such *Knowledge Production* may require and be supported through backward tracking that relates an account with learning, but again I need to be circumspect about the possibilities of illumination and causality (see Anderson and Jones 2000).

Let me take an example. McNulty (2005) begins his story of headship of Shorefields Community Comprehensive School in Liverpool by stating 'the school was in the worst of circumstances. We had a falling roll, poor examination results, completely dilapidated buildings, financial problems and the worst case of governor abuse of their new powers in the country' (p. 7). He completes the story by showing a turnaround in the situation: '**What a distance we had travelled in a decade!** From isolated, under resourced, devalued professionals working in appalling conditions in an area of profound social and economic disadvantage to this unapologetic, assertive, strongly collegial and visionary group who knew that attention was on them to play their part in the tide of regeneration sweeping the area' (pp. 257–8, bold emphasis in original). The account of the transformational process demonstrates the messiness and frustrations involved but also demonstrate the following:

Intentions: McNulty (2005) brings his experience to the challenges of the job, but also responds pragmatically to how his thinking and actions interplay. He tells the story of how some pupils asked him if the school was to become stricter with a new uniform, and he reflects thus: 'I did not regard myself as particularly authoritarian and had, quite frankly, given little thought to the issues the students had raised. This was, however, a great opportunity. **When students reveal their own expectations they provide an ideal starting point for improvement**' (p. 20, bold emphasis in original).

Rationales: these are delivery focused based on an explicit school improvement approach, where issues are about localized solutions to the outlined problems. Hence McNulty (2005) talks about the range of ways in which unity was created through systems and structures, and through cultural changes in relationships, with clear focus on positive messages internally and externally. Accounts are given for the reasons for what was being done, whereby professional resources are drawn upon, combined with the opportunities that presented themselves.

Narratives: these are *instrumental* in regard to how performance (from staff and student behaviours through to inspection grades) is the focus of change, with key learning messages from the experiences. The human element through stories is biographical not only with accounts of how a working consensus was established, but also how this was threatened through external coercion from gangs. The narratives are about urgency, intensity and being relentless 'we travelled on buses, broke up fights at bus stops, faced down local hooligans, complained to the police daily, petitioned Merseytravel, officers of the Authority, councillors and our MP to provide a dedicated bus service, and dealt with countless complaints from parents' (p. 84).

Outcomes: these are a sense of a road travelled over a long period of time, and as McNulty exits the job, there is a sense of satisfaction of having made a difference. This is brought home to him through both what he witnesses taking place and the external validation from Ofsted inspectors that 'the headteacher's leadership is extremely effective' (p. 257).

This one story is about how *experiential* resources are used, replenished and developed through *situational purposes* of needing demonstrable answers to seemingly endemic problems. There is no references list, but reading the story does illuminate how *positivist* and *behaviourist* resources are evident in how the situation is conceptualized and solutions adopted.

Functional

Functional purposes draw mainly from the *scientific* and *behaviourist traditions*. The intentionality is located in dealing with situations by proactively making changes, particularly by removing dysfunctions within the production processes. In Fay's (1975) terms, *functional purposes* are about using evidence and rules to control what people do, and using organizational science to predict outcomes. *Knowledge Production* is concerned with policy science through the implementation of new structures, systems and behaviours. The intention is to make interventions into *situational purposes* as a means of minimizing, co-opting or even eradicating the *experiential tradition*. Consequently, a professional can draw on scientific *knowledges* in order to secure necessary changes, where the urgency of change may claim a fit with experience, or make interventions based on a radical change imperative. The dominance of non-educational settings for this type of *Knowledge Production* means that education is a site where business models of change and development, with approved of behaviours, have colonized. The endurance of *situational purposes* has meant that more congenial policy science has been developed in the form of the Theory Movement in the 1950s and 1960s, and more recently through school effectiveness and its partner school improvement. The purposes are explicit with scientific language of efficiency and effectiveness, and *behaviourist* through work on cultures and teams, where professional researchers have recognized that need to examine the individual as leader within 'organisational functioning' (Evers and Lakomski 2013, p. 171, see also Lakomski 2005), and have presented compendiums of best practices (e.g. Hoy and Miskel 2013). Hence the underlying ontology and epistemology of *positivist* and *behaviourist traditions* have been translated and modernized into a form of predictive science for educational organizations that has been used to generate status for the profession through training and claims about causal links with outcomes.

Let me take an example. Goddard (2014) does not have a decade of crisis to articulate in the way that McNulty (2005) does, but there are some similarities in regard to biographical narrative regarding the *experiential traditional* resources that he articulates and which underpin his approach. In being the principal of Passmores Academy he gives an account of *The Best Job in the World*, particularly since he had come into the public domain through a TV 'fly-on-the-wall' documentary series, *Educating Essex*. Like McNulty (2005) he does not provide a list of references, but in describing his approach to school improvement and to leadership, he presents a form of transformation that is based on his absorption of *positivist* and *behaviourist traditional knowledges*:

Intentions: Goddard's (2014) main intention is to address the failure of teachers to aspire to headship, and he seeks to counter claims from teachers who want to stay in the classroom by arguing that the whole school is a classroom. The dysfunction of professionals not wanting to move into headship is key to a transformational project for the school and for the profession, where this is addressed through Goddard's (2014) argument that everyone in school is under pressure. In telling the story of doing an appraisal with the deputy he finds out that he is 'ruthless', and he justifies this on the basis of working on behalf of children. The head as leader, as the repository of leadership, does leading that is central to functionality, where the causal link of the principal with the conditions for learning is the key message.

Rationales: the delivery of reforms through localization is central to functional transformation, where Goddard (2014) provides a vision statement that locates the origins within *positivist* and *behavioural* sciences. Presented as a 'visual' vision and mission, he states: 'The first image I'd like you to visualise is an air traffic control tower. Air traffic controllers have no room for error. Their entire working day is structured to ensure they never fail. As professionals, they work in teams using the best technology available. Their decisions are checked and double-checked. This represents the excellence we strive to achieve' (p. 151). Following Leithwood et al's. (1999) promotion of the link between the 'high reliability organisation' and professional practice (see Chapter 3), Goddard (2014) has accepted the Taylorist approach to online production where cause and effect are close together as appropriate for a complex organization like a school. While this is not referenced in the book, it is possible to conjecture that Goddard's (2014) access to such thinking is through his documented links with the National College for School Leadership, a site of leadership training where Leithwood's research and recommendations have been very influential (Gunter 2012a).

Narratives: the coherent rationale underpinning the science of the school is delivery based on doing your best for the kids. However, this narrative is not linked to conceptualizations of the curriculum or pedagogy, but is linked to leadership behaviours. For example, Goddard (2014) presents 'The Five P's of Successful Leadership' which are listed as personality, passion, purpose, perseverance and pride, and he outlines his model of school improvement based on Gordon Ramsay's approach to turning around failing kitchens: 'The menu is obviously the curriculum. Schools suffer in the same way as do restaurants, when the curriculum is muddled, inappropriate or not focused on what's wanted or needed. Moving staff around is often what is required when you have dormant, unutilised talent' (p. 112). Overall, the link between his behaviour and the technology of outcome production means that the narratives are about delivery disconnected from the evidence about equity.

Outcomes: the account is different from that of McNulty (2005) who had to turn around a failing school in a crisis, but Goddard's (2014) account is more about ongoing transformation to the staffing, curriculum and building. A key focus is that of school ethos, where perception that things have got better is important. Measurement is a key focus of functionality, and Goddard (2014) is very clear about this, not least the personalization of the poor results in 2013. The main indicators of standards in England are public examination results, and there is an emerging tradition of removing headteachers. From Goddard's (2014) account it seems those around him supported him and the school through the crisis, where in this case subjective measurement of the leadership trumped the external data.

This one story illustrates how *positivist* and *behavioural* resources are used through *functional purposes*: some are descriptive of what needs to be done to enable continuous improvement, and some are normative about what ought to be done with predictions of outcomes based on implementing the right type of leadership. There is evidence of *experiential resources* in this story with some *situational purposes*, but generally the messages are less about responding to a crisis, and are more about how what has been done can be relatable to other professionals who can be inspired to take on the job and to be able to handle the endemic change imperative.

Realist

Realist purposes draw mainly from the *values tradition*, with an orientation towards understanding the realities of how people experience the organization and their work. In Fay's (1975) terms, *realist purposes* share the same *interpretive* conceptualization as *situational purposes* but with an additional emphasis on not only uncovering working lives but also examining what this means for values. *Knowledge Production* is concerned with the place of the subjective human within the social sciences, not only because relating change to values can explain why some changes succeed and others fail, but also because it gives parity of esteem to professionals and knowledge that otherwise could be marginalized, or rendered as 'followership'. Focusing on such purposes can be presented as a counterweight to *functional purposes*, where the realities of how people do the job and what the values are that underpin it can be challenged by asking: efficiency and effectiveness for what?

Let me take an example. Evans's (1999) project is to present an account of *The Pedagogic Principal*, where like McNulty (2005) and Goddard (2014) he is concerned with how the job gets done, but he also challenges the *Knowledge Production* processes that shape such accounts. He questions the idea that experience alone is appropriate and sufficient: 'What is called for is that quite different capacity to reflect on life, to develop a certain reflectiveness, a kind of self-reflectiveness that makes our life with children its object' (p. 124). He also rejects the Theory Movement legacy towards formulating a knowledge base, and having undertaken a doctorate in educational administration, he locates his own practice in relation to and within that of others who are participants in his project. Through his engagement with the research evidence which is fully referenced, he aligns with Greenfield: 'The work of this scholar and humanist educator influenced then and continues to influence the course and direction of my own work in educational administration' (p. v), and he goes on to say that Greenfield was the external examiner for his thesis. For Evans (1999), transformation is based on *values traditions*, where he sets out to examine and make a case for *realist purposes*:

Intentions: Evans (1999) begins with locating his position through a rejection of *positivist* and *behavioural science traditions* on the basis that there is a need to put values at the core of research; and *critical science traditions* on the basis that while values feature strongly such sources are not clearly or appropriately rooted in classrooms. In adopting *realist purposes* Evans (1999) is making the case for pedagogy to be the focus of *educational leadership*, where he sets out to shift attention away from abstractions towards practice where 'this study aims to show phenomenologically, *at the level of actual practice*, the important difference that pedagogical values make to the actual practice of educational administration' (p. 25, emphasis in original).

Rationales: Evans (1999) focuses on data where accounts of incidents generate perspectives that are presented as pedagogic moments where learning about leadership can take place in ways that are localized, but also show relatability to those who listen and engage. While McNulty (2005) and Goddard (2014) tell stories, what Evans (1999) does is to make the case that there is a need for 'descriptive, first-hand accounts of educational administration situations' (p. 27). This is because 'principals become storytellers' (p. 27) and through this process they enable the whole situation to be the focus of attention: 'The power of stories is that they engage us intellectually *and* feelingly, the head *and* the heart' (p. 27, emphasis in original). And, he goes on to say that such stories are meaningful because they generate a response: we empathize and question. In this way his rationales are democratizing as they invite and provoke contributions, where the stories about everyday incidents generate both a principal and a student perspective in ways that show different values and interpretations of the same situation.

Narratives: these are biographical and questioning in regard to the stories that are told and the challenges given to reveal the pedagogic moments of learning about and from the data. In doing so he makes the case for the rejection of a language and strategy that is based on *positivism* and *behaviourism* because the principal is actually turned into 'an organizational clinician or administrative technician than an *educator* in the full, deep sense of the word' (p. 128). Hence Evans' (1999) narratives are about how thinking through stories about practice can enable different perspectives, and hence his language is about education, doing education and experiencing education for all involved. Leadership is not about creating the conditions in which effective and efficient learning outcomes can be produced, but is a pedagogic process where reflexivity makes learning integral to relational encounters.

Outcomes: this is about both practice and research of practice, where Evans (1999) challenges the idea that principal work is separate from teaching and learning. He argues that educational administration is an extension of the classroom, where there is a need for a 'ground up' approach, and so the principal is a teacher, and is a teacher who is taught by children: 'This does not mean that we should be organizationally inept, only that we recognize that a strong administrative practice in education would be a practice suffused from the beginning by the impulse of pedagogy' (p. 129). Evans (1999) is careful to respect that principals work in difficult circumstances, where values matter a lot and where pedagogic learning is essential.

This story shows how *values* resources are used through *realist purposes*: at the core of this is the use of descriptive accounts of a situation combined with reflexive analysis to generate meanings. Hence while there is a strong affiliation with *experiential traditions* interplayed with *situational purposes*, the interrogation of the challenges facing the principal through values brings new and significant insights. Importantly, the historic legacy of the principal as moral guardian (Grace 1995; Brooks and Miles 2008) is visible, but how this plays out within context is an important contribution from Evans (1999), and is recognized as an agenda that is worth pursuing and developing (Richmon 2004;

Willower 1998). The struggle over values concerned with equity (as distinct from what Wright (2003) identifies as second-order values of organizational processes such as teamwork) is one that is exposed through conversational accounts, where some writers consider it as the basis for scholarly *activism* (see Leonard 2008).

Activist

Activist purposes draw mainly on the *critical science traditions* with a focus on the social, economic, cultural and political structures in which professional identities and work are shaped and developed. Such purposes focus on *Knowledge Production* that respects *values traditions* and *realist purposes*, with a prime focus on interrelating *experiential traditions* and *situational purposes*, with power structures that enable and disable agency, particularly in regard to professional practices that are raced, classed, gendered and sexualized. *Activist purposes* address situations through social justice strategies, where Smyth (2012) is a 'watcher' and Apple (2013) 'bears witness' to inequity and oppression, where both reveal a promise for alternative approaches to those that are normalized, by asking: normal for whom? In Fay's (1975) terms, *activist purposes* are not about accepting the silences (what has been 'shhed'), but there are forms of action where theory can be used to provide a language and an understanding that the person is not solely responsible for the situation they are in. However, as Hoffman (2009) shows, there can be a lack of agency with a sense of hopelessness and fear in acting politically within and external to the school. This requires not only illustrative cases and stories of what it means to do *activism*, but also a need to engage pedagogically with how change can and should take place, and how this makes sense to people because it is beneficial for the context in which the person is located. Recognition is given to how and why principals use their 'political acumen' in regard to social justice goals (Ryan 2010, p. 360), and this is particularly the case in regard to the ways in which race, class, gender and sexuality have been constructed and practised in such a way as to marginalize peoples and practices (Blackmore and Sachs 2007; Shields 2010).

Let me take an example. Winkley (2002) tells his story of headship of Grove School in Handsworth in Birmingham in ways that has resonance with those already engaged with (Evans 1999; Goddard 2014; McNulty 2005). There are common patterns of seeking to tell a story, to reflect on the story and to provide meaning for others to relate to and use. In reflecting on encounters with children, families and the community, he does illuminate the central location of pedagogy in how as a leader, doing leading and exercising leadership his orientation is educational, but he goes a step further. Importantly, he locates his twenty-three years as a head of this school to the wider context in which his practice is located. As a head who is concerned to work with teachers to develop the curriculum, he begins his headship at a time of a backlash against progressive child-centred learning. His educational leadership could be misinterpreted as interrupting traditional ways that parents like in favour of new ways that will produce illiterate and innumerate children. He completes his headship by locating the achievements at Grove School in relation to and in spite of the policy context that has made interventions in all schools as if they are endemically about to fail, where national standards are treating schools as if they are supermarkets, and where the key is 'commanding leadership, good test results, quality lessons based on clear blueprints' (p. 321). He identifies that while some test results show 'improvement', the attainment gap remains, and hence there is a need for a different way of thinking:

Intentions: Winkley (2002) brings his values and agency to the job, and his experiences as he grows into headship are used to inform his thinking. His *activism* is more than taking action, but is about questioning what it means to be a child and a teacher in a socioeconomic context of high levels of deprivation with resulting issues of crime. His intention is school improvement, where he engages with Rutter et al's (1979) influential text *15,000 Hours,* where the message is that schools make a difference, and he uses it to think out loud about the messages for teachers, children, resources and school ethos. Like Evans (1999) there is a concern about abstractions, and about the link between the utopian idea of the effective school and the realities of the context in which his predecessor talked more about survival than about improvement. Winkley's (2002) intentions are not about *functional purposes* for improvement, but the *activist* concerns to understand and work with the community in which the school is located, and to generate opportunities for inclusion.

Rationales: these are localizing and democratizing. While this account shares a problem-solving agenda, he also sets out to problem pose where he examines what it means to be a child in the community in which the school is located. Such children are part of a dynamic-changing context of the decline in manufacturing with resulting unemployment combined with immigration from former colonies: 'It strikes me, once again, how painful it must be to uproot yourself from one culture to enter another. Especially one that proves to be a mixed blessing: these invited guests are in no time at all seen as invaders' (p. 29). This sits alongside rationales that are about democratizing schooling, where the irony of how voice and inclusion rely on the leader is not lost on Winkley (2002). He has learnt that 'democracy in any organization and maybe especially in a school, seemed to me to need more than lip service. It was self-evident that people are infantilized in over-controlled environments. They grow emotionally and intellectually in proportion to the freedom they have to explore and fulfil their own potential. But this transformation requires careful managing' (p. 86). There is a sense in which there is a values-based political commitment underpinned with good management, rather than a business delivery plan with targets.

Narratives: these are biographical and questioning in regard to how the story of the school's change or 'revolution' over time is seen through his activist orientation to challenging what is the norm and how it might be different. So his stories are about the children, the staff, the parents and what it means to be beaten up at the bus stop or to have mental health problems worsened by poverty, and where the basics in life such as food, warmth, furniture are lacking but still vulnerable to theft. This leads Winkley (2002) to challenge the school improvement and effectiveness agenda: 'I was increasingly worried by the oversimplification of an argument that led conveniently to the view that poverty was an issue that could be largely ignored' (p. 253). He is talking about the 'no excuses' culture that has grown rapidly, and he counters this with narrative arguments: 'For even the most impassioned exponent of the education-can-solve-all-problems school had to admit that there was, in the end, some link between intake and academic achievement' (p. 253).

Outcomes: these are a sense of closure with some satisfaction at having brought dignity and caring to children, and in ways that have made a difference *educationally*. This is not benchmarked in regard to formal measurements, but based on a sense of what is valued: 'Pupils invariably seem not so impressed by the fact that you got them through a test or exam as by the fact that you *influenced* them and made them feel good about themselves in what seems, at a distance, unclear and mysterious ways' (p. 330, emphasis in original). There is something beyond data and national standards that is worth working for, and in this sense Winkley (2002) outlines his 'dissatisfaction at not having achieved what I think might have been achieved in more propitious circumstances, and regret that so much of my work has been such an exhausting struggle' (p. 330). In this sense, transformation is not based on charismatic control and visioning as a functional tool but on working to develop relationships in ways that enable pedagogies.

This story illustrates how *critical science* resources are used through *activist purposes*: issues of pedagogy and the curriculum are interplayed with children, staff, parents and community, and located in a wider structuring context in which aspirations and opportunities are sorted and resorted. Hence researchers are concerned with the curriculum and pedagogies, and how wider structures that impact on teacher and children's *Knowledge Production* need to be a focus of attention (e.g. López and Vàzquez 2008; O'Hair and Reitzug 2008; Thomson 2010b). This resonates with *activist purposes* in larger-scale projects such as democratic schools in New York (Apple and Beane 1999) and the community approach to education in Porto Alegre (Gandin and Apple 2003). What such studies show, including Grove School as a smaller scale study, is that there is evidence of *experiential* and *values* resources, and how they might be drawn on to respond to the need to meet the realities of the situation, but the commitment to *activism* means that such resources and purposes are deployed to connect the classroom and playground with heritage and context as sites where the school can make a different kind of difference.

Learning and development

The use of illustrative professional accounts regarding *purposes* enables an engagement with different intentions for *Transformational Leadership*: first, for *situational purposes* it is an individual response to events; second, for *functional purposes* it is technical interventions to control events; third, for *realist purposes* it is understanding the realities of events; and fourth, for *activist purposes* it is challenging the norms surrounding those events as *Transformative Leadership*. What those accounts also enable are perspectives about how the purpose of knowledge access and utility within professional practices are in reality multi-layered and not always coherent or obvious.

Knowledge purposes require a focus on how *knowledges* and *knowings* are being accessed and how such *knowledges* and *knowings* are actively being used to demonstrate knowledgeability. As Riehl et al. (2000) have shown this is integral to field debates, and based on previous case study work (McGinity and Gunter 2012a), this can be understood as: first, **delivery**, where approved of knowledge and knowing is assembled and applied, and this is evident in the *functional purposes* in both McNulty (2005) and Goddard (2014): second, **translation**, where knowledge and knowing produced in one setting is interpreted and transferred into education, and possibly in ways that may not be fully clear within accounts, and this is evident in the *situational* and *functional purposes* in both McNulty (2005) and Goddard (2014); third, **interruption**, where knowledge and knowing is used to question and challenge, and this is evident in the *realist* and *activist purposes* in both Evans (1999) and Winkley (2002); and, fourth, **alteration**, where knowledge and knowing is used to bring about change in the form of minor adjustments through to revolution, and this is evident in all four accounts of *knowledge purposes* but with some variations: McNulty (2005) and Goddard (2014) are focused on school improvement by relating situation with function, whereas Evans (1999) and Winkley (2002) are focused on *transformative* educational improvement by relating *realism* with equity.

This has implications for preparation and ongoing development. If preparation is in the form of training, then this assumes there is a body of knowledge that can be codified and transferred to the trainee, who can then predict outcomes through application, and so they can operationalize and see the correct outcomes. The *positivist* and *behaviourist science traditions* have been dominant in the field because they can be delivered; and where they cannot be directly applied then they can be translated and 'edufied' through language and the link with achievement. Bottery (1992) asks questions about borrowing, where he argues that translation is needed because schools are different and so a new business model 'must be moulded, adapted, re-invented almost' particularly since professional cultures require a respect for experience and training (p. 127). However, the *values* and *critical science traditions* would go further than making knowledge and knowing work and work better, not least because as Hodgkinson (1991) argues education is different. The *values tradition* requires *realist purposes*, and so Greenfield's (1978) contribution interrupted delivery and translation within *Knowledge Production*, where the emphasis is less about accommodating with business values and more about retaining fundamental educational values.

Critical science goes further, and questions whether such *values traditions* with *realist purposes* are also part of the problem, with a failure to ask serious questions about equity. For example, Ball (1995) argues for theory and its potency in bringing about alterations in thinking and doing: 'to engage in struggle, to reveal and undermine what is most invisible and insidious, in prevailing practices. Theories offer another language, a language of distance, of irony, of imagination' (p. 267). Giving recognition to interruption and alteration means that training is either not enough or not possible. The plurality in the field's knowledge resources suggests that professional learning needs to both give access and develop intellectual work in ways that support reflection on values, and critical engagement with social science theories. In addition, Eacott (2011b) makes the point that there is a need for more *activism* on the part of the profession and researchers to work on the relationship between education and leadership, not least because without such positioning *Knowledge Production* will remain outside of education.

Summary

This second layer of Actions means that *Knowledge Production* does not exist in the abstract but is or is not identified, accessed and used by *knowers* in relation to knowledgeability. This has implications for the location of *Knowledge Production* within a *knowledgeable polity,* not least through how the state actively or reluctantly intervenes in the 4Ks, and how politics and networks enable debates and silences in regard to knowledge mobilizations. How the professional is identified, trained, educated and accredited matters, particularly so in relation to the purposes underpinning such activity and how through this, the professional learns about *knowledge purposes.* Following Bourdieu (2000), there is a need to examine how professional practice as exemplified in the four accounts reveals a disposition to read, to think, to do primary research, or not. All four accounts show 'structured structures' in which practice was structured through biographical experiences, but importantly how 'structuring structures' illuminates differences through a predisposition to comply with school improvement training by Goddard (2014) through to a predisposition to claim agency with pedagogic improvement through a doctoral contribution by Evans (1999). In this sense *doxa* production is through the interplay between the agency and structure of *knowledge actors* within context, and in the next chapter, I move on to examine the *knowledge domains* that are being generated.

5

Knowledge Domains

Introduction

This chapter focuses on POSITIONS. Taking up a position is concerned with the production, protection and promotion of the *doxa* (Bourdieu 2000). Such truths are about engagement with *knowledge traditions* in relation with and to *knowledge purposes* in ways that produce claims about knowledgeability that enables exchanges. At this stage in the development of this intellectual history, my aim is to make transparent the plurality of truths within the field by scoping *knowledge domains* as the sites where *Knowledge Production* in regard to *traditions* and *purposes* plays out. I present four knowledge domains: *philosophical* where the focus is on *understanding changes*; *humanistic* where the focus is on *living changes*; *instrumental* where the focus is on *delivering change*; and *critical* where the focus is on *working for changes*. I examine how *knowledge traditions* as resources and *knowledge purposes* as intentions regarding those resources, interplay to produce positions for and about the truths of school leadership. In doing this I am mindful of the importance of change as a key feature of *Transformational* and *Transformative Leaderships*, and so I examine the implications of these four domains for how change is conceptualized and enacted.

Knowledge domains

The next layer of my analysis is about how *knowledge traditions* and *purposes* are manifest in the types of *knowledges* and ways of knowing that are evident within the field positions regarding knowledge claims. My work with Peter Ribbins enabled the development of *knowledge domains* (Ribbins and Gunter 2002), whereby we identified positions within the field regarding (a) the underlying ontology and epistemology; (b) the main concerns of those who locate here; (c) the methodologies and methods used; (d) the conceptual underpinnings; and (e) the key people and work taking place. This has been developed through a range of research (e.g. Gunter and Ribbins 2002, 2003a,b; Ribbins and Gunter 2002), and it has been tested out through analysis of teacher leadership (Gunter 2005b), reviews of research and theory (Ribbins 2003, 2006b) and conceptualization issues (Gunter 2005a). The outcome of this work has been developed in relation to the developing of this intellectual history, and is represented in Figure 5.1.

Figure 5.1 is concerned to illustrate positions regarding *knowledges* and ways of knowing in relation to: (a) *traditions*: this is represented by the vertical axis and is concerned to locate position according to whether the knowledge claims are about 'taking action' based on commitments to change and different forms of scientific knowledge, through to wider values and *philosophical* concerns about 'activity' through thinking and debating as integral to practice; and (b) *purposes*: this is represented by the horizontal axis and is concerned to locate position according to whether knowledge and knowing is about 'challenging' in the sense of problem posing as *realism* and *activism*, through to 'providing' in the sense of situational and functional problem solving.

The four positions as *knowledge domains* speak differently about change and how it is located within different approaches to 'transformation' within *Transformational Leadership*. I begin by outlining the four *domains*, before I go on to examine the implications for *Transformational Leadership*.

Understanding changes

This position is concerned with *philosophical* questions or the relationship between challenging and activities. Mainly this is focused on conceptual issues

Activity		
Philosophical understanding change	Humanistic living change	
Critical working for change	Instrumental delivering change	Provision
Actions		

(Challenge is labelled on the left side of the table)

FIGURE 5.1 *Knowledge domains (Developed from Gunter 2005a).*

such as: What does it mean to be and to do leaders, leading and leadership in education? And descriptive matters such as: What do we see and hear when we witness leaders, leading and leadership in education? In framing and approaching such questions the field tends to approach *knowledges* and *knowers*:

> *Knowledge traditions*: understanding is developed through mainly *experiential* and *values traditions*.

> *Knowledge purposes*: understanding is developed through mainly *situational* and *realist purposes*.

Consequently, the methodologies and methods used tend to be mainly through intellectual work, and, debate and argumentation within epistemic groups. Hence knowledgeability is located in the logic of ideas and arguments, which generate claims about the world as it is and should be. This can be seen as primarily about interruption and alteration, but philosophy can be used to enable delivery and translation to be located in values.

Illustrative of this position is Winkley's (Winkley with Pascal 1998) account as a primary school headteacher, where he talks about the increased emphasis on lists of standards and competences that enable the training of heads as distinct from preparation and development. He notes that the approach is technical and states that 'the real problem I have with it is that it is possible, it seems to me, to go through this kind of process, and still not be terribly good as a head'. His argument is that much of this can be picked up on the job or is the proper remit of support staff, where the concern for headteachers is in 'the creation of an ideas-creating school' that requires the professional to focus on learning (p. 236). This is what Hodgkinson (1983) identified as 'philosophy-in-action' (p. 2) where he argues that *philosophical* thinking and leadership are both possible, and they are worthwhile. Hodgkinson (1983) makes the case that all human activity is related to *philosophical* thinking because power and values are involved, but such thinking may not be recognized as relevant and so may be done by others at a distance from practice. Hence educational professionals need access to *philosophical* approaches in *order* to ensure that at least the thinking is done well and is located where the practice takes place.

Hodgkinson's work together with that of Greenfield's interruption to the Theory Movement through values is a strong intellectual tradition in the field, where *philosophical* matters are engaged with through debates about knowledge claims (e.g. Begley and Leonard 1999; Evers and Lakomski 1991; Riehl et al. 2000; Smith 2002), and those doing the job like Winkley (with Pascal 1998) raise these types of questions (e.g. Evans 1999).

However, *philosophical* work does remain a small part of the field, and it is the case that delivery has become more urgent than values-informed decision-making. Hence the promotion of *Distributed Leadership* as the counterweight to heroic forms of *Transformational Leadership* tends not to be based on *philosophical* thinking or ideas that are linked to fundamental values of humans within the organization, rather the approach is mainly functional with the caveat that any new model should not get in the way of delivery (Gunter et al. 2013).

Living changes

This position is concerned with human questions or the relationship between providing solutions and the realities of activity. Mainly this is focused on agency issues such as: What experiences do those involved in educational organizations have of leaders, leading and leadership? And, aesthetic matters such as: How can the arts help to illuminate and shape the practice of leaders, leading and leadership in education? In framing and approaching such questions the field tends to approach *knowledges* and *knowers*:

> *Knowledge traditions*: living is developed through mainly *experiential* and *values traditions*, with some *behaviourist science*;
>
> *Knowledge purposes*: living is developed through mainly *situational* and *realist purposes*, with some *functional purposes*.

Consequently, the methodologies and methods used tend to be mainly through a combination of intellectual and empirical work, particularly by giving voice to professionals to speak about what is familiar for them, what has gone well, what they think might have been done differently, and how capabilities have been challenged and developed. Examination of these stories tends to be by giving attention to behaviours, and to the functionality of humane problem solving.

Ribbins (1997b) outlines 'situated portrayal' as a methodology that he argues is different from, and more productive than, surveys by locating the headteacher within the organization as a humane practice, whereby a range of participants is expanded to include not only the headteacher but 'significant others' (p. 10) with a range of data methods – documents, interviews and observations. This leads to a range of projects: category one or the 'leader as incidental actor', whereby ethnographic work focuses on the school where the headteacher is part of the account but not the prime focus (see Ball 1981).

Category two or 'leaders in focus', whereby biographical and ethnographic work focuses on the headteacher in regard to the doing of the job (see Wollcott 1973). Category three or 'leaders as co-researchers' is a hybrid of the first two categories but has a distinctive feature whereby the approach is not only ethnographic and biographical but the relationship between researcher and researched is different whereby the headteacher is also a research partner (see Ribbins and Sherratt 1999).

Ribbins' (1997b) methodological work, together with that of researchers who have used and critically examined such approaches (see English 2006b), is an important contribution with a strong commitment in the field for ethnographic accounts of what people say and do. This is evident in Gronn's (2000) engagement with *Distributed Leadership* whereby he questions the status and potency of the leader as the causal initiator of vision, mission and practice. Gronn (2000) draws on Kerr and Jermier (1978) regarding substitutes for leadership. Teachers can and do have their own self-motivation, and are variously creative and routinized, and work within group norms whereby leadership may be attributed and temporary rather than always linked to roles and structures. Gronn (2000) is not prepared to dispense with leaders doing leading and leadership, and argues that practice is more than a form of learning as 'distributed cognition' (see Lakomski 2005). The associated link between problems and solutions is where the profession locates hierarchy, and so leaders continue to matter, but Gronn (2000) does show how distribution is not just the handing out of leadership from a leader but can be bottom up and can take place outside of the principal's scope of control. Here he reveals the situational and *realist purposes* within the habits, interdependencies and relational coordinations of activities with the possibility of spontaneity, that he calls 'conjoint agency' (Gronn 2003).

What this theorizing related to qualitative biographical and situational data does is to shift attention towards how and why work gets done within a division of labour, and how much of that process is related to the professionality and the professional interpretations of those who participate. Some studies can be longitudinal, where Møller et al. (2009) report not only on the importance of biography in relation to current practice but also how there are continuities and changes in how principals articulate what they do and why. Consequently, the issue of training can be raised, whereby the argument could be made that leadership as an exercise of power and influence over people may not be trainable but is developable. Importantly, the preferred ontology and epistemology of the person in a role are important: Does a principal with a degree in physics see the world differently and hence her/his job the same as one with a degree in English literature? Such a question is integral to *Knowledge Production*: randomized controlled trials for those disposed to laboratory experiments would be dismissed by those who are disposed to construct meaning through thinking, debate and collaborative research projects. Such matters have led researchers to examine the role of the arts in possible ways of generating reflection and reflexivity, through access to aesthetics (see Rapp 2002; Samier and Bates 2006).

Knowledge claims based on humane positions are based on a *doxa* of leadership as a lived life by those who are leaders and who do leading, where certainty and predictability may be problematic. This is recognized as important by those located as researching professionals (e.g. Evans 1999) and professional researchers (e.g. Ribbins 1997a); however, the current context in which practice is located means that unless such work is linked to *positivist* and *behavioural science* with direct *functionality*, it can be interpreted as indulgent and even be read as promoting an anti-change agenda.

Delivering change

This position is concerned with instrumentality or the relationship between solution provision and taking action. Mainly this is focused on evaluative issues such as: What impact do leaders, leading and leadership have on the outcomes from schools as organizations? And instrumental matters such as: What type of leaders, leading and leadership is needed to secure school effectiveness? In framing and approaching such questions, the field tends to approach *knowledges* and *knowers*:

Knowledge traditions: delivery is developed through mainly *positivist* and *behavioural sciences traditions*;

Knowledge Purposes: delivery is developed through mainly *functional purposes* but with some *situational* and *realist purposes*.

Consequently, the methodologies and methods used tend to be through measurement studies regarding causal connections between leaders, leading and leadership and student outcomes (e.g. Hoy 2012; Mulford and Silins 2011).

Day et al. (2009) report on a project with a remit to examine the relationship between pupil outcomes and school leadership. Such an approach is building on methodological work (e.g. Hallinger and Heck 1998; Leithwood et al. 2004; Robinson et al. 2008; Silins and Mulford 2002), whereby the case is made for a need for mixed methods used in schools over a period of time. While the UK government had invested in *living change* knowledge claims (e.g. Earley et al. 2002), this study claims a combination of literature work that establishes a baseline (Leithwood et al. 2006) with a range of quantitative and qualitative data that both shows correlations about perceptions of practice and provides accounts of those practices. Such an approach allows the team from a range of ontological and epistemological positions to make claims regarding 'statistically significant empirical and qualitatively robust associations between heads' educational values, qualities and their strategic actions and improvement in school conditions leading to improvements in pupil outcomes' (p. 2).

Methodological problems have generated gaps in knowledge, and in response to this there is a strong trend to translate what has worked in non-educational settings to schools, and so *Knowledge Production* can be highly *instrumental* through the application of exhorted good practice. In addition, there are those in elite positions in business and the school system who develop educational products where knowledge claims are popularized as necessary for improvement and effectiveness. Hence there are texts that have translated management into education (e.g. Handy and Aitken 1990), and leadership into education (e.g. Barber et al. 2011), where ideas and processes are communicated in bite-sized pieces and diagrams that can be easily interpreted and adopted. For example, Gray and Streshly (2008) confront, translate and promote Jim Collin's business model *From Good to Great* (Collins 2001), where school principals must have an 'unwavering resolve to do what must be done' (p. 6). This accounts for the use of the singular in the labelling of this *knowledge domain*; change is integral and endemic in this position, where sustaining a way of working is endemically subjected to new products that combine and recombine to produce 'new' but usually rebranded forms of practice.

Working for changes

This position is concerned with interruptive questions or the relationship between challenging and getting things done differently to the 'norm'. Mainly this is focused on critical issues such as: What happens when power is exercised as leaders, leading and leadership in education? And axiological matters such as: What does it mean for leaders, leading and leadership in education to support what is right and good? In framing and approaching such questions, the field tends to approach *knowledges* and *knowers*:

> *Knowledge traditions*: *working for change* is developed through mainly *values* and *critical science traditions*; and

> *Knowledge purposes*: *working for change* is developed through mainly *realist* and *activist purposes*.

Consequently, the methodologies and methods used tend to be mainly through intellectual, conceptual and empirical work, and debate and argumentation by individuals and within groups. Hence knowledgeability is located in arguments and data that reveal the situation in which professionals, children, parents and communities find themselves in, and by working in partnership alternative ways are developed and worked for.

Critical work tends to work for changes, by troubling existing *Knowledge Production* and the relationship with practices. There are two politically distinctive approaches towards the role of the state and public investment in 'common' and 'universal education':

Working for change from the right: I would identify this as a form of economic–political criticality that is concerned to promote neoliberal marketization in regard to public services, and hence the change that is being worked for is an espoused 'liberation' from bureaucracy through the removal of the state from educational services. The critique is ideological in regard to the failure of the state to provide the common school that is effective and efficient, and to provide universal education on the basis that children truant, and children who attend may not achieve what is required (e.g. functional literacy and numeracy) (Tooley 2000). State involvement has prevented higher standards, not least through how politics puts emphasis on deals rather than outcomes (Tooley 1995), and through investment in a professional teacher elite that is concerned with protecting its own interests through myths and arcane knowledge, and with demands for more investment (without accountability or responsibility) based on expansionist aims, and agreements that guarantee salaries disconnected from performance.

Chubb and Moe (1990) argue that the principal does not actually lead and might be considered more of a manager, and this attracts the compliant. However, in a market, the principal can be incentivized to be responsive with reward and censure, and this is particularly important for a school 'in flux' where competition means that there are 'attractive opportunities to move into new niches' which 'may require more dynamic, innovative leadership' (p. 57). Methodologically, there is a political standpoint with the use of data sets (e.g. published data on school outcomes), stories and accounts of change (e.g. Tooley 2009), and accounts by principals who are actively pursuing neoliberal change (e.g. Astle and Ryan 2008).

Working for change from the left: following Smyth (1989a) this is a form of social–political criticality that is concerned to challenge neoliberal ideology and criticality, through the advocacy of a reformed state and equitable public domain. Hence the change that is being worked for is equitable access to services and outcomes through a reformed state in the provision of publicly funded educational services. The critique is ideological in regard to how power structures promote advantage and disadvantage through how the intersectionality of class, race, gender, sexuality are recognized, challenged and eradicated through structural and cultural changes.

This form of criticality has been developed through major empirical projects as forms of policy scholarship that have examined policy texts, data sets and collected the stories of people's experiences of exclusion, and interrogated these through social theories of power. So Smyth et al. (2014) have identified 'five essential "doings" or anchor points' in such an approach: first, a form of *critical* ethnography through 'the need to *actively listen* to the lives of those who are the most adversely affected by the workings of power'; second, a form of political work, 'to take on an *advocacy position* ... towards developing a better life'; third, a form of relational esteem, 'to *represent* the lives, conditions and aspirations of informants in research in ways that are respectful and that do not end up doing further violence'; fourth, a form of self-reflexive theorizing, 'to sustain a continual *commitment to praxis* through challenging the manifest shortcomings of extant theory in light of the lives of informants ... and to draw on the best ideas from enlightened critically informed theorists'; and fifth, a form of political practice, 'to be *an activist* in working with schools, teachers, students and communities in producing "local responses" to globally generated issues – which means crafting the spaces in which people who have been marginalized can prudently and cogently *speak back* to the struggle for more just policies' (pp. 144–53, emphasis in original). What is right and good is to use politics to enable collective provision of shared needs such as education, and where the child can be educated not only for economic productivity but also for social, cultural and democratic participation.

Such research has focused on working with students (Smyth 2006a,b), teachers (Blackmore 1999) and principals (Shields 2010) in relation to socially just changes, and where the focus may not be school leaders, leading and leadership, but the problematics of what is happening to professionals means that these researchers make a contribution to understanding and explaining practice (see Gunter 2013a). In addition to revealing the problems that markets are generating in the public domain (e.g. Burch 2009), the field has developed leadership models where transformation is redefined from organizational compliance with neoliberal agendas towards bureaucratic reform and democratic goals (e.g. Apple and Beane 1999), and where practice within challenging contexts can be articulated as activist (e.g. Anderson 2009; Hatcher 2005; Hoffman 2009).

Knowledge claims based on *working for change* are based on a *doxa* of leadership as potentially maintaining or challenging established interests – such interests are identified and critiqued differently based on ideological position-ing about the state. The political right seem to be few in number in higher education in regard to the overt promotion of the market, where Tooley has been dubbed 'a twenty-first century Indiana Jones' (see Ball 2012), but busi-ness models about efficiency and effectiveness have been widely adopted in the field (see Caldwell and Spinks 1988, 1992, 1998), and in relation to profes-sional identities and practice (see Crossley 2013). The political left are located mainly in higher education, public administration and schools, where fund-ing from the social sciences enables research to be done that confronts the political right, the damage done to inclusion and reveals alternatives (Marshall and Oliva 1996; Smyth 1989). Such knowledge claims tend to be located in higher education provision of masters and doctoral degrees, where partner-ships with the profession sustain alternative claims for change than those promoted by the right as forms of neutral modernization.

Transformation and leadership

What is transformational about, for and within practice can be approached differently in regard to examining these *knowledge domains*, where leaders, doing leading and exercising leadership are able to transform something, whether that is people, systems, structures, and outcomes. By focusing on the contributions from different *knowledge domains,* the positions regarding *doxa* production that are evident in the field can be revealed, where a range of methodologies and methods can be opened for scrutiny:

> **Understanding changes**: following Hodgkinson (1983) that 'administration is philosophy-in-action' (p. 2, see above) then important insights can be made regarding the meaning of leadership and the relationship between practice and values. Importantly, there is little reference to *Transformational Leadership*, and interestingly change does not feature in detail and rarely in indexes. For example, Greenfield (Greenfield and Ribbins 1993) connects change imperatives with the drive to install scientific methods into practice, and is concerned that those who promote 'science' are doing so in ways that are damaging, particularly since 'many educational changes wrought in recent years begin to appear faddish and possibly ill-advised' (p. 38). What *philosophical* thinking, debate and the foregrounding of values do is to question the quality of thinking in the theorizing and practice of leadership, not least the shift from the organization to the individual. Greenfield (Greenfield and Ribbins 1993) argues that 'the individual is the building block of organization, not the building' (p. 58), and so change needs to be linked

to the person but not through processes of visioning and followership but through direct engagement with values. Hence there are ongoing issues to address, particularly between individual and organizational purposes, but there are no prescribed answers (Hodgkinson 1983).

There is no *doxa* production in the form of good practice or a model, because all is open to interrogation and questioning, but there is a *doxa* regarding how the person takes up a position based on espoused values that are reflexively engaged with.

Living changes: following Ribbins (1997a), the rapid changes through educational reform means that there is a need to examine the realities of principalship, what they do, what their experiences are, the challenges faced and the long hours of commitment. Change is recognized as endemic and so the imperative is to record in order to build knowledge about the doing of the job and how the role incumbent struggles with major issues, particularly values-based judgements. The texts that are produced can be read in a range of ways, but importantly researchers have increasingly read data by examining *Transactional* and *Transformational Leadership*. Day et al. (2000) show an acceptance of change and the role of transformational models in enabling success in a complex world, but they also go on to use their data to locate the study within the school improvement and effectiveness field, and in doing so propose a '*post-Transformational Leadership*' approach based on 'values-led contingency leadership' (p. 158). The demand for problem solving means there is an acceptance of organizational unity in the form of the self-managing school, and there is an imperative to abstract what is needed in the form of 'knowledge, qualities, skills or competencies that allow leaders to manage and lead successfully' (p. 171).

There is *doxa* production regarding what can be learnt from principals about how they do the job resulting in key messages about how the job needs to be done if they are to be successful in taking on site-based responsibilities, particularly the systems for increased performance and accountability.

Delivering change: following Hargreaves (1997) the rapid globally driven changes means that 'schools can no longer be castles in their communities' and also 'teachers (cannot) equate professional status with absolute autonomy' (p. 13). Consequently, it is not enough to think about what change means or to articulate the experiences of experiencing change, but instead the profession needs to learn to do change for themselves (or it will be done for and to them). The substance of the change is not the issue; it is the means through which change best takes place that matters. The technology of change can be through linear cause-and-effect models (e.g. Everard and Morris 1985), but the lessons of *living change* mean that there is a need to embrace how people understand and *feel* about change (Hargreaves 1994). Consequently, Fullan's (with Stiegelbauer 1991) contribution combines the rational and linear model of initiation, implementation and institutionalization with 'the phenomenology of change' or 'how people actually experience change as distinct from how it might be intended' (p. 4). Fullan (2001) builds on this by interplaying rationality with emotion by presenting how to lead through 'moral purpose, understanding of the change process, building relationships, knowledge building, and coherence making' (p. 137).

Doxa production is taking place, with the self-evident truth that change is endemic, and that to bring about the required changes requires a preferred approach to leaders, leading and leadership that is both leader centric which is *transformational* and leader relational by capturing commitment.

Working for changes: there are two positions here: (a) represented by Smyth (1989a, 1993a, et al. 2014) is a form of progressive radical transformation; and (b) represented by Tooley (1995, 1996, 2000, 2012) is a conservative restoration transformation.

Following Smyth (1989b) the rapid changes in education have used leadership as a 'seductive' idea and process to 'get school principals to take heed of research on "school effectiveness", and act as the visionary custodians they are supposed to be' (p. 1) in order to causally connect principals with improved outcomes. The demands for schools to change are recognized, but change imperatives, foci and processes are based on neoliberal and neoconservative ideas and the preservation of elite interests. While the philosophy of understanding is recognized as important, and the experiences of change by professionals are given direct attention, there is a rejection of change as a neutral delivery technology. Indeed technical transformations are 'rare' because the causes of school failure are more complex than the person in the top job (Barker 2005, p. 163). Therefore the approach to transformation is different: it is *transformative* and so it is less the property of an elite person who must deliver through the commitment of others, and instead is a communal resource that all can use in order to work on collaborative problems (Foster 1989). This is a form of counter-*doxa* production regarding how the self-evident truths of *Transformational Leadership* are not truthful or self-evident, and there is alternative *doxa* production regarding transformation that is socially, politically, culturally and economically *transformative*, and worth working for. Notably this *doxa* is focused on the curriculum and pedagogy, whereby access to learning and the recognition of difference are regarded as productive resources for teachers and students with parents and the community.

Following Tooley (2000) change in education has not gone far enough, and the transformation required is to remove the state and so return to a pre-welfarist economy. Hence *philosophical* thinking needs to be linked to the contributions of Hayek (1944) and Friedman (1962) (see Bottery 1992), humane accounts need to focus on the restrictions and frustrations of having to work within a rigid bureaucracy and *instrumental* delivery needs to be based on marketized systems and technologies rather than scaling up good practice across a state system. The case is made that 'the private alternative can blossom again if it is given the freedom to do so. It requires effort and space – for the family, for entrepreneurs and for philanthropy … there should be no doubt in anyone's mind that we don't need government schooling in order to satisfy educational demand' (Tooley 2000, p. 205). Therefore transformation is in how parents think about providing education themselves through choice of home schooling, and/or through private means (Tooley 2009, 2012). Rapid private and charity provision in developing countries is providing evidence of innovative and creative approaches that can be used to challenge the failure of the state to deliver in the developed world (Tooley 2000). The meeting of new aspirations and demands enables transformation in business through new products, companies and how the very rich can through philanthropy give back to communities.

There is *doxa* production that is a counter *doxa* by challenging the accepted norms of the state and dispelling myths about parents and choice, and there is a *doxa* of what Tooley (2000) calls the '3F's' of 'family, freedom and philanthropy', where leadership is located in families to choose, and in entrepreneurs and philanthropists to respond. Family and not the state is the core building block of civil society, and for what Tooley (2000) identifies as 'families who are dysfunctional' then philanthropists and not the state can provide support for children through 'substitute families', 'mentoring' and enabling choice as a practice (pp. 220–1).

All four knowledge domains consider that management is a process that is about doing, and while important for the organization and those who work within it, there is a sense that something more is needed. The *doxa* of certainty and predictability is located in Delivery, that can be constructed as undeniable, urgent and universal, where established power structures such as principalship can be co-opted to implement externally determined change, where principals are supplied with new ways of controlling the workforce and children through reworked vision and mission processes. Hence vision can be a technical statement through to an emotional commitment that can work in ways that discipline and build dependency. The construction of transformation as delivery enables critique of other knowledge domains as helpful (Living Changes) or irrelevant (Understanding Changes) or depending on ideological positioning either negatively or positively destructive (*working for changes*). The failure of delivery transformation to actually transform, or even recognition that much of the reforms may be a hoax (Ravitch 2014), means that the need to think otherwise through understanding, experience and *activism* remains on the agenda. The left–right tension remains in the field, and therefore links *knowledge domains* in regard to position to wider political and contextual matters, that I will develop in Chapter 6.

Summary

The construction of the four *knowledge domains* brings some clarity to positions within the field, and can help to generate understandings about how and why Leithwood et al.'s (1999) research and model building on *Transformational Leadership* is different from Foster's (1989) approach as *transformative*. Nevertheless, there are problems with the simplifications I have presented, where Ribbins (2003) reports on correspondence with Hodgkinson regarding our mapping work, with concerns raised about the authorial location of a research contribution within borders, and issues of equivalence – can *philosophical* thinking be the same as *instrumental* implementation? There are more issues, not least that there could well be sub-positions within each *domain*, the cross overs and hybrids in theory developing (e.g. Gronn's 2000, 2009, contribution to *Distributed Leadership*), and the way that positions can shift over time where *knowledge actors* may locate and relocate. Furthermore, there is increased recognition that some *domains* are crowded and busy (e.g. Delivering Change), and some are characterized as esoteric (e.g. Understanding Changes) and highly political (e.g. *working for changes*). This is why the location of *Knowledge Production* within a *knowledgeable polity* is important, mainly because such questions cannot be dislocated from the state, politics and networks. Methodologies and methods are about *doxa* production, and do not float free of investment and disinvestment by *knowledge actors*, including those in public office. Therefore the next layer of this intellectual history is about contexts, followed by *knowledge actors* in Chapter 7.

6

Knowledge Contexts

Introduction

This chapter is about POSITIONING. Having presented the interplay between *knowledge traditions* and *knowledge purposes* by examining *doxa* production and position taking within *knowledge domains*, I now go on to examine the structuring of positioning. The practices of researchers and professionals are located within and shaped by a range of *knowledge contexts* that constrain and enable in ways that are complex and embedded. I intend articulating four main 'meta-structures' as narratives that connect power structures to practice and practice to power: *Civic Welfarism, Neoliberalism, Neoconservativism* and *Elitism*. Each of these and their contribution to the shaping of intellectual histories will be examined, not least through the globalization of education policy processes and how public policies draw upon particular types of *knowledges, knowings, knowers* and *knowledgeabilities*. Again I will use *Transformational Leadership* as an illuminative example of how power processes shape thinking and discourse regarding what educational leadership is about and why it is important, and how it should be conducted.

Contexts

Identity formation and development within a reforming policy context continues to be a focus of research, with important outcomes regarding what it means to take up a position and to be positioned in ways that are historically and culturally rooted. For example, claims for more democratic ways of working in education have a stronger purchase in some countries than in others (see Moos and Dempster 1998); and whether a country is at war or not, and issues of development make a difference (see Harber and Davies 2006). Therefore the history of the field within the nation state is important, whereby the longer history in the United States of America (see Murphy and Seashore Louis 1999) compared with the United Kingdom (see Bush et al. 1999) and the links between the two (Gunter 2013b), matters in relation to the location in time of debates about *knowledge traditions* and *purposes*, and how *doxa* production takes place within *knowledge domains*.

There are a number of features of how this has been uncovered:

Political location: public institutions impact on positioning regarding the design, licensing and remuneration of educational professionals. This is evident in a range of accounts regarding how principals have had their work and identities challenged and changed through reform imperatives and training (e.g. Ravitch 2010).

Social location: how those who inhabit professional roles have grown up, trained and been appointed at a particular time matters in relation to how they see the purposes of education, their sense of professionalism (e.g. Weindling 1999), and how the intersectionality of class, gender, sexuality and race impacts on the self, the working life and citizenship (e.g. Courtney 2014).

Economic location: the workings of the capitalist system in regard to employment, wages and confidence impacts on the relationship between education and civil society, and hence the purposes of schools as integral to the production of the labour force (e.g. Tooley 2000).

An important feature here is how professional researchers and researching professionals engage with their identities in regard to *Knowledge Production*, where accounts of schools (e.g. Fink 2000) and by principals (e.g. McNulty 2005; Winkley 2002) show how this is played out. What is required of the profession, schools, children, parents and researchers is therefore at the core of analysis for and about positioning, and I intend approaching this through globalized and powerful 'meta-structures' that I have identified as: *Civic Welfarism; Neoliberalism, Neoconservatism* and *Elitism*.

Civic Welfarism

Civic Welfarism is concerned with social security through the state underwriting potential threats to personal, family and community well-being (e.g. illness, unemployment, homelessness, old age) combined with securing equity through developing approaches to collective rights and needs (e.g. education, health) (Kildal and Kuhnle (2005). It is an ideological as well as politically pragmatic project, where the strategy is located in an underlying principle of social security based on contribution rather than means testing and personal wealth, and signals a shift from dealing with the poor as an enduring problem towards a sense of solidarity and mutuality for all in a society (Beveridge Report 1942). The 'welfare state' is the institutional means through which such welfarism has been conceptualized, developed and enacted, and where diverse political cultures and histories means that states take a range of approaches over time, and this leads Goodin (1988) to confirm that 'the "welfare state" is not itself a single, unified, unambiguous entity. It is instead a ragbag of programs, only vaguely related and only imperfectly integrated' (p. 3). Ongoing deliberations about the boundaries between the state and civil society means that there are debates about what is settled and unsettled, not least as to whether the state expands and invests or retracts and disinvests. This is particularly the case in regard to the 'common school' for all children in a neighbourhood, whereby open access enables mixing and diversity to be recognized and enabled (Fielding and Moss 2011). Illustrative of this are accounts of particular types of schools (see Hatcher 2005), where Apple and Beane's (1999) *critical* narratives of schools in New York show that schooling is integral to democratic ways of life that can only be learnt through school as an experience. Importantly, this approach to schooling is a project that is worked for rather than bought off the shelf: 'Democracy does not present an "ideal state" crisply defined and waiting to be attained. Rather, a more democratic experience is built through their continual efforts at making a difference' (p. 14).

New Right ideology, manifest in Reaganomics in the United States and Thatcherism in the United Kingdom, attacked welfarism, with criticism made of professional groups and trade unions in regard to their power base to demand additional resources and benefits in ways that did not benefit the economy, and to their ability to protect their gains as 'a state within a state'. While major reforms continue to take place with a strong privatization agenda in public services, and challenges to the idea and reality of a society based on mutuality, the idea of welfarism and civic virtues remains a strong feature in research and commentary. Importantly, this tends to be scripted against New Right arguments and successive government legislation and policies, but the arguments for the public domain (e.g. Hind 2010; Marquand 2004; Judt 2010) and equity (Dorling 2011; Wilkinson and Pickett 2009) enable the case to be restated. The school and community as a site for democratic learning in regard to values, practices and conduct has generated an approach to *Transformative Leadership* that interconnects with working for social justice. A socially *critical* approach by researchers has generated notions and realities of transformation that link values to *activism*, where leadership is not an exotic power-over process of a special charismatic person but is a resource that all can have access to and can use. Such arguments are evident in accounts of schools that function differently from traditional hierarchies (e.g. Grubb and Flessa 2006), where as Smyth (1989b) argues, 'If schools are to be the critical and inquiring communities necessary for a democratic way of life, then the leadership within them will have to be more educative and pedagogical in various ways, rather than bureaucratic and authoritarian' (p. 5). Importantly, this has encouraged work that enables the intersectionality of class, gender, race, sexual orientation to be opened up to scrutiny in regard to access to and approaches to leadership (e.g. Normore 2008).

Neoliberalism

Neoliberalism is concerned with the accumulation and security of capital. The neoliberal 'project' is not homogenous or rational, and in identifying the origins and development of ideas and strategies, Dean (2014) argues it is 'a militant movement that draws its strength and gains its frontal character from that which it opposes' (p. 151). Indeed it feeds off and scripts strategy in relation to its own contradictions, it is in Thrift's (2005) terms 'always engaged in experiment' and so it is 'perpetually unfinished' (p. 3). So examining the relationship between ideas and implementation would not get a researcher very far, particularly since more productive analysis is located in enactments through entryism into public discourses (Dean 2014). Such instabilities and incoherence have been recognized by a range of researchers (e.g. Hall 2011), leading Gray (2010) to argue that before analysing impact 'one must first reconstruct it' (p. 52).

Such an approach reveals two main features, first, *capital accumulation*, where Harvey (2005) engages with Marx's theory of 'primitive' accumulation based on competitive markets underpinned by state security for money, property and contracts. Entrepreneurialism is presented as creative and modern, open to all who are energetic and resilient, and reliant upon those who sell their labour in ways that are flexible and expendable. Increasingly self-promotion through 'crowd funding' (e.g. Gofundme; Kickstarter; Indiegogo) is the means through which cultures of competition in order to 'stand out from the crowd' are normalized, and through philanthropy in the form of 'giving back' is the means through which cultures of choice about investment and notions of who or what deserves help become the conventional means through which social and cultural projects are removed from the public.

The over-accumulation of capital, where 'surpluses of capital (perhaps accompanied by surpluses of labour) lie idle with no profitable outlets in sight' (p. 149), leads to the second feature which Harvey (2005) calls *accumulation by dispossession* (p. 137). This explains waves of privatization from the 1970s, whereby surplus capital was made productive through the capture of public assets and services (housing, water, land, health, education). *Neoliberalism* is imperialistic both in the concrete and visible sense of the fusion of political and economic aims through the acquisition and control of land and resources to meet those aims, and as 'a more diffuse political-economic process in space and time in which command over and use of capital takes primacy' (p. 26). Consequently, ways of thinking about capital accumulation are not homogeneous, and so Thrift (2005) argues against a determinism of 'a grid of power relations ... which lie under the social landscape and dictate much of what it is about' in favour taking 'seriously the idea that capitalism is "instantiated" in particular practices' and so can be thought about as 'an impulse without determinate goals, a functioning which stamps particular forms of conduct on human multiplicity' (p. 1). Therefore schools can be bought, sold, closed, in different nation states, but the ideas can travel beyond ownership to infuse and inflect not only policy decisions and delivery in organizations that are not contractually owned by private business but also the communities and families that take on such forms of thinking and doing.

Neoliberalism has its origins in the writings of Hayek (1944) and Friedman (1962), with more recent development through Osborne and Gaebler (1993) and Bobbitt (2002), where 'the public domain has often been reconfigured from a shared, common space into a fallow, lethargic and unproductive space' (Ward 2012, p. 76). So in Harvey's (2007) terms change required a form of 'creative destruction' (p. 3) whereby structures, cultures and professions had to be rendered in crisis or 'not fit for purpose' and imbued with self-reverential 'provider capture' in order for dispossession to take schools and ways of life away from children, parents and families. The political project around these ideas and strategizing is summed up in Prime Minister Cameron's assertion that the Thatcher legacy means that 'in a sense we are all Thatcherites now' (Robinson 2013, unpaged). Such a statement is located in the logic of neoliberal ideas and dispositions transcending political parties in government, with four substantial trends: first, the exit of wealthy elites from public systems is being further encouraged through their globalized purchasing power for their children (Spring 2012); second, the idea of private (and indeed self) education for poor families is gaining momentum (Ball 2012); third, the idea of the school independent from local democratic processes as the best model for publicly funded education is growing through charter schools in the United States, academies in England and free schools in England and Sweden (Glatter 2011); and fourth, privatization that Hatcher (2001) describes as 'endogenous' whereby schools take on business cultures and practices, and 'exogenous' where schools trade as businesses (see Burch 2009; Callahan 1962), where the growth of 'for profit' discourses and vouchers within and for 'public' education is seen not only as expansionist but also as the means through which failing private schools can enter and shelter at a time of economic crisis (Gunter 2011).

As higher education develops entrepreneurial cultures and practices, then the private funding of research impacts on what can be thought, said and done, where Ward (2012) argues *Knowledge Production* has become 'formula and technique' (p. 127) and when combined with digitization and ICT then the 'Googleization of knowledge' requires what is known and worth knowing to be searchable or 'easily transportable and quickly sellable' (p. 127). The intellectual work for and about *Transformational Leadership* has been developed with this setting, where the school as an independent business is interconnected with forms of leadership that enables a shift from funding to bidding, from a system to entrepreneurialism, where the questions asked are focused on causal links between the leader and the led (e.g. Leithwood and Levin 2005). Business agency can work through the principal as inspirational with an impact on imagination, emotion and commitment (Gronn 1996). The notion and reality of vision and mission for the effective organization in the marketplace has entered policy, training and everyday practice (Gunter 2012a). This is a model that has been open to development, so that calls for innovation and modernization have had to handle professional concerns about working with children as distinct from other types of business, and so the responsiveness of this model has enabled those made accountable for performance to adopt it in ways that do not necessarily compromise their concern to improve learning outcomes and life chances. The protection of hierarchy means that this model has been popular with international organizations (e.g. IMF and World Bank) with a clear commitment from the OECD (e.g. Pont et al. 2008a,b). Therefore if schools are to be well led for the twenty-first century (see Stoll and Fink 1996), then there is a need for forms of leadership density (Sergiovanni 2001) so that leaders within the organization can take responsibility for performance, and executive leaders can lead within systems and chains of schools through takeovers (Hopkins 2007).

Neoconservatism

The label *Neoconservatism* is from the United States (and was originally used pejoratively) (see Goldberg 2003), and while those who developed *Neoconservatism* were anti-communist and displayed animus against the social liberalism of the 1960s, it is from the 1980s onwards that they impacted on policy, not least foreign policy strategy with the Iraq war (2003) and interventions to support pro-American governments. So democracy is promoted based on notions of freedom that are collective through liberation from autocratic theocracies and political oligarchies, and individual through alliances with neoliberal notions of a limited state.

In relation to education, *Neoconservatism* is concerned with traditional imaginings of how things used to be, and so 'seek a return to a romantic past where "real knowledge," morality, and supposedly stable social order existed' (Apple et al. 2009a, p. 10). Those who locate here have ideals in the sense of protecting and enhancing belief systems, but it is mainly a reactionary commitment to revealing what has been lost through major social and political reforms. For example, in 1993 the then UK prime minister, John Major, spoke to the Conservative Party conference about 'Back to Basics':

> In our schools we did away with traditional subjects – grammar, spelling, tables – and also with the old ways of teaching them. Fashionable, but wrong. Some said the family was out of date, far better rely on the council and social workers than family and friends. I passionately believe that was wrong. Others told us that every criminal needed treatment, not punishment. Criminal behaviour was society's fault, not the individual's. Fashionable, but wrong, wrong, wrong... . And now, we must have the courage to stand up and say so and I believe that millions and millions of people are longing to hear it. Do you know, the truth is, much as things have changed on the surface, underneath we're still the same people. (Major 1993, unpaged)

Hall (2011) describes such approaches as 'unfocused anxiety' (p. 212) where there is a need to bring 'social order' through how populism and the state work together, particularly through how Major is reminding people that they already have a persuasion towards these ideas, but are unable to voice them. The growth in security and militarization is connected to this, whereby surveillance combined with attitudes such as 'if you have done nothing wrong you have nothing to fear' acts as a legitimizing process (see Saltman and Gabbard 2011). The need to speak to and mobilize a 'silent majority' who 'know best' has resonance in western-style democracies, and so the imagining and myths are designed to speak to 'everyone' in ways that create an emotional and practical response about beliefs that most people hold, and those who have strayed can sort their lives out. This approach to moderation does not prevent alliances with those who Apple (2001) identifies in the United States of America as a separate conservative group that he calls 'authoritarian populists' who are 'religious fundamentalists and conservative evangelicals who want to return to (their) God in all of our institutions' (p. 11).

The normalizing claims made by neoconservatives tend to be on matters of personal morality in regard to the recognition of and extension of rights regarding abortion, same-sex relationships/marriage and contraception, and social morality in relation to crime, punishment and prison. The emphasis is on self-discipline in regard to agreed rules within traditional institutions such as family and community. *Neoconservatism* is therefore about reconnecting with enduring virtues, values and ways of life in which 'morality reigned supreme, where people "knew their place" and where stable communities guided by a natural order protected us from the ravages of society' (Apple 2001, p. 46). Hence there are arguments that women should return to the home to undertake their traditional role as wives and mothers; children should be taught obedience and respect for their betters and elders; sexual relationships other than heterosexual marriage should be denied and indeed criminalized; and social segregation (with the structuring of advantage and disadvantage) through class, gender and race should be accepted as the norm. Importantly, there is the use of binaries (them/us, me/you) together with the promotion of fear (e.g. 'Broken Britain' has become a popular discourse) through characterizing individuals and groups as the other, as a process of constructing danger and crises.

As an educational project it is best encapsulated by concerns about issues of pedagogy and behaviour, with solutions promoted through whole class teaching, strong discipline (including corporal punishment) and the use of school uniform as the means of controlling identity (see Boyson 1975). Indeed, links to traditional institutions such as faith, military and establishment is stressed, so that the right type of values and attributes are promoted, through forms of control regarding entrance and exit, as well as the curriculum and pupil conduct. Segregation operates through biology (boy and girls schools), faith schools and class (evident in fee paying for elite schools), inflected with race and ethnic divides within and between communities. The *Civic Welfarism* project is therefore subject to criticism, whereby the common school is condemned as a site of progressive learning rather than strong teaching of basic literacy and numeracy, new lessons (e.g. personal and health education) rather than traditional subject disciplines, areas of private matters (e.g. sex education) rather than respect for family life, and behaviours that relinquish adult responsibility for child care and control. Such criticisms are evident in how schools have been identified as in need of rescue or *Waiting for Superman* (Swail 2012), where private interests are presented as superior to condemned public schools in enabling and realizing individual and parental aspirations.

This is based on forms of school leadership whereby appointment and conduct tend to be gendered, classed, aged and raced – white, middle class, middle aged and male. *Knowledge Production* is based on belief systems about what works, anchored in power structures of faith, wealth and race – it is about knowing your place in the established order. Transformation is basically about retaining what has worked, and reinstating what used to work, with arguments about preservation and custodianship. Indeed, recent reforms with the use of 'academy' and 'college' labels for schools speak of notions of symbolic status and established meanings inflected with high standards, and the endurance of 'headmaster', rather than the full adoption of 'headteacher' to reflect the entrance by women into the role, is indicative of the power of neoconservative discourses. Importantly, New Labour spoke to this community in its first white paper, whereby in *Excellence in Schools* (DfEE 1997) they presented themselves as trustworthy with the nation's children by promoting testing, advocating setting and school uniform, and stressing the importance of strong leadership. *Transformational Leadership* based on the elite leader with charisma as captured by the neoliberal agenda of the principal as entrepreneur also speaks to neoconservative traditions. This is particularly through claims that a *Transformational Leader* cannot lead with and for change without due commitment to 'moral purpose' (Fullan 2001). Such claims speak to the secularism of economic privatization of the school as a business and to the spirituality of social privatization of the school as a community of like-minded people. This interconnects with *neoconservative* sentiments about established values and morality regarding the character of the leader, whereby Fullan (2001) stresses relationships in how the principal as *Transformational Leader* builds commitment to change.

Elitism

Elitism is concerned with the preservation of structural advantage, as evidenced through control of key political, economic, cultural and social institutions: 'The core of the elitist doctrine is that there may exist in any society a minority of the population which takes the major decisions in the society' (Parry 1976, p. 30). Consequently, alliances between neoliberals and neoconservatives are enabled through a shared 'elite project' regarding protecting and enhancing interests around financial, faith, military and traditional (monarchy and aristocracy) organizations. While such alliances are not hegemonic or stable, potential rivalries and competition are moderated through two main enablers for shared vested interests: first, that while there may be democratic accountability and participatory processes, it remains the case that 'the dominant minority cannot be controlled by the majority' (Parry 1976, p. 31); and second, while claims are made regarding aspirations and opportunities for all, and are supported with illustrative biographies of social and economic mobility and co-option, it remains the case that entrance and exit are closely controlled through schooling and marriage, cultures of taste and decency, together with geographies of home, work, leisure and consumption. The majority may be given access to 'mimicry' as a colonizing process, where elites regulate and control by creating aspirations about life, family, work and income, and where the 'othered' are enabled through makeovers, credit cards and lottery tickets to be 'almost the same, *but not quite*' (Bhabha 1994, pp. 122–3, emphasis in original). The majority cannot normally take advantage of tax havens, globalized private education, or networking with the powerful in Davos. This can be best illustrated by what Kettle (2013) calls 'Downton Abbey politics' (unpaged) where a person may gaze upon and through global TV ratings give approval to patriarchy, aristocracy and *noblesse oblige,* and as such enable the reassertion of previous settlements regarding the social, economic, political and cultural structures regarding who governs.

Research shows the increased need for a different type of worker in the form of a globalized service workforce in the form of a 'managerial and professional middle class' (Apple 2001, p. 11) of brokers and deliverers. The site where this is being played out is through the condemnation and dismantling of bureaucracy. Media owners have been crucial in the construction of stories and campaigns that illustrate this, where du Gay (2005) makes the point that 'given the prevailing political and moral atmosphere, it seems almost unimaginable for a politician, say, to stand for re-election on a pro-bureaucracy ticket' (p. 2). Indeed, while different political parties enter and leave government, the productive achievements and necessity of organizational systems for administering public money and services are not necessarily noted, but instead there has been a form of settlement about the need to 'roll back the state' and liberate people from the 'dead hand' of bureaucrats who follow procedures rather than act as entrepreneurs. Making bureaucrats redundant, combined with reprofessionalizing the residue as managers, has had a number of effects. Those who have left have taken public services into the private sector, not least by joining and setting up consultancy businesses, and those who have remained have taken on private sector identities and practices, and work symbiotically with the businesses that enable this (see Gunter and Mills 2016). Where the market does not penetrate, then communities and charities may pick up the pieces as a 'big society' and so services that were once provided by the public purse (e.g. local libraries) may be retained through local volunteers. Furthermore, larger projects (health, homes, welfare, education) can be enabled through philanthropy, where wealthy individuals identify what they would like to support, make an emotional commitment (the need to give something back) and fund targeted projects that bring private benefits (Ball 2008b; Reckhow and Snyder 2014; Saltman 2010). *Knowledge Production* is focused on the structural and social power to determine what is known and is worth knowing through an entitlement to think, say and do.

Underpinning this is a mixture of beliefs and evidence about the normality of elites through eugenics. Current discourses around the Darwinian underpinnings of the 'survival of the fittest', within neoliberal competition interplayed with the 'people like us' notions of *Neoconservatism*, are rooted in claims about the gene pool and blood. Schools are places of inclusion and exclusion, where people are sorted in terms of intelligence and testing that can be linked to stereotypes, and so 'eugenics (has) "done its work" and ensconced itself firmly within policy, in institutional and classroom practices, and in the language and concepts of teaching' (Ball 2013, p. 95). Consequently, elites have a right to rule, and have this ascribed to them through voting systems and acceptance of discourses, through breeding and being at the head of the pack. Examples in current politics are Mitt Romney in the 2012 US presidential election campaign who described 47 per cent of the American people as 'welfare bums', and London Mayor Boris Johnson who made the case for a return to grammar schools and intelligence testing on the basis that elites are at the top because they are cleverer, and 'in a competitive society "the harder you shake the pack the easier it will be for some cornflakes to get to the top"' (White 2013, unpaged). In relation to education specifically, there are eugenic claims by those responsible for leading major reforms, such as Sir Keith Joseph in the Thatcher governments of the 1980s, that are focused on problem teachers, problem children, problem parents and problem communities (see Ball 2013). More recently, Dominic Cummings, special advisor to Michael Gove, former UK secretary of state for education, has claimed the domination of genes in relation to educational performance, and so investments (e.g. Sure Start in England) are a waste of public money (Wintour 2013). Consequently, whether children can benefit from *civic welfarist* public education is integral to this argument, whereby the neoliberal residualization of basic skills necessary for economic production combined with limited neoconservative moral instruction for a good life becomes common sense, particularly at times of austerity and concerns over immigration.

As a leadership project the emphasis is on those who demonstrate excellence in leadership in regard to personal qualities, and even if discredited new incumbents can replace and convince. So education policy over the past thirty years has sought to identify and replicate the 'strong leader' through new forms of selection and training. While claims are made about attracting and appointing the best, in reality there has been a narrowing of the 'professional gene pool' through condemnation of particular professional values and practices in ways that suggest abnormality and degeneracy in school leadership, and acclaim for leaders and leadership cultures from elite organizations in business and faith groups. In this sense the fit between the person and the neoliberal and neoconservative agendas has restored demands for particular traits to be recognized. In its broadest sense this links to research that seeks to identify and categorize traits such as intelligence, determination, integrity and confidence (see Stogdill 1974) in ways that guarantee self-selection into and out of appointment processes (plus resignation by and dismissal of heads who no longer fitted is normalized), and supports policy strategies whereby the crisis in public education requires special people to rescue and to lead 'independent' schools. Models of *Transformational Leadership* not only fulfil neoliberal and neoconservative economic and social requirements, but also enable the elitist project to operate (see Leithwood et al. 1999). The emphasis on organizational improvement and effectiveness generated normative claims about what needed to be done, and who might do it, and while this created a recruitment problem the solution lay in the contribution of elites, not only in taking over and setting up schools but also in what Saltman (2010) describes as the 'corporatizing of educational leadership' (p. 79).

Trends in educational reform

The four 'meta-structures' generate narratives that can be distinctive but also can allow for accommodations and alliances:

Civic Welfarism: the state can legitimize and can provide universal rights and services such as education as public and shared;

Neoliberalism: the state can provide security and safe currency, but all education provision should be in the private sector;

Neoconservatism: the state can communicate and protect key moral messages, but all education provision is a family matter; and

Elitism: the state is a site that can be controlled through entryism, service and social connections (family, school, university) where private education can secure and protect this, and where public education can be a concession that is worth making in order to retain power.

The trends in western-style democracies since the Second World War have been through the dominance of *Neoliberalism* in alliance with *Neoconservativism* and enabled through *Elitism*. While *Civic Welfarism* has been a strong feature in the immediate post-war years, the trend from the 1960s onwards has been towards the private, where families and fortunes, and gaining the upper hand, are those that matter.

Change is enabled through a combination of the law, the leverage of money and the input of celebrity cultures, and it speaks a language with tones that are respectful of people and respond to their aspirations (Apple 2006). So while the *civic welfare* model needed reform, it did not happen fast enough or in ways that shaped the discourses, and educational professionals either left or complied or saw new advantages to respond to. The crisis within and for public education is wider than education but is an issue about the 'public', particularly disaffection from politics in civil society. Consequently, Fraser (2014) challenges the positioning of all activity within the market, and in drawing on Polanyi's arguments about 'fictitious commodification' she questions whether 'society can be commodities all the way down' (p. 5). Fraser (2014) problematizes markets by recognizing the dangers to social bonds and welfare if all is a private good to be traded, and indeed the severity of the current crisis is such because the various alliances have solidified into deep and mutually reinforcing social, economic and political cleavages. It seems that the interrelationships between *Neoliberalism–Neoconservatism–Elitism* have worked within in order to dismantle *Civic Welfarism*, and have used 'inclusion' and 'making a difference for children' in ways that cannot easily be resisted or reworked, and in doing so particular children have been advantaged at the expense of others. Research and publications have revealed this, but there is no golden age to return to, because as Fraser (2014) shows, the one-sided critiques of marketization have not always given recognition to how protecting people through the state actually 'neglects injustices *within* communities, including injustices, such as slavery, serfdom and patriarchy, that depend on social constructions of labour, land and money precisely as *non*-commodities' (p. 4). In other words, public service depends on care, dedication and commitment that operate on values and not money, and this has tended to be identified as necessary but low status, and is classed, gendered and raced.

This suggests that *Transformative Leadership* that is located within but challenges *Civic Welfarism* is a helpful way forward. However, while this intellectual history of the field has given recognition to the work going on in research and practice, it is relentlessly under attack. The dominant model is *Transformational Leadership* as a construction that is a product of the interplay between *Neoliberalism–Neoconservatism–Elitism*, and is intimately linked with enabling deal making to be worked through in schools, classrooms and homes. It is a model of leadership that has status through its links with esteemed people in distinguished roles in business, faith and society, and it is about preservation by being busy co-opting others into mimicry based on the anxiety of performance. There is a need to acknowledge what it means to calculate about the self, about others and to be calculated by others, where in Gorur's (2014) terms professional practice becomes '*a world-making process*' (p. 16, emphasis in original). Research projects about education policy show the way that social, economic and political networks operate to produce and reproduce such approaches to school leadership (see Olmedo 2014). This illuminates how in order to construct forms of leadership that speak to professional traditions and modernization imperatives, there is need to shift the site of *Knowledge Production* from the library to the principal's office, an office inhabited by paid contracted *knowledge actors*; the focus of *Knowledge Production* from thinking and understanding to acquiescence and delivery; and the presentation of knowledge from text to be thought about, to bite-sized bullet points to be complied with (Gunter and Willmott 2001). This has been done through discourses of relevance through to funding regimes, not least through how much practice is deemed common sense and does not need research. The funding of research is increasingly based on approved remits, methodologies and findings, with a trend away from location in higher education into charities, business and consultancy firms.

The field has the *knowledge traditions* (*positivist* and *behavioural science*) and *purposes* (*functional*) that can be read, combined and used to engage with *experiential traditions* and *situational purposes*, with position taking within *knowledge domains* that provide the instrumentalism and quasi science to construct, hybridize and make this form of *Transformational Leadership* work. Consequently, while the rhetoric is about access and opportunity, the approach to *Transformational Leadership* actually misses the point, particularly in regard to the need to confront social justice matters within *Civic Welfarism*. Other forms of *Transformative Leadership* that are located in *values* and *critical science knowledge traditions* with *realist* and *activist purposes* continue to work on social justice and inclusion, often under the radar, in ways that are reported as productive but can be positioned as esoteric or perhaps dangerous. Indeed, Bottery (2009) has shown how the ecological crisis questions all taken-for-granted forms of education, not least how the school is a consumer of scarce resources. Importantly, this generates questions about *Transformational Leadership* of a school in a competitive economy, and whether a green form of transformation requires a different approach to provision and conduct.

Bourdieu's (2000) thinking tools are helpful in conceptualizing these trends, particularly as his empirical work and theorizations are located in a rejection of determinism. The interplay between agency and structure is important, and the argument is that position taking through *knowledge domains* and positioning through *knowledge contexts* give recognition and respect to the person (as professional, as researcher) and the structured and structuring workings of power that shape, limit and enable. Determinism suggests a form of hegemony that could be impenetrable, and indeed the language that is used can suggest this with Thatcher declaring the TINA principle or 'there is no alternative'. In addition the logic of *Neoliberalism* and the entrenched locations of *Neoconservatism* and *Elitism* mean that crisis production requires solution provision that suggests hegemony, though how this plays out within different nation states needs to be recognized (see Bates 2008; Court and O'Neill 2011; Fitzgerald and Gunter 2008; Fitzgerald and Savage 2013). Hall (2011) argues that 'hegemony is a tricky concept', and he goes on to make the point that *Neoliberalism* 'is a process, not a state of being. No victories are final. Hegemony has constantly to be "worked on", maintained, renewed and revised' (p. 127). As such the layering and over layering within policy reforms may neutralize and may even extinguish aspects of *Civic Welfarism*, but there are resiliences with opportunities to fire back when cracks appear in striving to secure hegemony. Nevertheless, there is sufficient evidence to suggest a 'hegemonic project' (Hall 2011, p. 128), where Scherrer (2014) argues that 'staying power' is linked to how 'meta-structures' such as *Neoliberalism* not only generate advantage but help to protect such advantage for and by elite groups (p. 1).

Summary

This focus on *knowledge contexts* enables the relationship between *traditions, purposes* and *domains* to be examined in relation to a *knowledgeable polity*. I now intend moving this forward by following Jessop's (2014) analysis that there is a need for researchers to stop gracing such 'meta-structures' with a life of their own; they should not be allowed to 'function phantasmagorically ... as so many ghastly, ghostly, apparently free-floating symbols, images and icons' (p. 355). Instead, there is a need to focus on what people do, think and say, and 'instead, they would be seen as anchored in (and as helping to anchor) specific social practices, organisational routines and institutions, and/ or partly constitutive of specific social identities in the wider society' (p. 355). This is important because research shows that school principals position take and are positioned in time and over time in different ways (Grace 1995; Gunter 2012a), and so there is a need to recognize that some work against the grain even if it is difficult and can be personally challenging. In addition, research continues to take place that reveals and opens up spaces for criticality in ways that speak to those who have formal roles in public education (Gunter 2014), with analysis that shows that principals can play the game in savvy ways (Thomson 2010). Hence, while the *illusio* creates opportunities for particular dispositions to be revealed, and it is helpful to see how misrecognition works in the enactment of *Transformational Leadership* (see McGinity and Gunter 2012a), it is also the case that such research shows the complexities, tensions and concerns about position taking in relation to positioning. This requires the building of this intellectual history to now move into people, their practices and the networks they inhabit, shape and use.

7

Knowledge Networks

Introduction

This chapter is about PRACTICES of, by and for *knowledge actors*. Intellectual histories are located in the social, economic, cultural and political practices of *knowledge actors* such as politicians, officials, philanthropists, professionals, researchers, parents and children, as well as the general public. Leaders, leading and leadership in educational organizations exists through what is done and done repeatedly in formal and informal ways through everyday practices, and where *Knowledge Production* constructs and supports normality and interruption. This has been central to the construction of this intellectual history so far, where a focus on and interplay between *knowledge traditions, purposes, domains* and *contexts* means that I have examined but not given prime attention to the work and contribution of particular *knowledge actors*. This chapter takes the project forward by acting as a bridge, whereby I identify and scope such practices and how *knowledge actors* locate and struggle over claims through networks, and by drawing on Bourdieu (2000) I identify and deploy what I have come to call *regimes of practice* (Gunter 2012a). Following on, I then link this to Part 3 where a set of chapters provide details of particular *knowledge networks* that are variously outside, align with and make *regimes* work. Again I will use *Transformational Leadership* as a site through which to examine *regime* production and reproduction for and within school leadership.

Actors and networks

The field of school leadership is replete with *knowledge actors*, as people who claim to have knowledge through modes of knowing, and as *knowers* they have knowledgeability. Such *knowledge actors* can be identified as children, and parents, through to ministers and professors. They variously create, access, select, use and ignore *knowledge traditions, purposes, domains and contexts*, and in doing so, they engage in practice through thinking, talking and doing in a range of ways whether sitting at a desk or riding a bike. Furthermore, the complexity of lived lives means that humans are in a dialogic location regarding simultaneously being and doing as a researcher, parent, faith member and taxpayer. I am stating the obvious because there is a need to give recognition to not only how the field of school leadership is a busy, crowded and complex one, but also how this enables power processes to be made transparent. Indeed, the interplay between agency and structure produces position taking and positioning of advantage and disadvantage in the field through power processes (see Koyama 2010). The objective exchange relations within a field take place through the staking of capitals, where some capital is worth more than others, and where some groups or 'types' are worth more than others. Parents and children are worth more as 'choosers' of schools than as citizens, and principals are worth more as chief executives than as teachers. Such matters are integral to an intellectual history, but would require several volumes in order to explicate in detail. I therefore intend focusing primarily on research as a knowledge resource, and this will enable me to examine researcher practices through the interplay between power and production.

Following Bourdieu (2000) *doxa* production is a site of positions and positioning through the staking of capitals, and where the *illusio* is evidenced as 'a fundamental belief in the interest of the game' (p. 11). Two illustrative examples from within the professional research community can illuminate this:

School leadership in schools located in areas of economic, social and political disadvantage: different positions and positioning is evident, for example, for Cutler (1998) the school is a site for improvement, whereas for Gewirtz et al. (1993) it is where educational values are threatened by marketization. What seems to be different is that those located in improvement and effectiveness research conceptualize the issue as a methodological one, where Sammons (1999) identifies how children bring a 'dowry' or 'the mix of abilities, prior attainments, and personal and family attributes' (p. xi) that have to be separated out from the measured difference of school experiences. Consequently, children can be positioned as objects upon which elite adults impact (e.g. Leithwood and Levin 2005), and can be respondents in the improvement and effectiveness agenda (e.g. Rudduck and Flutter 2004). In contrast, those who focus on educational matters, focus on what children bring to school as a resource to be used pedagogically, where Thomson (2010b) examines and unpacks a student's 'virtual school bag'. Here the positioning of children enables work to be done on their self-exclusion from the system (e.g. Smyth and Hattam 2004) and how different approaches not only bring children back in but are also pedagogically powerful (Czerniawski and Kidd 2011; Fielding 2006; Mitra et al. 2012; Smyth 2006a,b, 2011b; Smyth et al. 2008).

School leadership in schools as organizations: again positioning can be different, whereby the realities of human interactions have led Hoyle (1982) to identify micro-politics as the 'dark side of organisational life' (p. 87) and to consider what this means for practice. Debates about the school as the site of dysfunction caused by humans with organizational histories is a feature of the field, where this can be handled by enabling principals to be better players (Lindle 1999; West 1999). Indeed, this has been taken up differently in the field by either counteracting the role of the leader in tension with the subordinate by developing a democratic and participative system (e.g. Blase and Anderson 1995), or by retaining the leader-centric role but ameliorating the situation through emotional intelligence as the means to enable principals to be resilient and communicate more effectively (e.g. Harris 2007). The interplay between the wider political agenda and how this is played out locally adds to the mix of complexity regarding what is a local issue and what has been provoked through external interventions (Ball 1987; Hoyle 1999; Mawhinney 1999). More seriously the failure to act has been raised by Samier (2008) who approaches the issue from another direction in regard to how people can be silent, and 'avoid responding out of fear or moral blindness' (p. 87). This is where the limitations of emotional intelligence are evidenced, not only by revealing how manipulation works (Hartley 2004), but also how 'being eternally positive' (Blackmore 2011, p. 225) means that emotion is disconnected from power structures (Zorn and Boler 2007), where injustice is unlikely to be confronted, and so 'leaders can … be unintentionally complicit in these injustices' (Blackmore 2011, p. 225).

These two examples raise issues about the framing of projects: what questions are asked, where the silences are and how this relates to how researchers understand their role and contributions. Each example is worthy of scholarly interest and funding, but not all are afforded attention, whereby in a *knowledgeable polity* dominated by the interplay between *Neoliberalism–Neoconservatism–Elitism*, it seems that micro-politics has been 'neutralized' through the promotion of emotional intelligence within leadership training. Furthermore, student voice is increasingly about consumption with more of an emphasis on 'exit' than 'loyalty' (Hirschman 1970), and where research is taking place it is usually more about functional conformity than about empowerment. The issue of the socioeconomic location of schools is given most attention, not least in England where governments and philanthropists have invested resources to commission particular projects that focus on improving the leadership of schools 'in exceptionally challenging circumstances' (Harris et al. 2006). The game in play in England is privatization, and the logic of that game is that researchers are involved in enabling public schools to be improved in readiness for corporate takeover or failed in readiness for closure with new providers entering the gap in the market. However, research has not only exposed the power processes underpinning this (e.g. Olmedo 2014) but also challenged the limitations of the *Knowledge Production* used to support policy strategies (e.g. Thomson 2007). Therefore there is a need to get underneath this and examine the nature of academic work.

Research projects that are undertaken in higher education are the product of a number of structures and influences in relation to the agency of and with the person as researcher (see for example, Tschannen-Moran et al. 2000): first, their interests and dispositions, regarding what matters to them and their ontology and epistemology in regard to methodology; second, their education and training, regarding the skills and knowledge that they have as a researcher, and how that links to their biography such as having worked in a school prior to entering higher education; third, their personal circumstances in regard to whether they are the sole or shared financial supporter for their family, and how this links to the location of a post, and the nature of the contract (long/short term; tenure or temporary, etc.) where issues of expediency and earning a living may be a prime motivator; fourth, their credentials in relation to appointment, promotion and tenure, where their espoused claims be at a particular stage in their career and how this impacts on applications and appointments; and fifth, how researchers have had experience of leadership roles in previous or current employment impacts on how they understand and engage with those who are role incumbents in the school system. My own work on the field in the UK shows that while all of these are a feature in the biographies of knowledge workers in higher education, such career emplotments are not necessarily linear or rational, where a number of early field members accepted pay cuts to move from school leadership into higher education, and where serendipity is a factor in being in the right/wrong place at the right/wrong time (Gunter 1999, 2012a).

A further layer of complexity is located in how research projects are related to a number of features of the university as a place of research activity. This is connected to how the university locates itself regionally, nationally and internationally, and so, for example, elite research-intensive universities will have demands and expectations on the professoriate regarding the type of projects, who are legitimate funders, the location of outputs and citations

(Becher 1989). The status of education matters, and as a 'rendezvous discipline' (see Breckman 2014) it does not have an agreed body of knowledge, methodology or list of esteemed output locations. At a time of high-stakes performance audits, this can be problematic, not least through how recognition works through rituals such as disciplinary citation, and the pecking order of departments. For educational researchers, this is visceral: on the one hand, they do not do bounded disciplinary work and so are deemed to be not scholarly enough, and on the other hand, they are too scholarly by being disconnected from the relevance of everyday practice in schools. In addition, the increased management of research has been charted and analysed (e.g. Fitzgerald et al. 2012; Smyth 1995), where notions of impact are not only helpful to educational researchers regarding partnerships with the profession, but also problematic regarding the demand to demonstrate world leading status. The economizing and politicizing of research remits, design, funding and management has generated tensions in academic work regarding whether it is 'about' or 'for' something (Young 2008), where some researchers outline their role is to help change happen (Sammons et al. 2010) whereas others counter this (Ball 1995). Hartley (1998) argues that intellectual work in general is being affected by current cultural and economic changes as they challenge the validity and coherence of knowledge, and so there is a need to examine how practice is shaped.

Epistemic groups

The field of school leadership has espoused networks that academics 'sign up to' in regard to the membership of learned societies through to friendship groups. These are sites where the stresses and strains of academic work, the 'hot topics' and the unfolding identity and purposes of day-to-day work are exposed and potentially confronted. Such networks tend to be called 'epistemic groups' whereby association is through shared ontological and epistemological questions and methodologies within *knowledge traditions, purposes* and *domains*, with identified sites for communicating and working on projects. This can be in the form of groups of academics within a 'school' of education, where a programme of research and teaching that has an espoused focus is core to identity and reputation. Wider than this is how people and their projects (research and teaching) are located within national and international networks, particularly through conferences, journals and other collaborative ventures.

There are three main epistemic groupings that make a contribution to school leadership: first, the focus on how the school as an organization works through the professional practices of teachers and administrators. This is known as EA and is visible through networks such as UCEA and BELMAS, and respective journals: *Educational Administration Quarterly* (EAQ), *Educational Management Administration and Leadership* (EMAL) and *Journal of Educational Administration* (JEA). Second, the focus on school 'improvement' as a change process and school 'effectiveness' as an organizational outcome. This is known as EEIR, and is visible through the International Congress for School Effectiveness and Improvement (ICSEI), and a range of journals, for example, *School Effectiveness and School Improvement* and *School Leadership and Management*. Third, the focus on power structures and how some reforms are damaging to public education, with claims made that EA and EEIR are complicit with this, and that there are alternative approaches to reform that are located in social justice claims. This is known as CEPaLS, and is visible through special interest groups within AERA, BERA, BELMAS, and through particular groups such as New DEEL in the United States of America, and a range of journals, for example, *Journal of Education Policy, International Journal of Leadership in Education,* etc.

Research about epistemic groups is not a prime occupation of field members (see Burlingame and Harris 1998), but the work that has been done tends to examine major shifts in *Knowledge Production*. As already noted, Greenfield gave a paper at the International Intervisitation Programme (IIP) in Bristol, UK, in 1974 where he challenged the ontology and epistemology of the Theory Movement: organizations exist in subjective practices and not as abstracted objective units of analysis, and therefore values matter more than predictive science. The wrath of the field is in response to what Bourdieu (1988) identifies as 'divulging tribal secrets' (p. 5), where Greenfield (1978) gives recognition to how the field ontologically and epistemologically could not handle debate as a practice:

> People ask me if the reaction bothers me. No it doesn't. The slings and arrows of academic warfare are not unpleasant. Somewhat like St. Sebastian, I suppose, I'd rather be in pain as long as the crowd understands what the ceremony is about. But it is hard just to be written off, ignored or buried. (pp. 86–7)

Greenfield's (1978) reflection on the paper is that he seems to have provoked 'an unfortunate battle in rather poor taste which somehow demeans theory and the past glory of the field of study' (p. 83), and he argues that his lack of an invitation to the 1978 IIP is connected to the inability of the field to engage in real debate. What matters is how his intellectual contribution is socially located, where people invest capital in careers and reputations that he realizes have been undermined. Hence his intellectual contribution is also politically located through how conflict is solved by personal attacks: 'The paper began to be talked about in unscholarly ways. I discovered something about my field: its pettiness, its calcified and limited vision, its conventionality, its hostility to dissenting opinion, its vituperativeness' (p. 247).

Hodgkinson (1993) encapsulates the impact of Greenfield's work, where he 'remains a stimulating irritant to the ranks of the professoriate. For some a burr under their saddles, for others a continuing inspiration' (p. xiv). Importantly, the scholarly debates wanted by Greenfield did take place (e.g. Culbertson 1983; Gronn 1985), and the impact of his paper was different in the United Kingdom compared with the United States of America (Baron 1980). Hence fields cross nation state borders, where the impact of Greenfield in England was that he was regarded as 'knocking at an open door' in regard to his intellectual contribution, particularly since early field members had sought out support from the United States of America but had concerns about the Theory Movement (Gunter 1999).

Such internal dynamics also speak to external borders particularly through objective relations with other epistemic groups, where struggles over recognition in the field can make claims and counter claims visible. Epistemic unity can be seen as integral to defending criticism from researchers in other groups, and were debates about *Knowledge Production* in the way Greenfield's contribution illuminates could be seen as 'letting the side down'. Nevertheless, the formation and development of epistemic groups is related to border disputes, and this can be visible in terms of how positioning takes place in support or against, and how claims are framed. There is friendly cross-border traffic (e.g. Harris and Bennett 2001), but there can be intemperate denunciation where there are complaints about the 'other side' where Chapman (2005) identifies a failure of sociologists of education to do more than give 'damming attacks' (p. 18). Overall, there seem to be four major areas of border disputes:

Purposes: Ozga (1992), Gunter (1997) and Thrupp and Willmott (2003) raise concerns about the direction and level of scholarship in EA and EEIR, with others questioning purposes through an examination of Journal outputs (Fitz 1999; Gorard 2005);

Conceptual: Ball (1990a, 1995) and Morley and Rassool (1999) raise concerns about the power processes within EEIR research as being about disciplining rather than empowering the profession;

Political: Ball (1990b), Blackmore (1999), Smyth (1989a) and Thrupp (2005) raise concerns about complicity of EA and EEIR in structural power relations that deny inclusion, with Slee et al. (1998) providing a range of evidence and arguments about the dominance but failure of EEIR in regard to students and disadvantaged contexts;

Methodological: Angus (1993), Coe (2009), Gorard (2010, 2011), Slee and Weiner (2001), Thrupp (1999) and Wrigley (2004, 2013) raise concerns about the technologies of data production within EEIR, with rebuttals from this community (Muijs et al. 2011; Reynolds and Teddlie 2001; Scheerens et al. 2001; Teddlie and Reynolds 2001).

Such engagements enable field members to stake claims about and for *Knowledge Production*, and can be visible in journals (e.g. Townsend 2001) where the critiques are laid out, but the 'rules of the game' can also be explored in terms of how the debate is conducted (Thrupp 2001). The substantive issue is the failure to reply (Thrupp 2001), and whether that is because certain ontologies and epistemologies prevent replies (e.g. Willmott 1999), and when replies do take place it is on the basis that 'we don't want to be like you' (Scheerens et al. 2001).

This focus on epistemic group formation and development is integral to an intellectual history, but such debates and activities do not take place outside of the wider social, economic and political contexts within a *knowledgeable polity*. Therefore how epistemic groups are objectively related to parents, children, business, faiths and government is in need of examination, and I do this through the identification of *regimes of practice*.

Regimes of practice

Epistemic groups may play insider–outsider games about purposes and methodologies, but they do so through playing with those in other locations within a *knowledgeable polity*. Indeed parents and children are automatically identified as beneficiaries, where research is done in their name. In addition, members of business, faith and government institutions may be members of such groups, and if not are seen as people who may be enabled by *Knowledge Production* or at least need to read and take heed of findings and analysis. Following Bourdieu (1990) this activity takes place in a field as a terrain that can be mapped in regard to the fields of power and the economy, and this is presented in Figure 7.1:

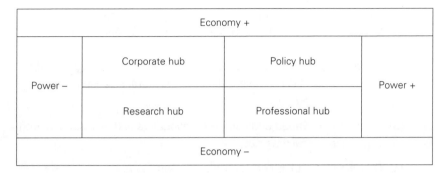

Economy +			
Power –	Corporate hub	Policy hub	Power +
	Research hub	Professional hub	
Economy –			

FIGURE 7.1 *Power hubs in Knowledge Production.*

Figure 7.1 shows that there are four main hubs that structure objective relations within the field regarding *knowledge traditions, purposes, domains, contexts* and *networks*:

Corporate hub is structured through the economy as the dominant power process. Studying this reveals that those who stake a claim here for recognition are business owners, consultancy companies, philanthropists, professionals and researchers who do the intellectual work in support of marketization of public services. This intellectual history of the field illustrates the following dynamics:

(a) *Traditions* tend to be *positivist* and *behavioural science*, with a strong emphasis on using and making interventions into *experiential knowledge*;

(b) *Purposes* tend to be *functional* and *situational*;

(c) *Domains* tend to be *instrumental*, combined with anti-state *criticality*;

(d) *Contexts* tend to be *Neoliberal* associated with *Neoconservatism* and *Elitism*; and

(e) *Networks* tend to eschew epistemic groups in favour of marketized 'what works' with the growth of EP that has links with EA and EEIR.

Research hub is structured through espoused independence from dominant economic and power processes. Studying this reveals that those who stake a claim here for recognition are professional researchers in higher education and researching professionals in practice (in schools, colleges, local and national administrations) who are doing postgraduate studies. This intellectual history of the field illustrates the following dynamics:

(a) *Traditions* tend to be respectful of *experiential knowledge* but the main emphasis is on *positivist* and *behavioural sciences, values* and *critical science*;

(b) *Purposes* are varied and can be *functional, realist, activist* and with some *situational* pragmatism;

(c) *Domains* are varied and can be *philosophical, humanistic, instrumental* and *critical;*

(d) *Contexts* tend to be *Neoliberal* associated with *Neoconservatism* and *Elitism*, but with a strong commitment from some *knowledge actors* for *Civic Welfarism*; and

(e) *Networks* tend to be located in epistemic groups but the growth of marketized popularism of what works means that some *knowledge actors* practice outside of their 'intellectual home'.

Professional hub is structured through a strong link to dominant power processes through employment in public institutions such as schools and local/state administration, but with independence from the economy through public ownership. Studying this reveals that those who stake a claim here for recognition are accredited professionals as teachers and role incumbents in posts such as 'Head of', 'Co-ordinator for' and 'Principal'. This intellectual history of the field illustrates the following dynamics:

(a) *Traditions* tend to be located in *experiential knowledge*, and how this interplays with access to and engagement with *positivist* and *behavioural sciences, values* and *critical science knowledges* through professional preparation and training;

(b) *Purposes* are primarily *situational*, but can be *functional, realist* and *activist*;

(c) *Domains* are varied and can be *philosophical, humanistic, instrumental* and *critical*;

(d) *Contexts* tend to be *Neoliberal* associated with *Neoconservatism* and *Elitism*, but with a strong commitment from some *knowledge actors* for *Civic Welfarism*; and

(e) *Networks* can be located in one or more of the three identified epistemic groups, but this may not be the case because of the endurance of *experiential knowledges* combined with the growth of marketized popularism.

Policy hub is structured through a strong link to dominant economic and power processes as a result of the mandate to govern. Studying this reveals that those who stake a claim here for recognition are politicians, advisors and officials in national/local/state governments, and this is located in their espoused commitment to represent the wider public, including a direct obligation to parents and children. This intellectual history of the field illustrates the following dynamics:

(a) *Traditions* tend to be located in *experiential knowledge*, and how this interplays with access to and engagement with *positivist* and *behavioural sciences, values* and *critical science knowledges* through access to experts;

(b) *Purposes* are primarily *situational*, but can be *functional, realist* and *activist*;

(c) *Domains* are varied and can be *philosophical, humanistic, instrumental* and *critical*;

(d) *Contexts* tend to be overtly ideological with the right and centre governments tending to be *Neoliberal* associated with *Neoconservatism* and *Elitism*; and left and centre governments tending to be *Civic Welfarism* with some links to *Elitism*; and

(e) *Networks* may or may not be located in one or more of the three identified epistemic groups, and may access popular models of the day.

I intend approaching this mapping of the terrain by presenting what I have identified as *regimes of practice* (Gunter 2012a) whereby objective relations through the staking and exchanging of capitals enable the power processes within *Knowledge Production* to be revealed.

Scoping of *regimes of practice* can be illustrated by Callahan's (1962) intellectual history, and his concern to explore 'the origin and development of the adoption of business values and practices in educational administration' in the United States of America between 1900 and 1930. In identifying a 'cult of efficiency' in the US education system, Callahan (1962) charts what he calls 'an American tragedy in education' by studying how Taylorist ideas gained currency. What he is able to demonstrate is a shift in the self-image of the school administrator and how the performance of pupils, the efficiency of the curriculum and school organization was conceptualized as a business function and product. What is being revealed in this study is a *regime of practice* that is anchored in the *corporate hub*, and which is based on *policy hub* support, *professional hub* commitment and *research hub* evidence and tools. *Knowledge Production* within the *knowledgeable polity* that is dominated by the *corporate hub* impacts on the *knowledge traditions, purposes, domains* and *contexts*, and where those located in other *hubs* are variously drawn in, excluded and absent themselves. In other words a *regime of practice* is a networked position in a field, where people associate and contract exchange relationships in order to develop and defend their interests.

My work on *regimes of practice* in the UK school leadership field in the 1990s (Gunter 2012a) shows three main regimes:

Government Regime: I labelled this the *new labour policy regime* (NLPR) that is anchored in the *policy hub* where ministers, advisors and civil servants in public office engaged in exchange relations with business, consultancy and philanthropists in the *corporate hub* selected headteachers and educationalists in the *professional hub*, and selected researchers from the *research hub*, where EEIR and the production of 'what works' entrepreneurialism and popularism were favoured.

Research Regime: I labelled this the *policy research regime* (PRR) that is anchored in the *research hub* where through research projects, located in social science methodologies and conceptual frameworks, the NLPR was subjected to scrutiny and critique. Alternative knowledge claims from within CEPaLS have been promoted through exchange relations between professional researchers and researching professionals from their respective *hubs*.

Practice Regime: I labelled this the *school leadership regime* (SLR) that was historically anchored primarily in the *professional hub*, with control over professional identity and work, and with people moving into higher education but revealing a sustained professional *habitus*. However, the privatization of education shows the strong positioning of the *corporate hub* in exchange relationships with the *policy hub*, and where professionals were expected to take on entrepreneurial dispositions and practices such as *Transformational Leadership*. Researchers from the EA and EEIR enabled this through exchange relationships within and for the NLPR. Those within EA who have resisted this have moved closer to the PRR through exchanges with CEPaLS researchers (see Gunter 2012a).

This analysis confirms Freeman and Sturdy's (2014b) conclusion that 'knowledge and policy ... (are) ... mutually constitutive' (p. 216), whereby the *policy hub* is crucial in regard to decisions about *knowledges, knowings, knowers* and *knowledgeability* within the *knowledgeable polity*. Investment through economic, cultural, social and symbolic capitals is crucial to decisions about what is known, who knows it and why it is worth knowing. Anchoring in a hub and drawing *knowledge actors* from other hubs simultaneously enables exchanges to not only show the dominance of particular knowledge workers in corporate, research and professional locations in *Knowledge Production*, but also how that dominance as a form of attributed acclaim shapes *Knowledge Production*. In doing so it impacts on internal debates, whereby Greenfield's (1978) challenge for *values knowledge traditions, realist purposes* and the *humanistic domain* has to be understood and explained through a context where *Neoliberalism* was under scrutiny by Callahan (1962), and where field members from other nation states had their practice shaped and structured through *Civic Welfarism*. Furthermore, it also impacts on external debates where critiques from within CEPaLS regarding *Knowledge Production* within EEIR and EA and regarding the limited and narrow evidence base could be sheltered through regimes that linked them with the *corporate* and *policy hubs*. This enabled professionals and professors to develop entrepreneurial skills as corporatized knowledge workers who fuelled popular ideas from business and faith interests, and policy skills as implementers brought into government institutions to lead and legitimize changes.

The dominance of *Transformational Leadership* as an appropriate school leadership model is therefore located in the formation, development and reformation of *regimes of practice*. The form of *transformation* produced in the interplay between *positivist* and *behavioural sciences* with *functional purposes*, and located in the *instrumental knowledge domain*, is rooted in the *neoliberal–neoconservative–elitist* context that structured the attack on *Civic Welfarism*, and drew on the legitimacy of EEIR and EA research to do this. Regimes anchored in the *policy hub* but also drawing in those who sought esteem and market interests from the *corporate, research* and *professional hubs*, invested in and worked and reworked this model for school leadership. Codification of the idea of the single leader, what leading means through entrepreneurship and how leadership is exercised through personal charisma combined with followership is now endemic in the practices, languages and imagination of trainers and their manuals, and how professionals present themselves to the world (in the media, to appointment panels and to auditors). When this model crashes, then it is regarded as an implementation failure and so contracts are not renewed, and where there are gaps in evidence, then role models who embody selected common-sense notions are used.

The translation of this codification often enables this effective and efficient model for excellence to float free from epistemic groupings as forms of 'good practice' that could be commodified as new products for sale, or passed on as popular approaches that professionals and professors could talk about, try out and be coached to fit into, and create a culture where thinking and talking otherwise is a heresy. While border disputes remain, the practices within the regime that have created this form of *Transformational Leadership* means that misrecognition is in evidence. Notably too much is staked in the model to accept *values* and *critical science* locations for forms of *Transformative Leadership*. The dominance of economic and power relations means that critique of these 'othered' approaches is enabled through the promotion of one best way that denies plurality, and that engaging in capital staking and exchanges outside of an original hub creates the opportunity to relocate. Hence professionals and professors learn to be consultants within the system and when made redundant they relocate within the *corporate hub*, where knowledge exchange based on fees rather than public service settings speaks to shared dispositions about privatization (Gunter and Mills 2016). This can work locally, nationally and globally, where knowledge transfer is facilitated through the production of a form of transformation that can be delivered by celebrity professors who can translate, localize and inspire. While such approaches are recognized as modern forms of imperialism, particularly from the north to the south (Connell 2007), the use of new technologies combined with the individualization of responsibility means that government regime members are hungry for solutions, and so are fed by and also feed *doxa* production.

Summary

This chapter has outlined the final layer in the construction of an intellectual history. The specific contribution has been to interplay the 4Ks with networks within a *knowledgeable polity*. Notably the association and exchange relationships between researchers in higher education with *knowledge actors* in other sites (schools, business, public institutions) can be explained through *regimes of practice*. Such regimes are formed and sustained through *hub* activity, where the contractual exchange relationships and shared *habitus* regarding the game in play have enabled *policy hub* and *corporate hub* members to dominate what is known and worth knowing about through the production and reproduction of *Transformational Leadership*. How networks of researching professionals and professional researchers have sought out/ ignored and been drawn into/excluded from such exchanges needs more analysis. Therefore, in Part 3, I intend deploying this five-level framework for an intellectual history in regard to four main networks, and in doing so, I am able to consider the exchange relationships within as well as external to their borders.

PART THREE

Dimensions of Intellectual Histories

8

Educational Administration

Introduction

Educational Administration (EA) is a label that is used by those who focus directly within and in relation to professional practice. Those who locate here often show a combination of a range of employment locations: professionals who work in educational organizations, and professionals who have relocated into higher education, together with those who locate their intellectual project and academic careers fully in higher education. There are field-specific cultures and traditions within particular countries, where, for example, the historical antecedence of agendas and projects reach back further in the United States of America than in a lot of countries, such as England. This is evident through the maturity of historical accounts (e.g. Gunter 2012b; Rose 1977), and how the United States has been an important source of intellectual resources for field development in other countries (e.g. Gunter 2013b), with cross-border collaborations (e.g. Crow and Weindling 2010).

Leadership

Leaders, leading and leadership is currently a strong feature of EA activity whereby the demand from global economic change, international league tables and national government modernization programmes on principals, the workforce and schools requires the field to endemically engage with human and organizational issues. While EA remains the overarching label for activity nationally and internationally, there have been processes of relabelling in some nation states from administration to management to leadership (Gunter 2004). The relationship between activity and branding is an important point, where one professorial respondent in the KPEL project states: 'You know ten years ago I was a Professor of Educational Management, now I'm a Professor of Educational Leadership. I'm not conscious that I'm doing much different from what I was doing then, to be honest.'

Starratt (2003) provides an overview in the North American field where he talks about how educational administrators 'exercise educational leadership' and what this means in regard to values and 'where schools should be going and what large purposes they should be serving' (p. xiii). It seems as if the same types of staff used to be managed (e.g. Bennett 1995) but are now implicated in leadership (e.g. Bennett et al. 2003), and in Starratt's (2003) terms this requires practice to be 'grounded in an articulate and compelling vision of schooling' (p. xiii). One professorial respondent for the KPEL project identified the shift towards leadership: 'There was a feeling that you're not going to bring things about through managerial leadership or transactional leadership, what was needed was a different leadership and that's been developed so that more recently we're talking about learning centred leadership.' The relationship between role (e.g. teacher, head of department, principal) and the power process used to conceptualize that role (e.g. administration, leading, leadership, management, performance) is a central feature, with ongoing discussions and thinking on behalf of, for and with the practitioner (e.g. Sergiovanni 2001).

The consistent message is that leadership is a power process that is about influence, and where there tends to be an acceptance of *Transformational Leadership* as a functional visionary process led by the principal, with modifications as new hybrids are developed. Like EEIR there is a tendency to make lists of the key features with common claims around vision, and control by building commitment and commanding followership:

> The effectiveness of the organization and of all of its members is likely to be enhanced when there is a clear understanding of and agreement about the purposes of the organization and about the mode or style of leadership in the different parts of the organisation. (John 1980, p. 8)

> The leadership problem, in sum, has three parts: developing a widely shared, defensible vision; in the short run, directly assisting members of the school community to overcome obstacles they encounter in striving for the vision; and, in the long run, increasing the capacity of members of the school community to overcome subsequent obstacles more successfully and with great ease. ... Turbulence will be the norm and not the exception. (Leithwood et al. 1994, p. 8)

Both extracts are different in time and context, but they are both concerned with the relational aspects of how people work together. Whereas John (1980) is located at a time of leadership styles, a decade later Leithwood et al. (1994) are working at a time where the focus is on transformation through vision as a motivator and controller of practice and attitudes. Change in the form of neoliberal and neoconservative reforms sustained by elite dispositions is a given, and so leadership is about enabling followers to accept and to embrace external demands, with some studies making transparent what it is like to do the job (e.g. Earley 2013). The high-stakes environment for leaders means that the field has drawn on business effectiveness solutions regarding organizational cultures with foci on capacity, competence and capability development that are located in relationships, mentoring and coaching (e.g. Robertson 2008).

Key texts can be recognized as milestones in the development of the field (e.g. Evers and Lakomski 1991; Halpin 1958; Hodgkinson 1978; Hoy and Miskel 2013; Greenfield and Ribbins 1993; Leithwood et al. 1999), and these suggest that there is a plurality within the field regarding knowledge claims and exchanges (see Donmoyer et al. 1995). There are those who seek to measure and examine causal connections through to those who seek to understand the realities of practice, through to those who aim to provide solutions for busy practitioners. Concerns have increasingly been on troubling the technicalities of organizational structures and systems towards values (e.g. Begley and Leonard 1999). This has been integral to shifting the field away from predictive models towards the purposes of professional practice, and how to work in ways that are productive and humane. As one KPEL respondent stated, while management and day-to-day activity is important, 'I do find myself writing about leadership because it's an important backdrop for what happens'. However, another respondent is concerned with the primacy of leadership: 'It's right that it should be made more explicit, but I do have concerns about the degree to which it has now come to dominate everything and everything has to be called Leadership'. Challenges to take this further in regard to issues of leadership as a power-over process have been undertaken by work on gender (e.g. Hall 1996; Shakeshaft 1989) and diversity (Lumby and Coleman 2007), and through conceptual work on power and leadership (e.g. Bottery 2004; Gronn 2010). However, this remains isolated, where courses, keynotes, books and social media continue to examine organizations and practitioners without due regard for theories of power, educational values and issues of identity (see Bates and Eacott's 2008 account of Australia). Importantly, such work has more association with CEPaLS (see Chapter 11), where there are border issues regarding intellectual and empirical locations of EA *knowledge actors* and their projects.

An intellectual history of EA

Here I provide a summary by deploying the framework developed in Part 2.

Traditions: EA *Knowledge Production* demonstrates evidence of *experiential, positivist and behaviourist sciences* and *values*.

Experiential resources tend to be located in the biographies and stories of those who inhabit professional roles. While there have been robust attempts to codify and present ways of intervening in actual professional practice variously using *positivist* and *behaviourist sciences,* and *values traditions,* the emphasis on how people experience the job and come to take up positions on the meaning of their practice is an important feature of the field. Indeed, it is argued that 'administration as science tends to ignore or marginalize the complex moral issues involved in administrative activity', (Starratt 2003, p. 5).

Much EA activities are unrecorded except in the heads of those who enact leadership, though some do put fingers to keyboard in order to give accounts (e.g. Evans 1999), and some work with researchers regarding their lives and working lives through biographies (e.g. Sugrue 2005), and ethnographies (e.g. Southworth 1995; Wolcott 1973). Indeed, living with a principal and/or having been a principal, is an important feature for researcher motivation, where Southworth (1995) notes: 'The literature, though insightful in some ways, fails to portray the essence of the experience of headship as I remember it and as I believe many heads I have worked with appear to experience the job' (p. 7).

Such accounts provide what Pascal and Ribbins (1998) describe as 'a rich and comprehensive understanding of the views and perspectives which individual headteachers bring to their work' (p. 7), and so the particular contribution can be opened up for scrutiny. This matters because much attention has been given to principals, and major investment in training and development is based on claims regarding their significance. Wolcott (1973) concludes thus:

> Yet there is no question that some principals exhibit more capacity for leadership in the job than others. They create a sense of purpose among a majority of those with whom they interact. They seem able to capitalize on the potential of the institution while others are rendered helpless by its limitations. I am not ready to go so far as one principal who insisted that the principal 'makes all the difference' in a school, but neither would I ever argue that he [*sic*] makes no difference at all. (p. 325)

The complexity and humanity involved in the job, and the sense that there is other work than leadership work is a valuable contribution, not least how a professional within a context (political, organizational, economic, cultural), at a moment in time (age, partner, family) develops and engages with identities.

While this tradition remains strong in regard to the resources that the EA field produces and draws on, it remains the case that other *knowledge traditions* are used to move the field towards more scientific (including behaviourism) and humanitarian ways (values), and as such there are tensions in regard to how and why this needs to happen.

Positivist scientific resources are located in the Taylorist tradition regarding the conceptualization of the human being, and how the leader's behaviour can be identified and measured. As Halpin (1966) notes, there is a need to shift from a rating of leadership towards 'the measurement of a group's description of its leader's behaviour' (p. 86). Such an approach is about the need for knowledge workers in higher education 'to try to develop useful theory in educational administration' (p. 3), and this was integral to what is known as the Theory Movement. This has a resilient legacy within the field through (a) the ongoing emphasis on the identification and measurement of leadership behaviours (e.g. Leithwood et al. 1999); (b) the focus on problem solving with the deployment of techniques for solutions (Hoy and Miskel 2013); and (c) the disconnection of theorizations from the realities and realpolitik of practice within context (Gunter 1997).

Such matters have been directly confronted by scholars, whereby Evers and Lakomski (1991, 1996, 2012) are working for a better science by making the case for 'coherentism' (Evers and Lakomski 1996, p. 10). The aim is to answer concerns about the eschewing of values in theory building and the challenges to certainty from postmodernism. What Evers and Lakomski (1996) focus on are 'coherence considerations' (p. 243) in regard to theory: 'fruitfulness, consistency, explanatory power' (p. 243) which enables the interrelationship between education and non-educational settings and theorizations to be engaged with. Importantly, they propose and examine the use of neuroscience and information theory as two fruitful ways of examining subjectivities and values within decision-making. Such arguments enable them to question the use of questionnaires to gather views about leaders doing leading and leadership, particularly because there is a need to take account of cognition and how learning takes place, rather than assume that the meanings encoded in language in questionnaires are read and responded to scientifically.

Behaviourist resources are interconnected with the demand for a science of educational administration, not only to predict outcomes from best practice but to handle the challenges of personal reflexivity and potential pragmatism. Hoy and Miskel (2013) build on the *behaviourism* within Simon's (1945) examination of *administrative behaviour,* and the productive efficiencies within Taylorism, by presenting educational administration as best conceptualized through systems theory. The focus on the input–process–output–feedback system enables the 'process' as the site of transformation to be examined, particularly through the deployment of business models and problem-solving case studies. Within the field, this type of approach has manifested itself in the promotion of particular approaches to the control of professional practice. Some of this is about individuals through an examination of motivation or on organizational matters such as structure and culture, with debates about collaboration or collegiality through teams. Like EEIR, *Transformational Leadership* is regarded as effective through questionnaire ratings, and following Bass (1998), it is argued that '*Transformational Leadership* can move followers to exceed expected performance ... (because it) ... generates greater subordinate effort, commitment, and satisfaction' (Hoy and Miskel 2013, p. 453).

Values resources are located in the arguments that professional practice is located within something more than the predictive capacities of the system and the control of behaviours. The human aspect of leaders, leading and leadership is nicely captured by Southworth (1995), who, in completing a major ethnographic study of a headteacher, concludes 'that to develop reflective, critical and ethical leadership, headteacher development should not be wholly devoted to technical matters. Heads also need to focus upon the ethical dimensions of their work and consider alternative ways of leading' (p. 215). Such an engagement for practitioners is difficult because of the challenges generated from the interplay between what they actually do and what they ought to do, and also because as Southworth shows humans get tired where reflexivity can be marginalized because they are on a 'treadmill' (p. 217).

Within the field of educational administration the place of values is recognized as integral to relational exchanges (see Begley and Leonard 1999), where matters of trust and ethics are regarded as central to the human and professional condition within educational practice (see Samier 2003; Samier and Schmidt 2010). Nevertheless, values remain controversial, not least through Ribbins' (1999) analysis that 'Simon did not deny the place of values in the world but ... believed that they were not susceptible to objective verification' (p. x). So, 'students and practitioners alike should restrict their attention to the worthwhile and realistic task of producing objective, value-free knowledge of what worked in the administration of organizations, rather than the pursuit of a self-indulgent, and ultimately, vain search for subjective and value-laden prescriptions of what ought to be done' (p. x). Nevertheless, Ribbins (1999) goes on to show how the Theory Movement had its doubters in the United States as well as internationally, and those who had been integral to the search for the theory such as Halpin and Griffiths had pulled back. It is generally regarded that the Theory Movement was in decline by the early 1970s, but it was Greenfield's paper in 1974 that finally confirmed its passing.

Greenfield's paper opened up the challenge for the field to develop a 'humane science' through recognition that 'administrators are essentially value-carriers in organizations; they are both arbiters of values and representatives of them' (Greenfield and Ribbins 1993, p. 149). Consequently, questions are raised about whether training is a proper site for the discussion of values, whereby Ribbins (1999) identifies some tensions among field thinkers about this, but agrees that practitioners are interested and do talk about such matters (see Begley and Leonard 1999). Hence such debates tend to be interlinked with *experiential* resources (see above) whereby practitioners talk in terms of what is important to them and how they are seeking to improve educational experiences. Greenfield argues that the drive for science in the Theory Movement 'offered them certainty in their choices while absolving them of responsibility' (Greenfield and Ribbins 1993, p. 164), and what the promotion of values within a humane science does is to return responsibility back to the field, whereby choice cannot be necessarily predicted.

Begley (1999) argues that this is because there are several propositions: first, that organizations are 'social constructions' whereby how people understand a situation is open to interpretation, and just because someone says this is the case, does not mean it is read in that way; second, people are not just resources to be deployed for organizational ends, but 'people and their well-being ought to be treated as ends not merely as organizational resources' (p. 2); and third, while there are advances in the natural sciences, not least in neurosciences, it is the case that 'they will only in the end explain the *how* not the *why* of human enterprise, and they will never be capable of 100 per cent prediction of human intentions or actions' (p. 2). Hence the underlying ontology and epistemology of administrative science, and the endeavours of Evers and Lakomski (see above), can only take the field so far; in the end the infinite variety of people and a sense of professionality are important, 'otherwise people are doomed to keep repeating the mistakes of the past over and over again' (Begley 1999, p. 2). Hence, values-based pedagogies are integral to preparation programmes rather than the design of training based on scientific certainties.

Purposes: The plurality in the traditions that EA draws on means that there are a range of purposes: *situational, functional* and *realist.*

Situational purposes draw mainly from the *experiential tradition* within the field whereby the intentionality of action is located in the stories of those who inhabit roles labelled leader and whose work is known as leading and leadership. There are a number of different approaches taken that can be said to have situational features within the accounts given: first, principals who write about their experiences of leading changes that they have been charged with delivering, with accounts of how they have 'dug deep' to draw on experiential resources in order to meet requirements (e.g. Stubbs 2003); second, principals who write about the situations they have found themselves in, and how they have sought to work their way through this (e.g. Arrowsmith 2001); third, principals who have been respondents in research projects and have given their stories through interviews (e.g. Ribbins 1997a), worked with a researcher in an ethnography (e.g. Wolcott 1973), or have completed doctoral studies (e.g. Evans 1999).

Functional purposes draw mainly from the *positivist* and *behavioural* traditions within the field, whereby the intentionality is located in the prescriptive models for change, together with the tools through which that change can be delivered. Such functionality of purpose with the focus on translation and delivery has commonalities with EEIR, and EP networks, where there are common roots in the shared traditions and some cross overs through collaborations and joint projects. Importantly, such functionality enables a conceptual fit with policy demands, whereby the insider cover of Hoy and Miskel (2013) shows the link between the case studies in the book and required leadership standards.

Functionality is therefore located in the provision of change models regarding the conceptualization of change together with the linearity of how this might be done. For example, Everard and Morris (1985) are concerned with eliminating dysfunctions as barriers to change, such as challenging particular attitudes and behaviours (e.g. 'What's this got to do with us?' or 'Haven't we tried this before?'), and developing more productive ones: 'In a meeting ... decisions can be influenced far more effectively by using the behavioural "process" of the meeting than by simply restating one's arguments, however sound they are. How we use our awareness of behavioural processes is a key aspect of managerial ethics? Do we use it to "manipulate" or to "facilitate"?' (p. 18). This focuses on the self in relation to others, with the need to learn and behave appropriately as a leader, such as developing competencies and capabilities in the 1980s through to emotional intelligence from the 1990s. It also focuses on others and how you as a person can talk with and work with others who you lead and line manage, and how you are accountable to those above you in the hierarchy.

The normative demands are strong, whereby education can and must learn from business, and in doing so must draw on the scientific traditions that not only enable behaviour to be controlled but also provide the methods for achieving such control. For example, quality processes from business had a strong impact on the field, with an intensive investigation into and the promotion of particular models (e.g. Total Quality Management), and studies of particular people's work (e.g. Deming) (see Sallis 1993). The 'leadership turn' from the 1990s with the focus on *Transformational Leadership* still retains the focus on relational matters but does so through leader-centric analysis, not least through the continued emphasis on making such a model more conducive. For example, Bhindi and Duignan (1997) focus on what they call 'authentic leadership' which links the self with others, where 'authentic leaders support people-centred practices and ethical standards that promote meaningful relationships and an organization that is based on authentic values' (p. 59). Normative functionality tends to invoke values in regard to organizational matters, but as Wright (2003) argues, there is a need to think more deeply, not least on the problematic relationship with vision and mission. This is what I turn to now.

Realist purposes draw mainly from the *values tradition* within the field where the intentionality of change is located in the realities of how this is experienced, and how this shapes the morality and ethics of decisions within context. Partnerships have been formed with local administrators and professionals, where one professorial respondent in the KPEL project talked about 'collaborative working with the local authority, seeking to celebrate and acknowledge good practice that had been undertaken in educational leadership and management'. Here researchers are concerned to collect the stories of those in formal roles as principals, and to use them to examine and expose the tensions and dilemmas of doing the job. Sometimes this is through interviews that are then used to develop themes with a researcher narrative that explicates and theorizes (e.g. Hall 1996), and sometimes this is through edited principal narratives that are structured through the interplay of the story and the questioning of the researcher (e.g. Ribbins and Marland 1994).

Such *realist purposes* confront change in relation to what it actually means to deliver externally determined agendas in the form of legal requirements through to guidance about good practice. Some accounts examine the realities of *functional purposes*, and what it means to be required to deliver change, and to translate espoused leadership practices in order to do this. For example, reports by principals (e.g. Arrowsmith 2001) and researchers (e.g. Lortie 2009; Sugrue 2005) show the range of competing demands, the contradictions faced by principals in trying to handle such demands, and at the same time recognizing personal and professional vulnerability in the face of high-stakes testing and location in a competitive market place. Keeping the school as an organizational system running smoothly and at the same time confronting this system to make changes, is a basic challenge to interplaying outcomes with a productive consensus. In addition to this, there is the prospect of not only having to introduce change that a person may not believe in, who knows it will not work, or may even be a short-term fad, but also having to front the change and convince the staff, children and parents of how 'there is no alternative' perhaps by demonstrating localized interpretations. This is why one professor talks about how 'we need to learn from experiences from elsewhere, but not simply to go through policy borrowing without careful consideration of applicability to the new context'. What *realist purposes* do is to highlight the realpolitik of the job, and how the local version of a reform is based on a sense of who the audience is that the principal is addressing and calculating trajectories and likely outcomes (Gronn 1996).

Domains: The pluralistic approach to *knowledge traditions* and hence purposes means that the main domains within EA are: *philosophical, humanistic* and *instrumental*.

The strong emphasis on *positivist* and *behaviourist science traditions* means that the purposes tend to be *functional* and so the *instrumental* domain is prominent. Such instrumentalism has a number of features: first, scripts, language and conduct codes (stance or 'body language' and presentation issues such as personal grooming, dress and accessories) that enable organizational and staff issues to be designed, thought and talked about in particular ways; second, diagnostic tools to predict, monitor and evaluate performance (e.g. use of Myers and Myers 1995); third, ways of doing work that are efficient and effective (e.g. time management, self-motivation); and fourth, organizational arrangements and cultures (e.g. roles, performance systems, data collection and analysis). The integration of the human side (e.g. behaviour, feelings, energy) with system demands (e.g. strategy, planning, outputs) is through the focus on leaders, leading and leadership as vision and followership, and on the beneficiaries of this through the location of rationales and narratives within professional concerns about children and achievements. There are a range of *instrumental* texts that enable this to happen, some are linked to the EEIR and EP products, but within the EA field there are illustrative examples of tips on functionality, with products that are designed to 'meet the needs' of practitioners in new and exciting times (e.g. Caldwell and Spinks 1992).

The EA field does have *knowledge actors* who seek to understand change through engagement with *philosophical* matters. This can be through those who focus specifically on this through research (e.g. Hodgkinson 1983) and practice (e.g. Winkley 1999) as intellectual work. Here the approach is to study and think about a situation and people, using *philosophical* methods that engage with questions of ontology (reality), epistemology (knowledge and truth) and axiology (values), and in doing so the thinking generated through this is deemed to be practical. For example, Winkley (1999) challenges the emphasis on instrumentalism used to deliver site-based management as educational reform in England from the late 1980s onwards, particularly since such matters can be learnt, and learnt quickly. For him the main issues in school leadership are to do with values and the ways in which these need to be thought about within the context of the curriculum and pedagogy. In this sense the process of thinking is *philosophical*, and connects directly with practice, and this relates directly with Hodgkinson (1983) who argues that 'administration is a value activity' because 'nothing is more important than values for they are the source of all meaning' where meaning is core to what leadership is about (p. 227). In this way, knowledge is used to interrupt, and if necessary to radically alter a situation, so that delivery is based on values-informed thinking and doing. Consequently, the approach to professional learning is through the use of theory to provoke and enable strategy, rather than training according to an agreed knowledge base.

Those in the EA field who are concerned to retain and develop *philosophical* matters as integral to practice tend to have strong connections methodologically to the *humanistic domain*. Living change is *humanistic* through the need to describe and understand what leaders do, and how they seek to develop meaning about this (e.g. Ribbins 1997).

Important for this approach to change are theorizations around power and the importance of micro-politics within organizations. This is what Hoyle (1982) identified in regard to personal histories, friendships and animosities, and the workings of gossip networks. Hence the capturing of what this means for those in the job is significant through the practical *philosophical* matters of thinking and doing, not least whether it is possible or even desirable to include this in professional training. Hoyle (1982) raises the significant issue of what it may mean to train someone to do micro-politics, and the ethical matters of learning to manipulate and control. Notably, Gronn (2003) raises this matter from another angle, whereby he questions that if leadership is about influence then why don't we call it that.

Contexts: within EA there is a historical and rooted allegiance to *Civic Welfarism* as the accepted way in which education is organized, but the adoption of business forms of management and leadership has demonstrated an acceptance of *Neoliberalism* and *Neoconservativism*, with some in the field acting as advocates for such changes.

A useful starting point is to consider how field members who focus on the lives and work of school principals tend to examine how their professional dispositions, as revealed through practice, and reflexivity about and for such practices, illuminate how they are 'made' within a context. In this sense, the context shapes and structures their work and hence what interests the field is how agency is related to and is located within this. Gronn (1999) is helpful through how he gives recognition to the talent pool in society and in the organization: 'Unlike an organization, people do not join a social system: rather, they are born into one' and for the organization, there is an opportunity because appointment panels 'are in the fortunate position of being able to pick and choose their memberships according to desired profiles' (p. 186). Examining succession planning means that continuities and shifts through generational change is given recognition, where retrospective accounts of doing the job enable this to be made visible in stories of change. Certainly an important contribution towards what this means for notions of 'professional' and 'career' is through the production of rational stages in a leadership career (e.g. Gronn 1999; Hart 1993; Pascal and Ribbins 1998) based on interviews. Weindling (1999) provides a digest of these approaches, and through the interplay with his data he suggests a six-staged model from pre-headship focused on preparation, to entry and encounter (first months), to taking hold (three months to a year), to reshaping (second year), refinement (years three to four), consolidation (years five to seven) and plateauing (years eight onwards) (pp. 98–9). How this links to the experience of externally determined changes that significantly determine new types of work and responsibilities is significant (see Gronn 2003), particularly since Weindling (1999) notes that headteachers in his study before the 1988 Education Reform Act were able to initiate most changes, but in the post-1988 world, the head has to internally manage externally determined changes.

The rapid and fundamental reform programmes that have taken place in schools and their systemic locations over the past fifty years are treated differently within the field. It is used to inform and enable understanding of the work and identities of principals, but there is another position where a substantial amount of outputs use change as a backdrop to create a *change imperative*. This tends to be in the form of narrations of changes, the demands made upon the profession, and hence the provision of leadership and management techniques and processes to be able to do the job. Hence the trilogy of books by Caldwell and Spinks (1988, 1992, 1998) are concerned to use current and futures thinking for and about the neoliberal context as a rationale for organizational and cultural restructuring of schools. Others take this as a given and promote business models against a backdrop of challenging change that the profession must and can respond to (e.g. Davies and Davies 2005), with occasional transparent glimpses of ideological location with *Neoliberalism* (e.g. Thompson et al.

2004). The tensions that are visible in this part of the EA field are in how the promotion of business tools and values can be related to the systems and *behaviourist* thinking underpinning the science traditions, and hence the adoption of, for example, 're-engineering' (Davies 1997). However, EA is also concerned to focus on the realities of doing the job, and hence a key message is that leaders, leading and leadership matter, and so the profession needs to embrace understandings and learning from research about leadership (Earley 2013). This paradox is central to how the EA community handles the relationship between how the context structures the drive for change based on 'knowledge for action', with the agency of the professional based on 'knowledge for understanding' (Bolam 1999).

Networks: the main formal networks are through EA organizations within each nation state, for example, UCEA in the United States, and BELMAS in the United Kingdom, with supranational networks such as EFEA and CCEAM. Each of these provides opportunities for meeting up and undertaking collaborative projects, to breaking down isolationism (Walker 1984). Indeed within the history of the field in the United Kingdom, there is a strong emphasis on early *knowledge actors* in higher education going out to meet up with and learn from those in North America and Australia who were part of a more established field (Gunter 2013b).

In the UK strong networking is located in the history of the field from the 1960s onwards with the formation of what is now called BELMAS, and how particular people such as George Baron and William Taylor brought people together to collaborate on professional needs at a time of rapid change, where learning was taking place based on international visits and conferences (Baron et al. 1969). Importantly, the UK networking was based on bringing professionals from schools and administration into discussion with those working in higher education, where there remains a strong emphasis on the field as inclusive of people located in different organizational sites (Gunter 1999).

A strong feature of the EA field is the codification of knowledge claims through the production of handbooks that illuminate cooperation: first, handbooks as state-of-the-field reviews and compendiums of knowledge claims (e.g. Boyan 1988; Murphy and Seashore Louis 1999); second, texts with and for professionals (Hughes et al. 1985). Such texts not only identify 'people', 'centres' and 'schools' as sites of field development, but through the commissioning of chapters (and sometimes the selection of pre-published materials) the knowledge base was scoped and fixed, and the leaders of key areas of knowledge were given an identity and status.

Particular people have become recognizable names in the field, and this book has given attention to those regarded as field leaders in their own nation and/or internationally. In this sense, networks are through how clusters of *knowledge actors* within a location can impact, not least how in the United Kingdom there has been a strong connection between the field and particular universities, where the Institute of Education in London is regarded as the historical home of the field through the work of Baron and Taylor (1969) (Gunter 1999). Conversely, Brooks and Miles (2008) show how in the United States of America the dominance of scientific management can be located through the engagement and influence of particular *knowledge actors* at Teachers College at Columbia University.

Knowledge production

The examination of the relationship between the demands for change, coping with change and delivering the change is through how EA associates with but is also distinctive from business and EEIR networks:

Theory: the concern is to identify and access resources that can support the practitioner within the school regarding organizational and professional matters (see Baron and Taylor 1969; Riehl et al. 2000). There are different positions regarding this: first, some EA *knowledge actors* seek to identify and translate business models for educational change (e.g. Davies et al. 1990); second, others see the social sciences such as sociology, political science and economics as enabling of the necessary intellectual work that is educational and linked to *philosophical* matters (e.g. Starratt 2003); and third, others provide resources for their 'fellow' practitioners (e.g. Caldwell and Spinks 1988).

Research: the focus is on developing an evidence base for the practitioner within the school. There are different positions regarding this: first, some *knowledge actors* conceptualize the school and practitioners as objects within a predictive system (e.g. Halpin 1958, 1966); second, some are concerned with measurement studies regarding the impact of practice on student and/or organizational outcomes (e.g. Hallinger and Heck 1998); and third, some are concerned to present the realities of professional work within schools, where there is a focus on the work of the principal (e.g. Lortie 2009) and their working lives and biographies through narratives and ethnographies (e.g. Southworth 1995; Wolcott 1973).

Preparation: there is a focus on principal preparation through approaches to training and development (e.g. Lumby et al. 2008). This has a number of features: first, the sharing of examples of how effective training and preparation takes place through on-the-job support and in-service professional development (e.g. Culbertson 1964; Hallinger 2003; Shoho et al. 2010); second, prescriptions for effective training and associations with business models (e.g. Caldwell 2006). Interconnected with this have been engagements with leadership centres, whereby the local investment in school leadership by governments and entrepreneurs is recognized as a positive development (e.g. Bush 2011).

Knowledge Production within EA takes the lead from professional needs, and consequently, the agenda has tended to be set by the immediate demands for practice where reform generates a leadership imperative. In this sense, EA is located within the *professional* and *research hubs*, and has found itself variously enabling or potentially trapped in regard to the demands of the *corporate* and *policy hubs*. Various government regimes have made demands on the profession, where EA has been a resource that has enabled *Transformational Leadership* to become a dominant model. However, EEIR is the most dominant resource, and as such EA has found itself lacking in capital value in the field. Those who are attracted by this have shifted towards EEIR and those who are concerned about this have shifted towards CEPaLS, where more critical work is being undertaken in support of the *professional hub*.

Summary

EA has a long and distinguished intellectual history in support of research and practice in the United States and more recently in other nation states such as the United Kingdom, and the brief examination of the 4Ks in this chapter shows plurality in regard to *theory, purposes* and *domains*. However, the impact of *contexts* shows that *networks* have increasingly experienced professional demands that are about enabling privatization. Hence within a *knowledgeable polity*, the role of the state and politics has created particular knowledge and practice imperatives that EA is concerned to respond to rather than critique. The idea of the Theory Movement remains influential, and it is evident either in the continued attempts to synthesize the plurality through the formation of a knowledge base or in sidestepping this and in retaining prediction and certainty that are evident in the continued dominance and rebranding of *Transformational Leadership*.

9

Educational Effectiveness and Improvement Research

Introduction

Educational Effectiveness and Improvement Research (EEIR) is a relabelling of what has traditionally been called School Effectiveness and School Improvement (SESI), where the shift from 'school' to 'educational' is 'a reflection of the wide breadth of topics that the field now covers' (Reynolds et al. 2014, p. 198). In other words, educational and teaching effectiveness is focusing on student outcomes operating at 'four levels: student, classroom, school, and system' (Muijs 2014, p. 243) with school and system improvement processes engaging 'within' the school, 'between' and 'beyond' schools (Ainscow et al. 2012, p. 6). Harris (2014) claims that work in this field is a 'formidable intellectual force' (p. 193) and Reynolds (2014) argues that school effectiveness, school improvement, and teacher effectiveness are now three 'strong disciplines in their own right' (Reynolds 2014, p. 195). The relationship or 'partnership' (Harris 2014, p. 193) between them is important, there are those who focus on determinants of effectiveness and those for whom change processes dominate.

Current EEIR has roots that Sammons (1999) claims are difficult to trace, but historiographies reach back into the rejection of claims by Coleman et al. (1966) that schools do not make a difference, with regularly cited texts (e.g. Edmonds 1979) that began the investigations into behavioural and organizational matters (see Chapman 2012; Sammons 1999, 2012; Sammons et al. 1997). The field has been scoped through retrospective identification of phases (see Hopkins et al. 2014; Reynolds et al. 2014; Scheerens 2014), with the prime concern focused on the classroom for teaching effectiveness, the conditions in school for cultural change, and the indicators of effectiveness for methodological robustness. Underlying the emergence and development of the respective areas of 'effectiveness' and 'improvement' are texts that outline and debate the field from within and make planned statements about the field: knowledge or the canon that is significant, claims about ways of knowing, and through citations and inclusion as authors in edited collections and journal special issues, those who are field players are recognized (e.g. Chapman et al. 2012; MacBeath and Mortimore 2001; Reynolds 2014; Teddlie and Reynolds 2000). Careers have been built with named chairs, and centres, where indicators of recognition include the ICSEI, the AERA Leadership for School Improvement Special Interest Group, and a range of journals, for example, *School Effectiveness and School Improvement; Journal of Educational Effectiveness; Journal of Educational Change; and School Leadership and Management.*

Leaders, leading and leadership

A study of field outputs shows that very clear claims are made from effectiveness and improvement researchers: Reynolds et al. (2014) identify 'effective leadership that was: firm, involving, instrumentally orientated, involving monitoring, and involved staff replacement' (p. 210), and by contrast 'ineffective schools have weak Principal leadership, a lack of emphasis on the acquisition of basic skills, a disorderly climate, low or uneven expectations, and inconsistent or no monitoring of student progress' (p. 214). School improvement researchers talk about how 'aspects of leadership are often intangible but we know that an effective leader has a vision and is able to convey this vision to different groups who are involved with the school including staff, pupils, parents and governors' (Stoll and Myers 1998b, p. 8). The articulated link between effectiveness and improvement is based on the former as 'the final picture' based on 'participatory leadership' as 'firm and purposeful' by a 'leading professional' taking a 'participative approach', and the latter as 'facilitating conditions' with 'headteacher as motivator and guide' and teachers 'as change agents' and involved in 'leadership roles and decision making' (Stoll and Mortimore 1997, p. 18). Direct connections are made between the 'effective leader' and the professional role of the principal (Sammons 1999; Stoll and Myers 1998b), where Edmonds (1979) identifies the principal as 'instructional leader' (p. 18). Sammons (1999) notes that while some studies identify roles other than the principal leading effective schools, the bulk of the evidence is about the principal who is 'proactive' and who can 'mediate' or act as a 'buffer' from unwelcome change (p. 197). Field members have sought to examine the relationship between leadership as a practice and context, with work on schools in 'challenging circumstances' such as urban areas (e.g. Ainscow and West 2006; Harris et al. 2006).

Rapid reforms focused on school standards in western-style democracies have generated a leadership imperative that is regarded as necessary and urgent: 'The quality of leadership can make a difference between a school which struggles and one which strives for the highest levels of attainment, between a school where pupils and staff are pulling in different directions and one where everyone collaborates and works towards a shared purpose' (Coles and Southworth 2005b, p. xvii). Indeed leadership is seen as one of the 'conditions for school improvement' (Hopkins 2001), and drawing on the IQEA project, the argument is made for 'vision building', leadership based on 'experience' and understood as a 'function' that all can participate in and in ways that prevent 'group think' (Hopkins 2001, p. 99). The gaze of field members has focused on a range of projects regarding roles such as subject leaders (e.g. Busher and Harris 2000) and middle leadership within departments (e.g. Harris 2001; Sammons et al. 1997), as well as wider evaluations of leadership (e.g. MacBeath and McGlynn 2002). Considerable amounts of work have been undertaken to develop models of leadership:

- *Transformational* as distinct from transactional leadership is a strong feature with emphasis on visioning, charisma, and commitment building (e.g. Leithwood et al. 1999).

- *Distributed Leadership* as a means of counteracting the heroism implicated in the transformational model with emphasis on what Sergiovanni (2001) calls 'leadership density' based on 'shared' and 'relational' exchanges within roles and delivery remits (e.g. Spillane 2006).

- *Instructional Leadership* as a focus on the link between organizational roles, and teaching and learning (e.g. Southworth 2002).

Major projects have taken place where leadership is a part of the study (e.g. Halton project in Canada, see Stoll and Fink 1996), and have been the sole focus of the study (e.g. Day et al. 2009, 2011; Hopkins 2007; Mulford and Silins (2011); Robinson et al. 2009).

One example is The Impact of School Leadership on Pupil Outcomes (IMPACT) project (Day et al. 2009) whereby perceptions of professional practice combined with student and organizational data led to the production of 'ten strong, evidence-based claims about successful school leadership':

- 'Headteachers are the main source of leadership in their schools.

- There are eight key dimensions of successful leadership.

- Headteacher's values are key components in their success.

- Successful heads use the same basic leadership practices, but there is no single model for achieving success.

- Differences in context affect the nature, direction and pace of leadership actions.

- Heads contribute to student learning and achievement through a combination and accumulation of strategies and actions.

- There are three broad phases of leadership success.

- Heads grow and secure success by layering leadership strategies and actions.

- Successful heads distribute leadership progressively.

- The successful distribution of leadership depends on the establishment of trust' (Day et al. 2010, p. 3).

In examining and developing the evidence base, the field has confronted how the impact of a principal as leader is mediated (Hallinger and Heck 1998), and that led the IMPACT project team to conclude that 'school leadership is second only to classroom teaching as an influence on pupil learning' (Leithwood et al. 2006, p. 3). Importantly, Leithwood and Riehl's (2003) analysis found that it is student characteristics that impact most on achievement (e.g. ability, motivation, socioeconomic status), and the next is classroom strategies (e.g. staff development). They conclude thus:

> Leadership effects are primarily indirect, and they appear primarily to work through the organizational variable of school mission or goals and through variables related to classroom curriculum and instruction. While quantitative estimates of effects are not always available, leadership variables seem to explain an important proportion of the school-related variance in student achievement. (Leithwood and Riehl 2003, p. 13)

This indirect approach is repeated in texts and asserted as important in school improvement (e.g. Harris et al. 2006), where international projects designed to chart and understand leadership effectiveness (e.g. MacBeath 1998) have sought to trouble the presentation of 'categoricals' of effectiveness in relation to the 'quixotic natures of schools' within local contexts (Riley and MacBeath 1998, p. 151). Indeed, parallel work is taking place about teacher effectiveness (Muijs et al. 2014), with projects on teacher leadership (Harris and Muijs 2003) and *Distributed Leadership* (Leithwood et al. 2009).

Even though work continues to take place on leadership outside of the principal role, the approach to leadership and its relationship to elite roles in schools remains a strong and enduring feature, where projects that scope and develop claims about and for other forms of leadership tend to be scripted in relation to the normality of a hierarchy. Hence *Distributed Leadership* tends to be engaged with in response to but not as a challenge to principal leadership, where the single person in the top role is retained and is conceptualized as the repository of leadership to be distributed from (see Gunter et al. 2013). There is recognition in the field that the relationship between leaders and leadership within structured roles in a pyramid does tend to be in Anglophone countries, in contrast to other countries (e.g. Scandinavia) where there is sufficient evidence to suggest different approaches. Hopkins et al. (2014) argue that such collective approaches mean that 'nobody exercises "leadership" in the sense that most educational systems would recognise the term; hence, there is little impact on student learning' (p. 267). Leadership as a resource for all to access and use irrespective of structure and roles is within the literatures (e.g. Foster 1989), and there are examples of schools that operate with different structures (e.g. Grubb and Flessa 2006), but these resources are not directly engaged with by the effectiveness or improvement knowledge workers.

An intellectual history of EEIR

Here I provide a summary by deploying the framework developed in Part 2.

Traditions: the intellectual resources developed for and used by the field tend to be mainly *positivist* and *behavioural science*, with some *experiential*.

Positivist scientific resources tend to be mainly a feature of educational and teaching effectiveness research, where a recent a 'state-of-the-art' review of educational effectiveness outlines the 'foundational questions' for the field: 'what makes a "good" school' and 'how do we make more schools "good"?' (Reynolds et al. 2014, p. 197). Claims are made that this work over time has established a 'discipline' (Reynolds 2014, p. 195) by generating 'a valid body of knowledge about "what works" at school, classroom, and increasingly at country and educational system level' (Reynolds et al. 2014, p. 216). There is evidence of internal charting of development and learning from this, where, for example, Scheerens (1992) examines the accumulation of evidence through a review of projects, methodologies and findings. Though the context-specific nature of the science makes predictability and transferability across systems challenging, and so there is interest in comparative projects (Sammons et al. 1997).

Claims for a science of effectiveness are based on establishing distinctiveness from those who work primarily in improvement: 'Quality cannot be inferred from intrinsic characteristics of processes. Effectiveness is apparent from education results' (Scheerens 1992, p. 79). Therefore the approach is to identify indicators of effectiveness, which are then used to measure and predict effectiveness, where, for example, Stoll and Mortimore (1997) engage with the importance of value-added measurements, and more recently Muijs et al. (2014) talk about 'the importance of the classroom level as a predictor of pupil outcomes' (p. 231). Considerable methodological developments have taken place with an increased emphasis on methodological precision, and these are listed by Reynolds et al. (2014) as: multi-level modelling; meta-analysis; structural equation modelling; growth curve modelling; mixed methods research (p. 204). Traditionally, the types of claims tend to be based on correlations that Scheerens (1992) argues are problematic in relation to causation, where experiments give more certainty. Indeed, the use of experiments through randomized controlled trials is recognized as an important feature in the field (Reynolds et al. 2014), and the association as a science with medicine is also recognized through a strong commitment to meta-analysis of evidence in order to support 'evidence-based education' (Reynolds et al. 2014, p. 200).

Behaviourism as a *knowledge tradition* is connected by effectiveness researchers to their scientific claims. Reynolds et al. (2014) note the identification of 'nearly 60 different behaviours by teachers in classrooms' (p. 212), and teacher effectiveness research is located in 'the study of measurable behaviours' with an emphasis on 'finding those behaviours that could act as reinforcers of student behaviours' (Muijs et al. 2014, p. 232). Therefore Muijs et al. (2014) identify that 'the most consistently replicated findings of teacher effectiveness studies conducted in different countries link student achievement to the quantity and pacing of instruction' (p. 232), and so attention is given to what teachers do in relation to time on task; and the organizational matters that enable this such as the length of the school day.

Claims by improvement researchers regarding science tend to be through the identification and impact of behaviours that underpin 'potentially testable theories of systemic change in education' (Hopkins et al. 2014, p. 257). Hence there are concerns to examine leadership attributes and behaviours in regard to organizational development and location (e.g. Harris et al. 2006). There are strong links with psychology, where Hopkins et al. (2014) use Lewin because of 'his emphasis on the influence of the organisation on the behaviour of its members' (p. 259). Such approaches therefore focus on relationships and culture, for example, Stoll and Fink (1996) advocate invitational leadership, and consider the presentation of self and how to build links with others.

In spite of this scientific and *behaviourist* approach, there remain some strong *experiential* resources within the field. For example, Hopkins et al. (2014) give recognition to the role of the practitioner through action research with Stenhouse and Elliott, and through school-based reviews. The KPEL project data from the UK shows that members of the improvement community are more likely to have begun their careers as teachers and leader professionals, and so their interests, methodologies and claims are linked to the professional concerns of people who they regard as their peers. This illustrates various improvement projects (e.g. Day et al. 2000; Chapman 2005), and the trend towards distilling key messages for professionals that speak to them in ways that connect with their professional concerns and identities (e.g. Fullan 1992). Importantly, the KPEL data from the UK contains accounts of some researchers who have also taken on major leadership and management roles within higher education, and they are concerned to examine how they might demonstrate their approach to effectiveness and improvement.

Purposes: the accessing and use of the *positivist* and *behaviourist science traditions* tends to be mainly *functional* (descriptive and normative), with some *realist* tendencies.

While case studies are used to demonstrate the complexities of securing effectiveness and improvement (e.g. Cutler 1998), the imperative to do something is a key feature of EEIR: 'The challenge is real because research findings demonstrate that some schools can make much more of a difference than others and that schools serving very similar intakes can give their pupils very different experiences and achieve different outcomes for their pupils' (MacGilchrist et al. 1997, p. 1). The identification, communication, evaluation, and development of data and ideas that can be used at local and national levels are therefore core to field purposes (Reynolds 2012). One school improvement field leader articulates how 'I have deliberately tried to locate myself at that intersection between, research and practice' where 'getting your hands dirty' with real-life world issues is not 'a very comfortable place to be, actually, you don't make a lot of friends there and you make a lot of enemies'. Others talk about how their work is 'applied' and 'collaborative', and 'generative' not only through the development of new ideas, but also with recognition of where the funds are to support such work.

Functionally descriptive outputs enable the evidence base for effectiveness to be made explicit (e.g. Sammons et al. 1995), and examples from research about and for *Distributed Leadership*, with texts that are about lessons learnt (Harris 2008; Spillane 2006; Spillane and Diamond (2007) along with accounts and assessments of the evidence so far (Leithwood et al. 2009). Integral to this are descriptions from the profession regarding their experiences, and so Jackson (2000) talks about the school where he was headteacher and the importance of the IQEA project in generating improvement, and other heads show how they have integrated EEIR thinking and evidence into their own postgraduate research projects (e.g. see Tomlinson et al. 1999).

There are also *normative* accounts within the improvement field where beliefs about what needs to be done can overtake the evidence base, and the effectiveness community are concerned about how 'enthusiasts can take on new ideas without recognizing the possibility that no effects may be shown, and may lack awareness of the need to create robust evaluation methods' (Muijs et al. 2014, p. 250).

The data from the KPEL project in the UK shows a strong concern to follow interests by individuals and within groups, but there is also recognition of funding and how they relate to government as funders and research users. A clear intention of effectiveness and improvement knowledge workers is to obtain funding, particularly where research and policymaker concerns are interlinked (e.g. Creemers et al. 2000). The rationales tend to be about 'making a difference' mainly through informing policy, with narratives about relevance and utility. Hence the drive for *positivism* and *behaviourism*, as the means of curbing *experiential* resources, is linked to the remit of commissioned projects and the demands for particular forms of data that communicate clear messages about policy impact and success.

Prior to New Labour taking office in the UK in 1997, Barber (1998) talks about how the then Conservative government had been responsive to school effectiveness research (e.g. the 1992 Ofsted framework was based on research), and in preparing for office Barber (1996), endorsed the effectiveness field, and by co-writing, he identified the evidence base and how it would be used to inform government policy (Reynolds et al. 1996). Once in office, key people from the effectiveness and improvement community were drawn into the policy process through appointed roles and commissioned projects. Importantly, there is evidence of the packaging of knowledge by state consultants and deliverers of reform (e.g. Coles and Southworth 2005a; Hopkins 2007).

This shared disposition revealed by those within and outside of government is evident in a range of ways, not least how critiques of government policy have been responded to. For example, Sammons et al. (2010) responded to Barker's (2010a,b) analysis by claiming that it is 'dangerous because they promote the view that policymakers and practitioners are powerless to effect positive change whereas considerable bodies of research provide valuable evidence on strategies to promote improvement and can enhance life chances for the disadvantaged' (unpaged). This 'servicing' arrangement between research and policy is a key feature of the narratives within the field, not least concerns about how research is sometimes not taken up (Reynolds et al. 2014).

Domains: the outcome from primarily *positivist* and *behaviourist* resources and actions linked to application and implementation at government and organizational levels is the location within mainly the *instrumental domain* with some *humanistic* claims about change.

The disposition towards the production of scientific evidence, often based on *behaviourist* assumptions, has three main *instrumental* outcomes: first, children and teachers are constructed as objects upon which those in leader roles impact, where teachers and children are usually positioned as in deficit. For example, Muijs et al. (2014) present a model for how knowledge is built through teaching and learning by identifying what students need, and then what knowledge and skills teachers need to meet those student needs. Second, and connected to this objectification of behaviours and organizational conditions, is a tendency to extrapolate key factors: Edmonds (1979) presents *Five Correlates of School Effectiveness*; Sammons et al. (1995) present *Eleven Factors for Effective Schools* (see also Sammons 1999); MacGilchrist et al. (1997) presented the *Nine Intelligences* that make up the Corporate Intelligence of the Intelligent School; Muijs et al. (2014) present *Eight Factors for Teacher Effectiveness*; and Hopkins et al. (2014) present *10 Features of Highly Effective Educational Systems*. The interplay between 'needs' and 'factors' requires a change process that is engaging and compelling, and so a third outcome is the use of metaphors (sometimes mixed): (a) machine metaphors such as 'levers' (Hopkins et al. 2014, p. 269), (b) building metaphors such as 'doors' (Stoll and Mortimore 1997, p. 15), and (c) medical metaphors regarding 'organisational health' with a sense of diagnosis and recovery (Hopkins et al. 2014, p. 259). This is based on the organization as a unitary object that can be a machine, and where behaviours can be controlled through levers, and breakdowns require a shift to organic thinking through attribution to the body and 'health'. This is consistent with theoretical assumptions based on systems theory, whereby the input–process–output model is used for machine and biological understandings of a problem that needs to be and can be fixed.

The production of functionally descriptive (this is what the situation is), and functionally normative (this is how the situation needs to change) *instrumental* texts are structured by the reform agenda. Hopkins et al. (2014) note the impact of major reports on change, for example, *A Nation at Risk* report in the United States in 1983, and interventions such as the OECD International School Improvement Project (ISIP) (Hopkins 1987), and how these give recognition to improvement and effectiveness data and processes, but also the limitations on the link with the student outcomes. Improvement and effectiveness communities are stimulated, enabled and validated through policy requirements, where Hopkins et al. (2014) identify the development of a 'how to do it' agenda, where there is clear evidence from field outputs of the acceptance of policy change with a commitment to providing resources for professionals to bring about the required changes. In order to deliver functional unity, the school is variously 'empowered' (Hargreaves and Hopkins 1991) and 'intelligent' (MacGilchrist et al. 1997), with improvement based on various control technologies such as school evaluation (e.g. MacBeath and McGlynn 2002; Ramsay and Clark 1990), student voice (e.g. Rudduck and Flutter 2004), and planning (e.g. Hargreaves and Hopkins 1991; MacGilchrist et al. 1995). A particular feature is the provision of strategies and tools for the removal of dysfunctions, both within the organization, but also within the system through a focus on what has become known as 'schools in challenging circumstances' (e.g. Harris et al. 2006) and on 'system leadership' (Hopkins 2007). Often think pieces with normative claims of how the changes are the right thing to do are made, particularly by writing texts that professionals can read and use, as workbooks. For example, Harris and Lambert (2003) provide not only a prescription for the 'what', 'how' and 'why' of leadership but also use a capacity questionnaire plus benchmarking factors for self-assessment. Interestingly, it seems that reform is necessary where de-politicized change processes have been designed to support the change leadership (Fullan with Stiegelbauer 1991; Fullan 2001).

Often underpinning *instrumental* texts is a *humanistic* domain. There is sense that change is about people and their experiences, and there is a need for a conceptualization of the human as subject and not just as an effectiveness determined object. Day et al. (2000) use stories to outline the work of school leaders in ways that show the importance of relationships, and the tensions and dilemmas involved in handling externally driven change. So projects that include interviews with professionals are in evidence, and with a focus on how to work with people to enable them to understand the need for the change and how to do it in ways that are developmental. This underpins key school improvement texts (e.g. Leithwood et al. 1999; Hargreaves and Fink 2006; Stoll and Fink 1996), where leadership models are presented in ways that speak to professionals who have traditionally worked in structures and cultures that are simultaneously hierarchical (transformational, *Instructional Leadership* models) and collegial (distributed, sustainable leadership models). The complexity and tensions involved in this are recognized with solution packages that enable professionals to locate themselves within the outlined 'problem' and then how to sort the situation out. For example, Stoll and Fink (1996) relate 'invitational leadership' to a typology of schools: moving, cruising, struggling, sinking, and strolling. In a moving school that is effective and improving, the key issue for leaders is 'to maintain the momentum', whereas in a cruising school there are signs of decline that may not be seen, where leaders 'need to demonstrate' what needs to be done. A strolling school is not improving fast enough and so 'the leader must expect, express and model a vision of "greatness" for the school'. Struggling schools want to change but need 'direction and planning', whereas sinking schools are in danger and so need 'strong and rigorous' intervention (pp. 115–16).

Context: the four main *knowledge contexts* impact on the *traditions, purposes* and *domains* outlined above through a predominance of *Neoliberalism, Neoconservativism* and *Elitism,* with a residualization of *Civic Welfarism.* While those who have created and developed the EEIR field often have their origins of their careers within a civic-welfarism context, a review of activity and approaches to *Knowledge Production* shows a general and often unacknowledged acceptance of the neoliberal and neoconservative discourses.

A study of EEIR texts tends to show an acceptance that change is happening that generates a solution-imperative agenda. Description of reforms suggests an acceptance of a crisis in public education with the emphasis on standards and international league tables, along with restructuring through site-based management and 'independence' (see Hopkins et al. 2014). The privatization of public education is not critically examined, and indeed, there are some examples of researchers aligning very explicitly with neoliberal choice and marketization agendas (e.g. Hopkins 2007).

The main approach to the spread of managerialism as a means of making retained public services more business-like is to make human practices more effective and efficient through scientific claims and interventions into behaviours located within *functional purposes* and *instrumental* products. As one effectiveness researcher said to us in the KPEL project – 'ideas and data are more important than teachers', not least it as argued because most of those who locate here have never worked in a school. However, within the improvement community biographical legacies mean that there is sense of knowing about the realities of schools, and so there are some *humanistic* trends that tend to be located in a residualized *Civic Welfarism* agenda of re-professionalizing peers who they work in partnership with in schools and local administration, and through a focus on the needs of children. For example, Hopkins et al. (2014) emphasize how field development is linked to 'a more specified approach to educational reform by transforming the organisation of the school through managing change in the quest for enhanced student achievement' (p. 264).

On balance, the push–pull of government policy is based on elite status, where neoliberal and neoconservative ideologies and strategies tend to dominate. Changes in the funding of universities in England mean that as one improvement researcher articulated, 'you go where the money is'. Therefore EEIR *knowledge actors* served Thatcherite governments pre-1997 and post-2010, and Thatcherite-informed governments between 1997 and 2010. The inclusion of EEIR researchers in government (in what I have called the *new labour policy regime,* Gunter 2012a) through either contracted appointments (e.g. Barber and Hopkins in the Department, Southworth in the National College) and/or commissioned projects (e.g. Day et al. 2009) means that the emphasis is on research *for* rather than *about* policy. Illustrative of this is Hopkins' (2007) development of system leadership within government, and how neoliberal data, measurement and ranking systems (e.g. PISA) generate a need for system leadership in ways that make it a saleable product (Hopkins et al. 2014, p. 268).

Funding for research does come from the social sciences through, for example, ESRC funding in the UK (e.g. Ainscow et al. 2006). However, the main funders outside of government-commissioned projects tend to be philanthropic and consultancy organizations, where Hopkins et al. (2014) note the importance of the Wallace Foundation (Leithwood et al. 2004) and Aga Khan Foundation, with references to studies undertaken by McKinsey (e.g. Mourshed et al. 2010). The relationship between remit and funding, or the business motive underpinning *Knowledge Production* from consultancy firms, is not troubled.

Networks: the main networked groupings that locate here are those who work in EEIR, who also influence EA and EP.

The EEIR network is made up primarily of two main sub-groups: those who work on effectiveness at whole school and teacher levels, and those who work on improvement processes through activity that examines change and leadership. These areas of interest are distinctive with key texts and field reviews (e.g. Chapman et al. 2015; Sammons 1999; Teddlie and Reynolds 2000; Hopkins 2014) but are also linked through projects that seek to examine interconnections (e.g. Day et al. 2009) as well as conferences (e.g. ICSEI).

Both improvement and effectiveness researchers are located in western-style democracies, though the KPEL data show a strong UK–European connection between effectiveness researchers. Handbooks and edited collections also demonstrate institutional locations and links (e.g. Chapman et al. 2012; Teddlie and Reynolds 2000), and within the UK (Reynolds et al. 1996) and Canada (Levin 2008) there is a strong connection with government.

Historically, the London Institute of Education has been an internationally recognized site for effectiveness work, through the leadership of Peter Mortimore and The International School Effectiveness and Improvement Centre (ISEIC), where statements of aims include developing knowledge and the links between effectiveness and improvement through school-based projects, and collaborative partnerships (HEIs, LEAs, consultants and government) (Stoll and Mortimore 1997). The former Cambridge Institute of Education was a site of school improvement researchers, not least the home of the Improving the Quality of Education for All (IQEA) project (Hopkins et al. 1994; Hopkins 1996).

Knowledge production

The status of leaders, leading and leadership within the EEIR field as an area of interest and research activity is ambiguous. While there are key projects (e.g. Day et al. 2011) and reviews (e.g. Harris 2005a), it is teacher effectiveness and not leadership effectiveness that is singled out for the most recent state-of-the-art review in the field journal *School Improvement and School Effectiveness* (Reynolds 2014). It seems that leadership is being put in its place where Hopkins et al. (2014) regard it as *one* of the features in an effective education system, and Reynolds et al. (2014) argue for 'the integration of leadership, its characteristics, and its future possible changes fully into the field, since it has been seen as a stand-alone issue, and there needs to be studies where leadership is integrated within a model of school effectiveness which is theorized and takes into account the ways in which leadership interacts with other key school factors' (p. 218).

The debates within this EEIR network tends to focus on the drive to generate the evidence base through the science of effectiveness and the descriptive conditions for improvement. Within the KPEL project interviews, field members gave recognition to concerns, not least how the biographical experiences of effectiveness researchers outside of schools meant that they were delayed in reaching the classroom as a prime focus of research. The development of effectiveness and improvement research has therefore taken place over time and within context, and so the evidence base is developing rather than fully secured.

There are three aspects to the challenges this raises within the field: first, the KPEL interview data shows a distinctive approach to the building of methodologically robust data, where those who locate primarily in effectiveness studies are concerned with developing a scientific approach and so talk about methods, measurements and claims, whereas the improvement community begin their approach with the needs of professionals and schools, and how they are concerned to support this and how their encounters *in the field* generate new and interesting questions for investigation; second, the KPEL data show that the majority of those who locate in improvement and effectiveness projects do not see leadership as a central concern for their work with some concerned about the overemphasis on leadership; indeed most respondents locate themselves in relation to teaching and learning, the profession, change processes and organizational studies, and yet these same respondents have led and worked on major leadership projects and have contributed to the evidence base; and third, the tension between the state of the evidence base and the demands from the professional field for support has generated a situation where normative recommendations are made for the adoption of leadership practices without the evidence on the basis that the field cannot wait for this green light (see Harris 2005b; Leithwood et al. 1999). Internal critique in print is rare within EEIR, but Muijs (2011) investigates how there is a tendency to jump from the idea to prescription without the evidence. He examines the orthodoxies of *Transformational, Distributed* and *Instructional Leaderships*, and this leads him to conclude 'that leadership does make a difference to organisational effectiveness and even to pupil performance' and 'there is some evidence that Transformational and *Distributed Leadership* in particular can contribute to organizational effectiveness' (pp. 54–5), but he goes on to argue that 'what is equally clear is that the research base is far weaker than many of the claims made for these forms of leadership, and indeed for leadership development' (p. 55). Interestingly, he does not mention names or projects within EEIR where this has been a feature.

Knowledge Production within EEIR tends to take the lead from an integrated imperative from policy and practice: policy requires effectiveness and improvement, and so professionals require appropriate models to change their practices. The funding of projects from governments and agencies establishes priorities and remits, where collaborative networks between those in government and those in practice and higher education enable synchronicity in agendas. Consequently, while EEIR is located in *research* and *professional hubs*, it is the exchange relationships and funding from within government regimes that shift their attention towards *policy* and *corporate hubs*. The *Knowledge Production* that has been undertaken as part of this process at national (e.g. Day et al. 2009), and supranational levels (e.g. Leithwood et al. 2004; Pont et al. 2008a,b), has capital value staked with and valued by governments and philanthropists, and so other networks such as EA and EP have drawn on and used these findings. *Transformational Leadership* is strongly located in these endeavours: it has been designed, legitimated and commercialized through knowledge exchange and claims within and for government regimes, and this has reached into other networks and activity in such a way that to think otherwise is unlikely to be on the agenda.

Summary

EEIR has a recent but influential intellectual history from the 1970s onwards, where the emphasis is on knowledge building and methodological robustness. The brief examination of the 4Ks in this chapter shows duality but interconnectedness in regard to *theory, purposes* and *domains*, where effectiveness seeks the functionality of science, and improvement is concerned with learning from and improving practice. The impact of *contexts* on education policy and the close linkages with *networks* shows that EEIR continues to make a contribution to privatization, with support for key policies such as choice (Hopkins 2007). Hence within a *knowledgeable polity*, the state and politics has invested in EEIR methodologies and *knowledges* as the means to improve standards, and has therefore funded the design and promotion of *Transformational Leadership*, along with rebranding through *Distributed* and *Instructional* hybrids.

10

Entrepreneurs and Popularizers

Introduction

*E*ntrepreneurs and *Popularizers* (EP) is a label that I have adopted in order to frame and give recognition to intellectual work that is a product of the market, where epistemic identities may not feature strongly because the emphasis is on trade. By 'entrepreneurs' I mean people who trade knowledge and know-how regarding who leaders are, what they do and how they might do it differently, and in this sense they popularize particular types of knowledge and ways of knowing (Ball 1995). By 'trade' I mean the processes through which knowledge is shared informally, through to more formal ways of financial exchange through contracts and fees, and how this impacts on the design and delivery of leaders, leading and leadership as a 'product' (See Rowan 2002). In addition to behind the scenes interrelationships, not least vouching for each other as trusted knowledge workers, generally the emphasis is on commissioning and contracting according to a remit rather than primary peer-reviewed research. In addition, some people access, combine and package ideas independently of research or data collection, and popularize models of leadership through books, training and cascading. Those who are located in higher education (within EA and EEIR) who move into and out of business networks, tend to eschew overt epistemological matters in regard to this activity.

This is difficult to map, but it is possible to identify important examples: first, those who hold positions of power in international organizations, governments or business, and who 'speak' and 'write' approaches to leaders, leading and leadership into existence; second, employees of higher education institutions who produce books and webpages that synthesize and popularize particular approaches, not least business models are presented as modern and modernizing; and third, private sector consultants from large international companies through to individual 'sole traders' who work with the profession. Some of these people work close-to-practice within schools through to those who are at a distance both from the school and the nation state where that school is located (see Gunter and Mills 2016). Therefore the examples I give could seemingly be an eclectic array of references, but at the same time there is evidence of a sharing of territory and dispositions, and also some networked links that are both public and behind the scenes.

Leaders, leading and leadership

A characterization of this area of field activity as 'catholic' on the basis of people, interests and organizational location is a truism, but at the same time, there is evidence of a shared elite narrative regarding the importance of leaders, leadership and leadership, and what it means. For example, in promoting the distillation of reading and thinking about 'what makes a good school', Taylor (2009) states that 'good leadership can be driven by an inspiring individual, but that alone is not enough; it also requires teamwork' (p. 5). The emphasis here is leader centric, but also supported by an elite cadre of role incumbents who are focused on delivery (see also Taylor and Ryan 2005). Such notions of the individual and team doing 'good' and 'strong' leadership are widespread features of what is communicated for the transformation into effective and successful schools.

Historically, the necessity and normality of the organization with leadership integral to entrepreneurship is located in business texts. The message is one of relentless transformation. Bestselling books by Collins (2001), Covey (2004) and Senge (2006), with clear messages of the importance of linking attributes to outcome delivery, have impacted on school leadership where Collin's claims about how a business can shift from *Good to Great* has been reworked for education (see Gray and Streshly 2008); as have Covey's *Seven Habits of Highly Effective People* (see Tooley and Howes 1999); and Senge's *The Fifth Discipline* (see Senge et al. 2012). The borders between business and education are increasingly permeable with principals promoting business ideas and methods (see Astle and Ryan 2008; Crossley 2013), and where Michael Barber tells the story of his movement between the profession, higher education and government (Barber 2007), and how he has developed this into a saleable global product (Barber et al. 2011).

The identification of the importance of business ideas as a means of enabling site-based management to work effectively in western-style democracies has been a key feature of field outputs, whereby from the 1980s onwards a range of publications have enabled the profession to become more business-like in their behaviours, thinking and language. A range of approaches to site-based management supported shifts in professional practice away from the classroom towards budgets, marketing, human resources and organizational culture, where neoliberal reforms generated accounts of principals doing new work (e.g. Crossley 2013). This is supported with specific approaches to strategy and 'how to do it' primers and workbooks for busy professionals (e.g. Davies and Davies 2005). Now the trend is to move beyond the enculturation of professionals as entrepreneurs towards their replacement by effective leaders from other services (e.g. DfES/PwC 2007) and increasingly by corporate entrepreneurs who can create for-profit educational services (e.g. Sandler 2010).

How those who package and sell leadership develop their knowledge is often not visible. When such learning goes public through what is said to a person in their office, what is on a presentation slide, and what is written in a blog, it can be difficult to chart but how and why the interplay of ideas, language and practice has been described. For example, Anderson (2009) witnessed a model of leadership presented by the New York City Department of Education. He states that 'they are seeking a linear, cause-and-effect pathway from leadership preparation to student achievement scores that is evidence-based' (p. 172), and he goes on to say how there are 'vendors' who are selling their leadership product:

Their claims are predictable. That effective leadership can be empirically defined and that it is – contrary to misconceptions – more science than art. In fact, their potential buyers will be happy to discover that they have identified 21 key leadership responsibilities that are significantly correlated with higher student achievement. Not surprisingly the company has a stable of consultants ready to fly to your school district and in-service your administrators in this cutting edge leadership science. (p. 172)

There are similarities here with the EEIR and aspects of EA, and a study of consultancy in the field (Gunter 2012a) shows the diversity: from those who are in higher education and seek to generate 'third stream income' by advising and working with government and schools through to major companies who develop and market their leadership products internationally. Networks of people in different organizational, employment and geographical locations are interlinking and working on the idea and reality of leadership in ways that enable the circulation, adoption and acceptance of the same type of approach. Hence a principal in any part of the world may adopt a 'new' way of undertaking professional practice that has been developed within business and has its origins in globalized networks of knowledge exchange and legitimacy (see Caldwell 2006). This is what Thomson et al. (2014) have called the *transnational leadership package* (TPL) whereby what sutures together the demands by governments for higher standards with on-the-ground practice in classrooms is leadership. Ideas and those carrying those ideas (in books, online, at keynote lectures, at professional development workshops) circulate the locality and the globe with similar electronic presentation slides and claims: 'The TLP provides a kind of (largely) Anglocentric policy ... (of) ... flat-pack of policy "levers" that will produce the actions and effects that count in national elections and internationally testing. While modern but cheap, it is worth "buying into" largely because to be seen as different is risky' (p. xi). Hence *Transformational Leadership* as essential for risk-taking and contractualism within the market remains a consistent feature, with campaigns about 'new and improved' through various hybrid products such as *Distributed* and *Instructional Leadership*.

An intellectual history of Entrepreneurs and Popularizers

Here I provide a summary by deploying the framework developed in Part 2.

Traditions: the identification of *knowledge traditions* is difficult, largely because those who talk about and bring leadership and followership into the preferred way of delivering an efficient and effective school do not usually provide the intellectual origins beyond the business gurus that they have adopted, or their experience of being in business themselves. Indeed, one strategy that is used is to undermine those who seek to examine and debate knowledge claims, particularly as a means of removing barriers to markets in training programmes, but more often than not what is said and written just does not consider such matters as worth engaging with. However, claims are made that demonstrate *positivism*, and in the main, it is largely *behaviourist*. For example, Wilkins (2014) uses the observations he made as an international consultant regarding school leadership to both promote the certainties of data along with the 'capacity-building' necessary for people to feel, understand and enact change (p. 123).

Such approaches have been illuminated by Anderson (2009) who identifies that 'there is little sense of leadership as anything but a series of behaviors and dispositions that lead to rising scores on standardized tests. A more narrow view of educational leadership is hard to imagine' (p. 172). An accepted way of securing this is through a list of statements regarding attributes, know-how and skills (see English 2003; Gunter 2012a). For example, PricewaterhouseCoopers undertook a review of school leadership for the then UK Labour Government in 2007 (DfES/PwC 2007) with a clear focus on behaviours:

> An important aspect of this study involved identifying leadership models that are effective in terms of raising standards of pupil achievement. A key element of this relates to the characteristics of effective leaders, i.e. the attributes and behaviours exhibited by successful leaders, irrespective of the organisational model or structure within which they are operating. Indeed, a strong message from the literature on leadership in the private sector is that, although corporate structures matter, they do not matter as much as the behaviours exhibited by the leaders of the organisation. A similar message emerges from our research; the behaviours of school leaders have a greater influence on pupil performance than school structures or models. (p. viii)

They then connect this focus with other government-funded research (Leithwood et al. 2006), before going on to present a list of effective leader behaviours based on discussions with the profession, where it is claimed that effective leaders:

- Adopt an open, consultative and non-hierarchical approach – distribute leadership responsibilities effectively;

- Are approachable and visible throughout the school;

- Communicate effectively with all staff;

- Take performance management of staff seriously, and provide clear development pathways for staff; and

- Understand classroom practice as well as the role of the school in the wider community (DfES/PwC 2007, p. ix).

The case is then made that such behaviours can be shaped and structured through models of leadership, not least that 'although leadership behaviours are generally more important than leadership models, the development of new models can be one of the *conduits* through which the right leadership behaviours are fostered' (p. ix). Consequently, the structuring of behaviours through what are identified as established but out-of-date approaches along with emerging new models is a central feature of the report. In Ball's (2010) analysis this 'leadership knowledge' is interrelated with its use within policy design and delivery (pp. 126–7). The literatures that are drawn on tend to be EEIR where the underlying knowledge claims are accepted, and the approach to the issue of leader, leading and leadership adopts the assumptions of 'improvement' and 'effectiveness'. The interrelationship between a large private consultancy company and a government department shows a shared belief system in the efficacy of leadership as a means of changing practice, and how this has impacted on the methodologies and the intellectual resources that are drawn on to conceptualize the project.

Purposes: the accessing and use of the *behaviourist traditions* tends to be mainly *functional*.

The emphasis on behaviours – what principals do, how and to what effect, and how they might do this differently through adopting a leader identity, leading actions and leadership processes – has a focus on enabling the local delivery of standards to be efficient and effective. Indeed, there is a strong emphasis on removing dysfunctions, particularly through how problems are identified and solutions promoted. There is often slippage between description and exhortation to make changes through the adoption of normative 'good practice'. This is evident in government (e.g. DfEE 1998) and business approaches (e.g. Caldwell 2006), where the networks of entrepreneurial knowledge workers enable and support product development (e.g. Crossley 2013). For example, the OECD has invested in the production of leadership knowledge through projects and reporting, and the summarizing in easily accessible formats (Pont et al. 2008a,b). The functionality of this work is enabled through the adoption and popularization of EEIR approaches, legitimation through citations and with the contracting of knowledge workers to undertake the project. Importantly, the authoring and the production of the evidence base for these reports show associations and shared dispositions between people from the OECD along with business and consultancy.

Functionality is evident in the conceptualization of leadership as integral to improvement and effectiveness, and through the slippage between formal role titles and generic 'school leaders' so that all, as the audience, are captured by the tone and content. Importantly, there is an emphasis on how education needs to fit with economic, political and social demands, particularly through 'futuring' and scenario building, and how leadership is an important means for delivery. The claim is made that

school leadership has become a priority in education policy agendas across OECD and partner countries. It plays a key role in improving school outcomes by influencing the motivations and capacities of teachers, as well as the environment and climate within which they work. Effective school leadership is essential to improve the efficiency and equity of schooling. (Pont et al. 2008a, p. 32)

And, the outcome of this analysis is that the authors identify 'four main policy levers which, taken together, can improve school leadership practice' and hence 'these should help governments to decide how to prepare and build high quality leadership'. The four are '(re)defining school leadership responsibilities, distributing school leadership, developing skills for effective school leadership, and, making school leadership an attractive profession' (p. 32). In addition to essays that examine each of these recommendations, there are selected case studies (Pont et al. 2008b) that promote the EEIR knowledge worker's ideas of system leadership that is concerned to secure functional improvement and effectiveness. Finally, functionality is enabled through the writing of a normative executive summary report that exhorts readers to adopt the key messages, where the language and claims make the relationship between ideas and actions clear and obvious (OECD 2008).

Domains: the outcome from primarily *behaviourist* resources and actions linked to application and implementation at government and organizational levels is the production of mainly *instrumental* with some *humanistic* change knowledge domains. Humanism is located in how prescription can be linked back to the experiences of selected professionals who are presented as demonstrating the right type of needs and solution provision (e.g. Pont et al. 2008a,b, PwC/DfES 2007). But the training and cascading of what is required, and how this links to business opportunities to provide learning resources, means that there is a strong emphasis on quick and simple guidance and support. This is how much of the intellectual work undertaken in EEIR and EA is distilled and presented as 'how to do it' texts, where the experiences of the author(s), their disposition for business solutions and the imperative to help the profession handle the privatization agenda are combined to produce *instrumental* models of change. In this sense, the interruption and alternative futures promoted by anti-state researchers such as Tooley (2000) provide the discourse around choice and accountability in which these solutions are normalized.

Illustrative of this instrumentalism is Barber et al.'s (2011) text: *Deliverology 101. A Field Guide for Educational Leaders*, where the case is made for the implementation of reform as the crucial missing part of change processes, and the reason why most reforms leave people disappointed. Inspirational politicians are used to establish the urgency and need for change, where vision is integral and project management enables the securing of outcomes. This book is the product of the interplay between Barber's time in government and in McKinsey & Company through the authorship and the production of a *Knowledge Production* template (see Rasiel and Friga 2001). The text 'speaks' directly to the reader to enable them to know what is relevant to them and how to read the 'field guide'. The separation of the 'system' or strategic leader from the 'delivery' or operational leader is Taylorist in conception, meaning that the 'delivery effort' is shared but the 'direction-setting' of the system leader ensures that 'aspirations' and 'strategy' are provided. In short, the role of the delivery leader is 'to understand what is in place, push to improve it if necessary, and then build upon it' (p. xvi). The key features of making this happen are the setting up of a delivery unit, staffing with the right type of people, a focus on the collection and use of data, and how to keep delivery on track through targets and monitoring. The emphasis is not just on the technicalities and techniques of structures, roles and management processes (e.g. planning) but on cultural change through how thinking, talking and action is shaped by and reshapes practice. While this deliverology primer is presented as speaking to a US audience, the potential exists for it to be transferred from context to context, with tweaking and development.

Context: the three main contextual structures impact on the *traditions, purposes* and *domains* outlined above through a predominance of *Neoliberalism* and *Neoconservativism* underpinned with *Elitism.* Such a context tends to be presented as demanding and urgent, where there is an imperative for the right type of leaders, doing the right type of leading and leadership to be in post and taking action. For example,

> The next two years provide a once-in-a-generation opportunity to transform public education in America. If that opportunity is seized …. This moment has been created by an administration that prioritizes education reform: by the $100 billion for education in the federal stimulus package, including almost $5 billion for the "Race to the Top Fund"; by the emergence of an increasingly shared national agenda focused on standards, accountability, data, human capital, and reducing school failure; by the growing interest in international benchmarking in the United States and the emerging understanding around the world of the characteristics of successful system reform. And while the economic crisis is a challenge in so many ways, it is also a spectacular opportunity to recruit more and better people into teaching, if the right kinds of programs can be developed. (Barber et al. 2011, p. vi)

The emphasis on outcomes and not structures means that private and public are elided (see Barber 2007; DfEE 1997), not least in ways that those who promote themselves as deliverers can be enabled to enter the 'system' and provide schools. So in England, the academies programme is based on the idea that private wealth and knowledge can be used to improve student outcomes, not least that school leadership can be made more effective through good advice and role models (Gunter 2011).

Those who speak authoritatively about school leadership tend to be those who are directly located in neoliberal (e.g. entrepreneurs, philanthropists) and neoconservative (e.g. philanthropists, faith groups) contexts, and those who are directly connected with and/or dependent upon such interests (e.g. members of governments). Grace's (1995) identification of the endurance of two nineteenth-century structuring influences on school leadership: the use of a dominant and elite person to communicate and monitor the normalized morality of school owners (*Neoconservativism*), and the promotion of entrepreneurial identities, dispositions and practices for that elite person (Neoliberalism), is very pertinent to current reforms and discourses. The tensions tend to be about the alliance between the two rather than appropriateness, and this tends to be resolved through how individuals work to resolve it. For example, principals talk about how they have embraced and promoted the neoliberal agenda (e.g. Crossley 2013), and there are accounts of how knowledge located within and for corporate elites is coming to dominate (Ball and Exley 2010).

The corporatization of education has impacted on leaders, leading and leadership. There are a range of studies that demonstrate how and why corporate elites have set out to frame the purposes, rationales and narratives of who leaders are, what they do and why they do it. This is about how the public system is characterized as failing with the solution through markets (e.g. Koyama 2010) combined with the actions of individuals and networks to develop markets (e.g. Spring 2012). A specific focus is on leader identity, selection, attributes and behaviours, training and accreditation with a strong trend towards the establishment of centres of excellence (Gunter 2012a; Ravitch 2010). The influence of particular individuals can be crucial and here I will reference Saltman's (2010) examination of the Eli Broad Foundation in the United States of America. His research shows how private knowledge and interests are dominating the who, what and why of school leadership:

> A central priority of the Eli Broad Foundation is to recruit and train superintendents and principals from outside of the ranks of professional teachers and educational administrators and, related to this, to shift administrator preparation away from universities and state certification to the control of outside organizations that embrace corporate and military styles of management. . . . At the core of these initiatives

has been the neoliberal celebration of private sector and denigration of all things public. In this view, educational leadership is imagined ideally as corporate management, and the legacy of public educational administration is devalued. (pp. 80–1)

What this example illustrates is what English (2003) characterizes as 'cookie-cutter leaders for cookie-cutter schools' (p. 27) whereby the standardization of leadership is about restructuring and reculturing public education as a means of opening up to markets. How this works out within philanthropy is through initiatives that speak to issues that 'we' can all 'buy into' such as student achievement, and presents solutions that are seemingly sensible. Saltman (2010) shows how there is a link between training and student outcomes, and argues that 'this way of thinking about teacher and administrator preparation exemplifies this resurgent positivism and its anti-intellectual bent. In this view, there can be no place for educational study that does not result in test score improvement ... so educational theory, sociology and philosophy of education, curriculum theorizing, pedagogical theory, – approaches in education that address the underlying assumptions, ethical, historical, and political aspects of what is taught and learned – none has a place in the "valued-added" perspective because all that matters is "delivery" of "content knowledge" through the use of the "best" "instructional methods"' (p. 90).

Networks: this is a challenging analysis to undertake because formal networks that have been identified in the construction of this intellectual history are not a feature. However, while rich and powerful individuals do work as sole agents, there are examples of people who associate and exchange knowledge and provide legitimacy. Furthermore, as already identified there are those who locate in EEIR and EA who also inter-link and network with private interests, for example, Tony McKay is director of the Centre for Strategic Educational Thinking (CSET, Melbourne) and has been the president of the ICSEI.

As already cited, there is important work on interlinking and associations by people in different organizational locations and remits have been done by Ball (Ball 2007, 2008a, 2012; Ball and Junemann 2012). In relation to leaders, leading and leadership, this has been undertaken through the description of networked links and the development of theorizations of those links (e.g. Ball 2010; Gunter 2012a). The sources I have used in this chapter are interesting illustrations that show collaborations and exchange relationships, not least through how reports and co-authoring teams are created and deployed in *Knowledge Production*. Here I intend presenting Future Leaders in the UK as an example.

Future Leaders was set up in 2006 to provide leadership training for school leaders located in areas of deprivation, and it began in London and has spread to other regions, with '330 Future Leaders working in more than 240 challenging primary and secondary schools across England, impacting upon over 225,000 pupils'. The main message is:

Our mission is to raise the achievement of children, regardless of background, and to provide them with equal choices and opportunities in life. By developing a network of exceptional school leaders, we are transforming challenging schools and working to eradicate educational disadvantage. (The Future Leaders Charitable Trust 2014, unpaged)

The assertion is made through a statement that 'we believe' that 'evidence supports that effective, inspirational school leadership can eradicate educational disadvantage – school leaders improve teaching and learning indirectly and most powerfully through their influence on staff motivation, commitment and working conditions'. This message is then communicated through five bullet points:

EVERY CHILD
All children can be successful, regardless of their background

NO EXCUSES
Every excuse is a step on the road to failure

HIGH EXPECTATIONS
Children, staff, schools and communities will live up to the expectations placed upon them

LEAD LEARNING
The most important things that happen in schools happen in classrooms

NO ISLANDS
When great school leaders work together, anything is possible
(The Future Leaders Charitable Trust 2014, unpaged).

The criteria for admission are clearly stated in relation to the situation in which a school is located, with inspirational stories of principals and schools who have benefitted, and claims are made about impact projects undertaken by those who sign up. The new Talented Leaders Programme is focused on workforce deployment, where it

matches exceptional leaders to areas of the country most in need of better school leadership. Successful candidates recruited to a headship position will commit to transforming their school, remaining in post for at least three years. Heads will receive a relocation package, coaching support and tailored training from The Future Leaders Trust's Headship Institute, alongside a £50,000 Leadership Sustainability Fund to be used to secure improvements and to build a stronger leadership pipeline within their schools. The support of ministers will make this a prestigious programme, and this is your opportunity to make a real difference to an area that needs you most. (The Future Leaders Charitable Trust 2014, unpaged)

The people and organizations outlined as supporting and underpinning Future Leaders demonstrate the formation and actioning of networks between organizations, for example, Whitehall, Absolute Return for Kids (ARK) and the Specialist Schools and Academies Trust (SSAT). So Future Leaders is a node with networks that spread nationally, where ARK is an education charity that is involved in the provision and ownership of Academies, and also internationally through how ARK has schools and other services abroad. Importantly, these networks are layered and interconnected in other significant ways, and again where the reach is complex and related to private interests. So the board is made up of headteachers, ARK, SSAT, with a clear link to *Teach First* which provides a two-year leadership development programme for those who wish to move into teaching, and at the end the teachers may continue or exit.

Future Leaders is linked with particular organizations, with a list of partners that draw from a range of organizations, and how the charitable status means that income flow is an issue that is upfronted:

As an independent charity, **The Future Leaders Trust** relies on essential monetary, in-kind and advisory support to continue to tackle educational disadvantage. We are supported by our sister organisation, **ARK**, and by the **National College for Teaching and Leadership**, which funds the Future Leaders flagship programme. Over the past six years, we have also received monetary or pro-bono support from **Barclays Capital**, **Barclays Wealth**, **Deutsche Bank**, **McDermott Will and Emery**, **UBS** and **The Fidelity Foundation**. Our supporters have made it possible for us to introduce many exciting changes, but we don't want to stop here. We have ambitious plans for the future – particularly for our regional growth, new primary provision, growing online network and support for our burgeoning number of headteachers. We are looking for organisations with a philanthropy agenda, aligned with our mission and capacity to fund growth and new projects or to support us with their expertise and resources. In return, we commit to using contributions in the most efficient, effective way, and to keeping our partners updated on our progress, doing everything we can to make their employees part of our journey. We will be transparent, open to questions, and dedicated to the partnership's aims. (The Future Leaders Charitable Trust 2014, unpaged)

This is an interesting illustrative example of how entrepreneurship and popularization are creating new partnerships and organizational arrangements to promote a particular leadership product. No independent primary research evidence is presented on the website regarding the claims being made, and no links are made to research reports or experts as the approach is based on beliefs and the capitals of those who have staked their careers and interests in this product.

Knowledge production

Knowledge Production takes place as a business process: an idea, manufacturing, marketing and sales. Therefore claims can be based on evaluations as 'speedy work', where in the KPEL project a consultant from an international firm talks about how they completed a major project on school leadership much faster than someone from higher education, and 'they generally tend to be reasonably well written and written in plain English and addressing issues that policy makers are interested in'. In addition, knowledge products can be located in personal beliefs and witnessed accounts of best practice, and this is evident in speeches through to websites, for example:

Politicians: Excellent leaders create excellent schools. Secondary schools need strong leaders at all levels, enabling them to provide a rich and diverse curriculum taught by professionals committed to success for every learner (Clarke 2004, p. 25).

Philanthropists: Mayor Richard M. Daley and Chicago Public Schools (CPS) CEO Arne Duncan joined the Chicago-based Academy for Urban School Leadership (AUSL) to announce an investment of $10.3 million from the Bill & Melinda Gates Foundation to support the turnaround of chronically underperforming district schools. AUSL will use the funds to transform three CPS-selected high schools over the next several years and expand its teacher residency program me (Bill and Melinda Gates Foundation, Undated).

Principal: The critical nature of leadership: without emotionally intelligent leadership and dogged determination fuelled by perpetual optimism and positivity distributed throughout the school sustainable improvement at the level achieved would not have proved possible. The cultural shift was achieved first by winning the hearts and minds of the staff and students and recognizing that ultimately 'influence' and not 'power' is the higher-level leadership concept. Adopting a high task–high people approach to leadership enabled the introduction of crucial developments without undue delay (Yellup 2013, p. 273).

Unions: Research informs us and our instincts tell us that successful school leaders are people who provide vision and direction and who hold values which are reflected in the life of the school. The vision may vary from place to place and the values will be distinctive to the headteacher and the school, but the combination of good leaders, clear purpose and strong values is a powerful formula when it comes to securing school improvement (Hill 2006, p. 58).

Such knowledge claims are located in experience, and communicated with a lexicon that is both descriptive and judgemental, for example, 'excellence', 'successful' and 'strong', and to challenge this by opening them up for debate would dilute the potency of what is being claimed that leaders, leading and leadership can achieve. This is summed up by a consultant in the KPEL project who talks about the 'new' imperative:

Well, I think the whole history of management development and leadership development has been very much flavour of the month stuff. And if you read, eventually a message that's put across looks a bit past it's shelf life and passé and people don't listen to it as carefully as when it came out. But if you can put it in new clothes, still have exactly the same notion, but use different words to describe it, people think 'oh, this is new'. So they'll read about it as though it was new, but if you actually analyse it to its root meaning, it is actually the same. And I think that's a good way of progressing, because you've got to keep up people's interest in improving all the time.

The relationship between the producer and the recipient is complex, but is summed up by another KPEL consultant respondent, who talks about how business models are 'picked up' because they can speak to what is already known. Therefore, this consultant identifies the powerful influence of Covey (2004) as an example, and how it is legible for the professional because they are steeped in *behavourist science*: 'Leadership is about behaviour isn't it really and that's significant really. ... I'll never forget the first Leadership Programme for Serving Headteachers (LPSH) we did when we had school leaders who'd never ever had any feedback, so here we were doing 360 degree appraisal for the first time, you know, it's breakdown time for some heads. I can remember a head, who said, 'I've been seventeen years ahead and nobody's ever told me. If anybody had told me that this is what my behaviour was doing, I might have done something about it. How awful!' And it's devastating when people get that kind of feedback'. Here the reception and realization of learning that challenges the *experiential tradition* validates the importation of a business model.

Knowledge Production within EP is both responsive and proactive in relation to consumer demands from government through to the profession. This happens independently of policy where EP is concerned to enter public education as a new market, but it is also the case that business strategy has been enabled through links to the *policy hub*. This is through the funding of projects, the invitations to give advice and to speak at major professional events, and the reading of key texts by ministers and officials. Consequently, EP *knowledge actors* are located in the *corporate hub* but are key to government regimes through the symbolism of modernization and 'can do' practices. This makes links with the *professional* and *research hubs* through consultancy contracts, and collaborative projects very potent. The *corporate hub* is integral to government regimes, the EP networks exchange knowledge with ministers and civil servants, and other networks within the regime such as EEIR, and hence share dispositions, languages and connections. This is not necessarily a planned or rational process, but there is a *logic of practice*, 'which is the product of a lasting exposure to conditions similar to those in which they are placed, they anticipate the necessity immanent in the way of the world' (Bourdieu 1990, p. 11). Therefore the construction and communication of *Transformational Leadership* as a preferred model is located in such exchange practices, and consequently the government regime is a site where people from a range of occupational locations can interconnect and play the game. Those from EEIR and EA who are successful in this game, can learn about EP activities, and so the cross over from public employment to private consultancy is learnt and eased.

Summary

EP has grown rapidly from the 1970s onwards, where the emphasis is on combining and recombining knowledge into packages and products. The brief examination of the 4Ks in this chapter shows an acceptance of particular approaches to *theory, purposes* and *domains*, where trading is based on the sale of the *doxa* of certainty and predictability. The impact of *contexts* on education policy and the close linkages with *networks* shows that EP is directly located in privatization. Hence within a *knowledgeable polity*, the role of the state and politics has enabled EP approaches to grow rapidly as a the means to improve standards, and where people who have been in government, schools and universities have crossed over into the private exchanges to promote new knowledge products. The design and promotion of *Transformational Leadership* is enabled by EEIR and EA research, but it is popularized by private *knowledge actors* as integral to the autonomous school as a business.

11

Critical Educational Policy and Leadership Studies

Introduction

Critical Educational Policy and Leadership Studies (CEPaLS) is a label that has been adopted to enable a focus on research that locates professional work and organizational development within wider power structures. Such criticality is located in approaches where there is a focus on the realities of working lives in schools, with some taking a social, political and/or economic critical perspective to such realities with a commitment to working for a more equitable approach to access, experience and outcomes of educational services. There is an ideological rupture in this form of criticality whereby the right is anti-state and is working to privatize education, and the left has pro-collective approaches to educational services where a reformed state has a significant role to play. As the right is directly involved in the entrepreneurialism and the popularization of branded leadership goods in the consultancy and training marketplace engaged with in Chapter 10, I am going to give prime attention in this chapter to critical work that challenges this dominance and reveals different approaches.

This is a territory where a range of contributions can be located, but as there is no specific network, or journal or conference, there is no formal epistemic historiography that can be drawn on. This is a community that tends to locate their research contributions in education policy journals (e.g. *Journal of Education Policy*) and radical educational administration journals (e.g. *International Journal of Leadership in Education*) with special interest groups in major national research networks such as AERA, BERA and BELMAS. There is evidence of groups of researchers and emerging networks (see for example, Bogotch et al. 2008), and there is a history of contributions that can be brought together, charted and considered regarding *Knowledge Production* and school leadership. So in this chapter I intend drawing on a range of work that: first, critiques approaches to leadership studies undertaken by EA, EEIR and EP; second, presents alternative evidence and theorizations of leadership; and third, undertakes research into public and education policy which means that the prime focus is not usually on leadership but contributes to leadership studies. In doing this, I intend scoping the research from three main communities: those who work on power structures in organizational leadership, and hence consider issues of class, race, gender and sexuality (e.g. Blackmore 1999; Jean-Marie and Normore 2008; Tooms and Alston 2008); those who work in policy studies and hence examine leadership as part of a range of concerns (e.g. Anderson 2009; Gunter 2012a); and those who have networked in order to generate an identity and contribution such as New DEEL in the United States of America (Storey and Beeman 2008), and CEPaLs within the BELMAS network.

Leaders, leading and leadership

Critical researchers aim to recapture the word 'transformation' in support of *Transformative Leadership* in order to make it mean more than the aggregation of test scores with performance judgements about a person, a group or organization. In Lingard et al.'s (2003) terms, the focus should be on 'leading learning' (p. 2), where 'student learning, academic and social, is the core imperative of school leadership … social learning should engage students in a globalized awareness of citizenship and civic participation which embraces difference' (p. 2). CEPaLS research is concerned to undertake such counter hegemonic work in regard to the ongoing restoration of control technologies in schools and higher education. The strategy is twofold: to expose the capture of leaders, leading and leadership by *instrumental* managerialists within EEIR, EA and EP, and to present alternative thinking and evidence about the relationship between leadership, learning and democratic practices.

What is identified in various project texts is a concern to confront and deconstruct leadership as a form of office holding with charismatic approaches regarding 'salvationist' (Smyth 1989b, p. 4) claims, together with the 'great men' of history 'who "make" history through their use of power and resources' (Foster 1989, p. 40). Work often focuses on leading and leadership as the property of the person inhabiting an elite role and usually deferred to as the leader (see Gronn 1999), and whose history is written by those who have an interest in air brushing out the people who actually did the work. Indeed Foster

(1986) argues that much of what is presented as leadership is not leadership but is 'essentially various theories on how to manage the firm' (p. 176). Twenty-five years on from this, Eacott (2011a) is sustaining the argument by concluding that 'education is arguably losing its voice in the policy arena' (p. 81).

Transformational Leadership as identified and promoted through EA, EEIR and EP activities is therefore critiqued as 'a static one-directional view of leadership in which the superordinate or leader leads an anonymous, unquestioning mass of subordinates or followers' (Watkins 1989, p. 9). Consequently, the person who is the leader and those who are rendered followers serve and conserve the power structure rather than do something new in the way that the modernization agenda often claims. While stories, myths and symbols can be manipulated to suggest change and participation, in reality the power remains in the leaders' office (Angus 1989; Bates 1987; Watkins 1989). Hence leadership 'obscures' (Watkins 1989, p. 11) the power relationships that are going on, and acts as a barrier for aspirations (Blackmore 1999), particularly because 'practical concerns' have come to matter more than 'social and cultural aspects of education' (Angus 1989, p. 78). Significantly, dangers are present through the imperative to do rather than to think, where the potential exists to 'cross the boundary between the advocacy of a particular vision or value system and the exercise of arbitrary power' (Angus 1989, p. 77).

Foster (1989) argues that '*Transformational Leadership* has gone from a concept of power to a how-to manual for aspiring managers' (pp. 45–6), and so there is a need to recapture that power process. The starting point is by locating the educational organization within a wider context, with a need to focus on the argument 'that if schools are to be the critical and inquiring communities necessary for a democratic way of life, then the leadership within them will have to be more educative and pedagogical in various ways, rather than bureaucratic and authoritarian' (Smyth 1989b, p. 5). *Transformative Leadership* is therefore different to that pursued by EA, EEIR and EP: 'Leadership is and must be socially critical, it does not reside *in* an individual but in the relationship between individuals, and it is oriented toward social vision and change, not simply, or only, organizational goals' (Foster 1989, p. 46). What this means is that leadership as a 'power-over' process through influence and authority is just that, where perceptions of the vitality and normality of the transformational charismatic leader are based on the ascribing of status as *the leader* rather than the reality or necessity for it (Gronn 1999). When this is recognized as a potentially democratizing process then all can be leaders, can do leading and exercise leadership. This recognizes that all (including all staff, and parents and students) have agency that can be used to illuminate a situation, contribute to a discussion, take on tasks and functionally sort something out because 'leaders become followers and followers become leaders in the ebb and flow of organizational interaction' (Watkins 1989, p. 28).

Leading and leadership as a shared resource means that how schools are thought about, designed and experienced can and should be different. Angus (1989) argues that 'the critical movement from critique to change may come when it becomes clear to participants that current social and educational arrangements, and the relationships between schooling and society, are neither neutral nor natural' (p. 88). The shifting of attention from organizational leadership to educational leadership is therefore integral to such a change, with a refocusing on pedagogy and the values and relationships that enable and sustain this (e.g. English et al. 2012). Consequently, researchers are concerned to present cases of difference that have historical as well as contemporary legitimacy, for example, schools where the approach is democratic through how children have a key role in decisions about the curriculum, learning and assessment (Apple and Beane 1999).

The technology of hierarchy is challenged through research that examines different models of co-principalship (e.g. Court 2003), with questions about redesign that are less about the attributes and charisma of the sole leader and more about the shared knowledge and resources with teachers as responsible educators (Thomson and Blackmore 2006). Research by Wohlstetter et al. (2003) shows that in Los Angeles the most effective leadership took place in networks or 'families' where there is a strong connection between leadership, organizational capacity and performance. It is argued that there is a need to interconnect, support, communicate and buffer the 'family' from too much turbulence in the policy context. They argue that leadership is a form of architecture with the building of teams and interconnections through brokering information, and so central to success are political processes. Other research is more radical, or in Davies' (1997) terms schools can be 'headless', where Grubb and Flessa (2006) studied ten schools in the United States and found examples of rotating principals where decisions are made in teacher committees, and one case where four people run the school without a principal. This type of research examines how things get done in schools in ways that go against the grain of traditional hierarchies, and also suggest that the advocacy of distribution has the potential to shift from *instrumental* delegation towards forms of power sharing that have productive anarchic possibilities (Gunter et al. 2013).

An intellectual history of CEPaLS

Here I intend to provide a summary by deploying the framework developed in Part 2.

Traditions: the intellectual resources developed for and used by the field tend to be *critical science*. It is the case that *experiential,* and *values* *traditions* are evident but these tend to be linked to a theory of power that connects the realities of the job and values to issues of inclusion and exclusion, and how professionals and researchers position themselves as activists. There is much engagement with *positivist* and *behaviourist science traditions*, but this tends to feature as a focus of critique.

What *critical science* means is located in Fay's (1975) conceptual contribution of building on and developing interpretive research through examining the 'felt needs' of people and 'that a great many of the actions people perform are caused by social conditions over which they have no control' (p. 94). Therefore *experiential traditions* are accessed in relation to how people do the job, and in particular how *values* are challenged through the tensions of the economic bottom line in relation to commitments to public and inclusive education (e.g. Ball 1990a, 1994; Thomson 2001; Thomson and Blackmore 2006). Consequently, research 'seeks to uncover' (Fay 1975, p. 94) the structures which aim to determine practice, and how practice actually takes place within the sites where such structuring is targeted (Thomson 2008).

In this sense, *critical science* is not directly oppositional but is concerned with exposing and examining the interplay between agency and structure, where structures dominate realities and imaginaries of practice: first, social criticality is concerned with the way people are advantaged and disadvantaged; second, political criticality is concerned with the way people are included and excluded from participation in the polity; third, economic criticality is concerned with access and deployment of resources, and the structuring of poverty; and fourth, cultural criticality is concerned with access to the arts with structures of taste and recognition. The social sciences are an important intellectual resource regarding strategic analysis (e.g. Wilkinson and Pickett 2009), and theories of power (e.g. see Rawolle et al. 2010). Furthermore, *critical science* is political in how the uncovering of a situation enables dissent and the production of alternative ways of practice, and hence there is a strong concern with scholarly *activism*. This raises questions about who a researcher works for, and who a researcher owes their loyalty to (Anderson 2009). If professionals and researchers are to take a stand on educational issues then 'advocacy leadership requires a *critical* theory of participation, one that identifies and defends those versions that ultimately aim toward membership in a more just and equitable society' (Anderson 2009, p. 118, emphasis in original).

Such *activism* is based on the interplay between a situation and how theories of power can bring illumination and understanding. This is by reporting on the relationship between power and social justice (e.g. Anderson 2009; Bogotch et al. 2008; Normore 2008; Smyth 1989), with specific attention to forms of social injustice (e.g. Blackmore and Sachs 2007;

Courtney 2014; Fitzgerald 2014; Lightfoot 2008; López and Vàzquez 2008; Tooms and Alston 2008). Foster (1986) argues that 'critical theory, as used here, means just that. No solution is presented, only the suggestion that the effort is worth the energy.' (p. 13). In this sense leading and leadership is intellectual work: it is not about 'improvement' and 'effectiveness' as technologies of confession and control (Ball 1990b), because this is based on 'a traditional and limited notion of "what counts" as education ... (and) ... is reinforced by the repetition of mundane, low-level skills which ignore the interests of pupils, richness of the mind, or a spirit of inquiry' (Angus 1989, pp. 66–7). Instead there is recognition that whoever is in a role and/ or whoever is participating in decision-making needs to think as well as do, and needs intellectual tools and professional preparation rather than training in order to help them think: 'Critique is not only a result of leadership but is constitutive of those practices: leadership always has one face turned towards change, and change involves the critical assessment of current situations and an awareness of future possibilities' (Foster 1989, p. 43).

Leaders, leading and leadership in education is a site for such *critical science* through projects that examine the realities of how people experience their work, and how this is linked to wider power structures. This position is summed up by Blackmore (1989) who argues:

> The universal individual central to this perspective of leadership is modelled upon men's experience. Hierarchical relationships are considered to be the 'givens' of 'rational' organizational life. Leaders display attributes and behaviours, possess moral virtues and principles, which are generally associated with 'masculinity'. It is a view which has effectively displaced women in educational thought, and therefore rendered women invisible in administrative practice. ... Currently it is epitomized in the view of school principals as corporate managers. (p. 94)

This is at the core of the challenge to the *positivist* and *behaviourist traditions* that have been adopted and pursued by EA and EEIR. In debating the conceptual and empirical resources that research needs to be based on, Bates (1989) identifies a 'parody of natural science' (p. 133) located in reification of the rules of prediction as 'a calculus of "leadership behaviour"' (p. 135). This is more than a failure of method to show a causal link between leaders and impact, but is based on a way of thinking that has failed because 'there is no calculus of leadership in the offing' (p. 134). Consequently, the use of *positivist* and *behavioural science* has produced a scientific gloss without a scientific methodology, with a failure to produce a body of robust and convincing evidence (Eacott 2011a; English et al. 2012; Gorard 2010). However, in spite of this, failed models continue to be developed and repackaged, where *Knowledge Production* does not do what researchers set out to do, but this does not seem to matter as they keep on doing it (Angus 1989; Watkins 1989).

Purposes: the accessing and use of the *critical science tradition* means that purposes tend to be mainly *realist* and *activist*, with some *situational* tendencies.

Foster (1989) outlines this active approach that interplays with the realities of doing the job and how you want to do the job that is based on: first, leadership must be critical, where human practice in history, currently and the future must not be received and acted upon, but must be actively critiqued, challenged and resisted; second, transformative not just at grand moments in history but more often it is through everyday actions; third, educative, where those who do leadership are teachers, and this is mainly done through stories that enable traditions, changes and aspirations to be articulated and examined; and fourth, ethical, where relationships between people in an organization based on power must be more than 'personal morality' regarding means and ends, it is about how leadership is the 'cause' of moral education through challenges to the accepted way of doing things (Foster 1989, pp. 55–6).

Within the field there is work that illustrates how *realist purposes* underpin research; for example, there is a growing body of research in the UK that lays bare the realities of what it means to do headship in England. For example, Ball's (1987, 1990a, 1994) study of education policy provides detailed testimony from professionals about the fabrication of school autonomy with 'new' forms of leadership, where he concludes 'we may perhaps no longer be asking whether the head is a good leader, but whether he or she is the leader at all' (Ball 1994, p. 88). With a broader remit, Thomson (2009) examines the problem of supply of future principals in western-style democracies and shows how risky the job is. Through using a cultural reference to the Harry Potter books, she shows not only how principalship is hierarchical but also how Dolores Umbridge has a *functional purpose* in opposition to Dumbeldore's moral purpose around access and enabling learning. Thomson (2009) concludes that in 'putting forward a representation of headship as a job which requires a heroic leader capable of holding the Dumbledore of charismatic leadership together with the Umbridge of bureaucratic conformity, the writers of headteacher advertisements may very well deter the very person who "fits" their real needs and desires' (p. 61). In other words, the focus on succession planning within the organization will not resolve the situation where principalship is increasingly regarded as a toxic job. This type of critical analysis links the *realism* of a situation with interpretation and arguments that connects with *activism*.

Activist purposes are about how people work to change the situation by going against the grain and demonstrating that alternative approaches can work and work well. Where Brooks (in Bogotch et al. 2008) states 'one of my great hopes is that educational leaders are destined to become social rights leaders ... my great fear is that these same leaders are doomed to repeat individual and collective behaviors that contribute to school systems that have at times been rightly characterised as "evil" – hegemonic, discriminatory, unjust, and unfair' (p. 1). Such aspirations in the face of ongoing concerns are reflected in studies of children and voice, and teachers and principals how they work within and for the community (Crowther 1997; Jean-Marie and Normore 2008; Mills 1997; Mitra 2008).

An important strand of work is focused on teachers as activists (e.g. Lingard et al. 2003), where Smyth (1989c) argues for 'situated pedagogy' (p. 200) where teachers can begin with the realities of their practice, and consider the power processes within *Knowledge Production* and seek to examine how such knowledge can be both challenged and used, and how other forms of knowledge might be recognized and included. The underlying message of this research is that 'leadership lies not on the position *given*, but in the position *taken*' (Foster 1986, p. 15, emphasis in original). The argument being made is for *activism* within and for change that is open to all but can be located in what Blount (2008) calls the 'affected status group' (p. 36) such as women, BME, LGBT, who engage in awareness raising and securing changes, and how this form of leadership is more than 'an axe to grind' (p. 36) but is social justice leadership.

This means that *Knowledge Production* has political purposes where the interplay between data and power structures requires professionals to think about the school differently. Where 'political alliances of leaders may have to be built among superintendents, principals, teacher leaders, union leaders, student leaders, and community leaders in order to defend the democratic goals of public schooling against those who wish to replace political democracy with a logic of the marketplace' (Anderson 2009, p. 13). While the literatures show examples of doing this, it remains challenging: How can principals do this when their work is structured by *Neoliberalism*? Schools have to compete and not form alliances of resistance, and principals can lose their jobs if they do not demonstrate performance. Anderson (2009) is helpful here in his arguments for a 'double-consciousness' whereby a person sees the self as the *Transformational Leader* through the eyes of dominant groups, and so the educational professional can resist attempts to change their identity. Consequently, *activism* is by understanding the self and how relational networks can be used for the type of education that is *transformative* (see Jean-Marie and Normore 2008).

Such *activism* is also supported through the limitations and indeed failure of business models, and functionally efficient and effective *Transformational Leadership* that does not deliver. Indeed, Foster (1986) asks: 'What happens to the field of educational administration when the grand theory does not materialise?' (p. 18), and so while the Theory Movement has long since passed, the knowledge claims of a predictive theory of leadership for improved standards endure. The purposes of *critical science* are to keep on demonstrating this and to expose the rebranded versions of leadership as a hoax (see Ravitch 2014). Such interruptions are enabled through analysis such as that made by Dimitriadis (2012), who identifies how failed business models can equate with failed education models such as NCLB, where the adherence to constructing a predictive science based on 'bottom line calculations' (p. 120) means that *Knowledge Production* is disconnected from the real lives of those who are meant to benefit.

Furthermore, this *activism* also challenges how 'hierarchical leadership is inevitable in large organizations' (Rizvi 1989, p. 207). Rizvi (1989) draws on Dewey to make the point that 'humans are a species that creates itself through accretion of its values, customs and culture, which are both reproduced and transformed through education' (p. 225), and for education to be creative then 'teachers need to devise experiences which involve making available to each student the opportunity to make a contribution to the enrichment of cooperative life' (p. 225). This is a process that is public and social, and while there are challenges to this – it is something that is worth working for. In this sense, technical *functionality* is important, not least budgets and systems have to be legal, but *functionality* is more than delivering predetermined outcomes. For example, Rizvi (1989) considers the reform of education in Victoria, Australia, where democratic possibilities are more rhetorical than substantial. Indeed, the functionality of the self-managing school has been opened to substantial critique (e.g. Smyth 1993), where the impact is one of the 'self-damaging school' through the inequities that have been generated (Smyth 2011, p. 104). It seems that the interruption of other *Knowledge Production* is an ongoing requirement for scholarly *activism*, particularly because it is based on asking fundamentals about *Knowledge Production*: 'What knowledge is relevant to advancing both practice and scholarship? How do we decide/debate what is relevant knowledge? How do we debate the value of methods of enquiry?' (Eacott 2011a, p. 108).

Domains: the outcome from primarily *critical science* resources interplayed with actions concerned with interruption and thinking otherwise for and with the profession, means that position taking is mainly the *critical* or *working for change domain* with some *philosophical* and *humanistic* claims about change. Let me begin with the latter two domains, in order to support the case of the prime location as working for social justice that is inclusive.

Critical science researchers do acknowledge and draw on *philosophical* contributions, where Codd (1989) argues that *'educational* leadership is a form of philosophy in action ... it is an area of philosophical practice' (p. 157). The moral issues underpinning the accessing and distribution of resources within a school requires tough thinking, as indeed does teaching as a process that is struggled over. In this way, there is some border convergence with EA, where Foster (1986) cites Hodgkinson (1978) regarding 'philosophy-in-action' and how this might be regarded as esoteric as working and running a school is about practical control and not debates, but he argues 'this is the point exactly: philosophy involves a set of beliefs about how the world is structured, and administrators, knowingly or not, put those beliefs into practice. Whenever an administrator writes a memorandum or lifts a telephone, he or she acts on an underlying philosophy of administration, developed over time through experience and training. Reflection on the underlying assumptions and philosophy provides self-understanding and that, in turn, may provide a better administration' (p. 19).

What is different from EA is the way that *philosophical* thinking is interrelated with practice that is focused on challenging accepted power structures, and requires an approach that is not about systems and structures but is linked to the wider meaning of education and how this begins in the classroom:

> Educational leadership entails commitment to a set of educational values and principles for practice which should be embodied in the curriculum itself. These values and principles do not constitute a body of doctrine or a particular set of beliefs, but rather a disposition towards rational reflection and deliberative action which is fundamentally philosophical in action. (Codd 1989, p. 161)

This focus on values links with the *humanistic domain* regarding the experience of change, where, for example, Lingard et al. (2003) report on the Queensland School Reform Longitudinal Study (QSRLS) (1998–2000). An account is given of the development of Productive Pedagogies and *Productive Assessment,* where like EEIR (Leithwood et al. 2006), recognition is given to how 'teacher practices contribute much more than, for example, principal leadership practices' (p. 9), but unlike EEIR the focus is therefore on teaching and learning.

Lingard et al. (2003) recognize the realities of practice without equating 'the notion of leadership with the characteristics of individual leaders, particularly principals, and instead (aim) to understand leadership in terms of the social relations of schools ... while allowing for the individuality of principals and the particularities of each school, we were concerned to build a more general analysis of leadership in schools, without falling into the trap of setting out algorithms of "right practice"' (p. 83). In drawing on Bourdieu's thinking tools, they present case studies that enable them to reveal the *habitus* of those who do leading and exercise leadership, where dispositions within leadership as a social practice show the importance of relational exchanges. Importantly, at a time of rapid reform, it is how professionals handle external demands while keeping the prime focus on teaching and learning that is crucial. Following Bourdieu (2000), this is about the 'game' in play: 'We argue that the skill of leadership is to influence the game and achieve the goals of the school through the many moves required by the field. We suggest that leadership *habitus* reflects on the game and the goals, both specifically and generally, shows concern for the multiple dimensions of the school while playing the game as a whole, and words to "do the most good" with moral will' (pp. 124–5).

This combination of *philosophical* thinking as a key methodology and combined with qualitative data from ethnographic work enables *critical science* to interplay thinking, data and theory to bring new insights. One fruitful area is how leadership as a practice is conceptualized, not least because *Transformational Leadership* is based on 'an under-theorised conceptualisation of strategy' (Eacott 2011a, p. 94). Critical research continues to show that agency within EEIR and EA forms of *Transformational Leadership* is failing the profession, where strategy is much more political than is given recognition for, and where values in relation to power and trust need to be the focus (Gunter and Hall 2013; Samier and Schmidt 2010). Importantly, this raises questions about preparation for formal professional roles in schools (Anderson 2009; English et al. 2012), where notions of training are problematic in the face of the need for intellectual work to be developed. Not least that as Anderson and Jones (2000) have shown, when professionals do practice located research they then develop wider interests in primary research. Partnership projects that enable a range of *knowledges* to be pooled demonstrate that the *working for change* approach is based on methodological approaches to agreed questions, and data gathering and analysis that connect localized practice to wider systemic structures (e.g. Brown et al. 2008; Mitra 2008; Normore and Blanco 2008). Consequently, while professional researchers use social theory (e.g. Bourdieu is used by English et al. 2012; Gunter 2012a; Lingard et al. 2003; Thomson 2010a), research professionals do as well (e.g. Bourdieu is used by Addison 2009).

Contexts: CEPaLS is concerned to restore a reformed and vibrant *Civic Welfarism* as the context in which public education can thrive, and as such research not only examines and debates this but also exposes the damage done by *Neoliberalism*, *Neoconservativism* and *Elitism*.

The contribution of *critical science* is to demonstrate that the research field within and for school leadership may be high volume with major investments by governments and their agencies into projects and strategies, but overall it is a 'moribund' field (Smyth 1989b, p. 4) because the answers are sorted, and hence there is only implementation to be concerned about. Training professionals to implement is failing education, where Stevenson and Tooms (2010) make the point that the field cannot continue to disconnect 'the macro-political economy' from the realities of practice or ignore it in professional preparation/development programmes.

This is exposed by CEPaLS' researchers in relation to examining professional practice within the shifting dimensions of the state where Grace (1995) in the UK shows how the historical antecedence of Victorian headmaster tradition is in tension with the post-Second World War participatory headteacher who sought to be 'first-among-equals'. The Neoliberal reworking of the headmaster into the entrepreneurial CEO has generated different positions, and with major moral questions regarding practice (Courtney and Gunter 2015). While research shows that the attack on the provision of public education is misguided (e.g. Ravitch 2010), the shift away from the state as a positive feature of rights provision and protection has been charted (e.g. Gewirtz and Ball 2000). Importantly, English (2008) examines the implications of this for the preparation of leaders, based on 'right-wing money ... aimed at wresting the preparation of educational leadership away from universities and a socially activistic agenda, and a resurgence of white racism (genetic determinism), homophobia, and the remasculinization of educational leadership positions, notably in the principalship and the superintendency where the numbers of women are increasing after a long period of gender discrimination' (p. 146). It seems that the state is being reworked through neoliberal and neoconservative agendas as the regulator of standards, where in Gronn's (2003) terms there is 'designer-leadership' and 'designer-leaders' (p. 7) and how standards, know-how and behaviours are structuring professional identity in negative and toxic ways: 'Standards can be characterised as solutions in search of problems, in that they prescribe anticipated, legitimated and programmed responses to societal and organisational possibilities yet to be realised' (p. 10).

The restoration of the state as progressive in relation to rights and the provision of public education are difficult in this context. This is not only in relation to the exposing of the damage being done as the state is pushed out, but also how there are legacies of problems with state provision. This could be about how the case for the common school has not been made particular well, and it could be as Apple (2006) argues there is a failure of scholarly activists to speak to the aspirations of parents and communities. Significantly, there is evidence that those who support public education have had to leave local administration in order to pursue their agenda, where research into the rapid growth of private consultancy businesses illustrates a paradox of public sector-inclusive values being worked for in private knowledge-exchange relations (Gunter and Mills 2016).

There is something more than this that needs addressing, notably that *Civic Welfarism* has been sustained by elite groups that may espouse inclusion, but have found the defence of the welfare settlement difficult in regard to issues of gender, race and sexuality, and how class works to sort and resort in ways that exclude. Reform was much needed in regard to public education, where those in support of public services were found wanting in regard to handling and firing back to the attack from *Neoliberalism* and *Neoconservativism*. In addition to this, these elite groups controlled entry and opportunities, for example, the entry of women into the professoriate in higher education in general, but our field, in particular, remains an ongoing issue of equity (Mertz 2009), and the dominance of men in the field may be an explanation for why, in Hall's (1996) terms, we still sit at separate tables where projects are designed and books continue to be written without any regard for gender discrimination. Indeed Rusch and Marshall (2006) show how *working for change* in relation to gender generates different positions, and while there are opportunities for 'teachable moments' there is also evidence of misrecognition in relation to equity. This makes working for the democratization of, for and within *Knowledge Production* as a legitimate agenda for change rather problematic, not least because it requires *activism* rather than *instrumentalism*.

Networks: the main networked groupings here are primarily the *critical* leadership community who directly focus on and examine school leadership, and those who work on public and education policy and hence examine school leadership alongside and within wider remits.

Networking is evident through editorial boards of major journals that focus specifically on leadership, for example, *International Journal of Leadership in Education*, and through those where education policy scholars locate their work and who may examine issues of school leadership, for example, *Journal of Education Policy*. There are research interest groups in major national networks, such as the CEPaLS group in the UK, and the New DEEL group demonstrates a strong identity of researchers who are concerned to work for democratic forms of leadership. In the UK those who work on education policy, and who may or may not examine school leadership, have a strong link with Europe, particularly through a shared interest in sociological enquiry.

A strong feature is through policy projects that examine issues of public policy with a focus on government and governance, and through this the school as an organization can be examined. For example, the work of policy sociology is significant, not only through the framing and debates about methodology and contribution (e.g. Grace 1995; Lingard and Sellar 2012) but also by examining the context in which educational professionals are located and in which such professionals undertake their practice. undertake their practice (e.g. Ball 1994) and how such analysis can support professionals as intellectuals (Gunter 2005b). This is enabled not only through journal articles and special issues, but also through major handbooks (e.g. Apple et al. 2009b). The independence of this research from the remit of commissioned projects is regarded as significant by this field, where research council funding in the UK is an important indicator of excellence and integrity.

Importantly education policy scholars do not primarily focus on school leadership, and so while there are important connections with *critical* leadership researchers there are border controls. For example, the New DEEL network in the United States of America is concerned to 'change the direction of educational administration away from an overly corporate and controlling model towards the values of democratic and ethical behavior' (Shapiro 2008, p. 288), and as such concerns about NCLB are examined (e.g. Storey and Beeman 2008) but links with policy sociology as an intellectual resource do not seem to have been made.

What this analysis of networks illustrates is what Glatter (1979) has identified as a key feature of the field in the UK, where the question is whether educational administration is one field or two. The point being that there are those who focus on the school, and those who focus on wider policy issues, where Glatter (1979) argues that there is one field, but there is a continuum in regard to where your starting point is: school or policy. And even if your starting point is the school, an issue raised by one professorial respondent in the KPEL project is whether you position yourself mainstream within EA or raise questions about such a position: 'The school leadership and management tradition in this country has been perhaps not as critical as it could be. ... And I think sometimes we have been so bound up with school leadership that we haven't always looked beyond the boundaries. And so I suppose I have discovered a role, and one that suits me and is appreciated by some, and I don't think I'm a popular writer with everybody. And I think it could be relatively easy to ignore the kind of stuff that I do. I think I find a boundary, as I was saying before, where I read beyond the field and then try to bring it in, and sometimes it hits the mark and it stirs people up. And sometimes it makes them uncomfortable, and sometimes it's ignored.' This can be evident through citations and conference agendas, where the networking dispositions of those involved in critically examining school leadership from a policy or organizational perspective are different, and there is also a need to examine how this works within and outside of the nation state.

Knowledge production

CEPaLS is concerned to examine how power works through policy and within the working lives of professionals and children in schools and wider communities. In doing so, the field produces and draws on: first, case study projects that examine the impact of power structures on working lives and identities (e.g. Gewirtz 2002; Normore 2008); second, case study projects that present *critical* leadership at work in everyday practices (e.g. Bogotch et al. 2008); and third, explanations that connect empirical data with power processes through the use of social (e.g. Thomson 2010a) and political (e.g. Gunter 2014) theories. Debates take place directly not only within the intellectual contributions of those who directly locate in studies of leaders, leading and leadership, but also from within policy studies that impact on thinking, design and engagement.

Here I intend examining this in relation to the issue of relevance, where the irrelevance of *Critical Science* is central to neoliberal and neoconservative discourses, and often voiced through EA and EEIR networks. One professor respondent in the KPEL project engages with this differently: 'A lot of educational research is policy-driven, and I don't necessarily mean that in a pejorative way, but I think it has consequences for the way it does or doesn't get funded because the problem with policy-driven research, as opposed to policy-relevant research, is the policy-driven research can in two years be of no interest to anybody, whereas policy-relevant research, by focusing much more on processes, can still be of interest even when the particular policy has disappeared.' In other words, what is relevant are the issues that researchers and professionals continue to focus on, as different from research that may be funded but is 'driven' by policy and so is expendable 'fast food' data and analysis. However, at a time of speedy research, the issue for CEPaLS is how this is handled in regard to contributions and what it means to 'make a difference' within practice. Another KPEL professorial respondent confronts this through how his *critical* research connects with professionals in ways that are welcomed and engaged with: 'It is educational leadership and it is about trying to get the best sorts of practices for the best sort of student learning outcomes. It's not simply about managing and representing the school and the marketplace in particular ways, and so on.'

What this means is that CEPaLS has to confront 'relevance' for the professional who is working within the negative conditions identified by policy researchers. For example, Ozga (1992) is so critical of the 'how to do it' books for the field that she does not review them but provides a terse condemnation of the intellectual poverty in the field. While other researchers may agree, Angus (1994) shifts the issue away from book publication as a site of concern, to making the point that policy researchers need to understand why the profession turns to such texts in regard to their professional practice. Indeed, understanding what it means to do leading, leaders and leadership requires empirical work, and possibly shared projects with the profession. Indeed one professorial respondent in the KPEL project states: 'I think one of the illusions that many academics have is that what they do makes a difference and I don't think it actually does. ... You have to look at serious social forces and that means collective action that the teachers unions are able to take, and so if one wants to contribute towards resisting what seems to me to be attacks on the interests of ordinary people in education, and among them teachers, then it's those sort of social forces that one has to try and relate to.' In this sense, the professor has to come out of the library, and this connects with Beachum's (2008) argument about whether justice issues are ones that ordinary people can recognize or is this a job that is 'couched in abstraction and only accessible to scholars and philosophers who can decipher its complex meanings for the mediocre masses' (p. 39). Such elitism in *Knowledge Production* (and elitism that is gendered, classed and raced) leads Jansen (2008) to ask whether theories 'openly and directly grapple with the ordinary, the everyday, and the commonsense' (p. 148). It seems that those who do *activism* are in a minority, and learning to do it is deep within a biography rather than through the seminar room; 'they stand out, precisely because they are bent on resisting commonsense' (p. 149) but this is difficult work because 'they are worn down by the sheer scale of administrative minutiae and managerial impositions that everyday narrows the space for liberatory pedagogy' (p. 149).

Work continues to be done on this, not least on how the realities of networks between the academy and schools, professional researchers and researching professionals are problematized and productive strategies developed (e.g. Apple 2013; Smyth et al. 2014). Gaining access to and sustaining research within educational sites are challenging and need to be opened up to more scrutiny (see Gunter et al. 2014), where Jansen (2008) goes on to argue for recognition of 'imperfect practice' (p. 155), or how people may do and say the wrong thing, will struggle to understand, but it is the commitment to keep working at social justice issues that matters. While we may have a commitment to democratizing *Knowledge Production*, we need to examine whose knowledge we are privileging, particularly in relation to respect for how the 4Ks may be thought about differently in relation to oppressed groups, colonized communities and through forms of knowing within indigenous communities that may not be given recognition (see Blackmore 2010). Indeed, words such as democracy and democratizing tend to be inflected with intrinsic goodness, with laudable aims about inclusion and reworking power, but this may be questioned. For example, Brooks (2008) argues that even if there is a belief in democracy, how can it be developed in organizations such as schools where those with the power have to relinquish it, and 'to use their powers (in) the professional relationships with *others*, who are different' (p. 111, emphasis in original).

The approach to be adopted cannot be turned into bullet points of solutions, where the case is made for intellectual work 'by transforming teachable moments into socially just moments (through questions, critique, and experiments), the disparate histories of races, classes, and genders may be seen in the contexts of today's struggle for people to learn' (p. 111). One such teachable moment is through how Leonard (2008) raises the aftermath of Hurricane Katrina in the United States, and what this means for what is relevant for practice. Overall, what it means is that what is trainable is limited to basic techniques (chairing meetings, writing a plan), and what is needed for leaders, leading and leadership that is about, for and within education is preparation and education where the social sciences and postgraduate research are a resource to support aspirations for social justice (English et al. 2012).

Knowledge Production with CEPaLS tends to focus on the interplay between policy interventions and the working lives of professionals and children, with a specific social justice agenda to examine how advantage and disadvantage are constructed through both everyday practices and elite agendas. In this sense, CEPaLS tends to be located in the *research hub* with strong links to the *professional hub*, researchers and professionals make research partnerships to support intellectual and empirical projects that impact on practice. This tends to focus on the limitations of and damage done by the *corporate* and *policy hubs*, with projects that seek to examine the activities of government regimes in regard to *Knowledge Production*. Hence CEPaLS is concerned to not only expose *Transformational Leadership* as an elite project, but also to work for *Transformative Leadership* as a process that is inclusive and concerned to make changes within everyday practice as well as the wider system. In doing so, CEPaLS recognizes the lack of capital in the field in relation to government regimes, though work with schools and communities is often (and necessarily so) under the radar, where capital can be revalued through stories of local changes and ongoing struggles for recognition and parity of esteem.

Summary

CEPaLS has a long and distinguished intellectual history that is within and against EA and EEIR, and is located in analyses of education as a site for the research of public policy. The brief examination of the 4Ks in this chapter shows a commitment to challenge, work against and work for different approaches to *theory, purposes* and *domains*. CEPaLS is concerned to examine social, political, economic and cultural injustices in society and how they are endemic within schools, and how this need not be the case through examples of major reforms nationally, and change strategies within localized policymaking and *activism*. While *contexts* shows that particular *networks* such as EA and EEIR have had their projects funded and have impacted on policy, those within CEPaLS are seeking to reveal this, and to develop different types of networked relationships with the profession. Hence within a *knowledgeable polity*, the role of the state and politics may have created particular knowledge and practice imperatives, it is the case that CEPaLS is concerned with knowledge and practice that has a contribution to make beyond the urgent. In doing so, a *knowledgeable polity* is a site for research, where the aim is to expose the corporatization of the state, politics and particular networks. Hence *Transformational Leadership* is examined as an elitist project that structures the practice of school principals as subordinate deliverers of privatization. Cases from research projects not only reveal this but also present other ways in which leaders, leading and leadership can be conceptualized and enacted, particularly through *Transformative Leadership* models that are inclusive and communal.

Conclusion: Developing Intellectual Histories

Introduction

In this final chapter, I provide a summary of an approach to an intellectual history of school leadership, and in taking a pause through the completion of this text I conclude by examining potential agendas. In doing so I take Sungaila's (2008) argument seriously that a history of the field is actually about the future, and so an intellectual history as a form of *Knowledge Production* within a *knowledgeable polity* is in the here and now, but primarily it is about how practices continue to unfold in libraries, offices and classrooms. In doing so I am mindful that the field has to confront some tough issues, and this is not new as Rapp (2002) notes the frustrations of the field as just not seeing what is going on, or at least not talking about what needs to be surfaced. In this sense I am following Furedi (2004) who argues that 'a civilised intellectual institution teaches its members how *not* to take criticisms personally, and how *not* to be offended by uncomfortable ideas' (p. 77, original emphasis). Consequently, this book should be unsettling at the very least, but it should also enable the field to confront its present through its past, and engage with some serious issues that could lead to the death of the field as a site of primary research that is enabling of professional practice. I begin with a current cultural example as a way of thinking about this, before going on to examine the implications for the field.

Breaking Bad

In the global sensation that is the US drama *Breaking Bad*, the viewer can watch sixty-two episodes over five seasons about Walter White, who is a chemistry teacher:

> When he is diagnosed, as the series begins, with terminal lung cancer, his terror (his existential, male, white-collar terror) focuses not on the prospect of his own death, but on how he will provide for his family. A chance

encounter with a former student, Jesse Pinkman – a classic dropout nogoodnik with a sideline in drug sales – sets his unlikely career as a drug baron in motion. As his alter ego 'Heisenberg' (the name of a knowing echo of that icon of uncertainty), Walter has chemical skills that enable him to cook some of the purest methamphetamine the world has ever known … and the rest, as they say, is history. (Wagner 2014, p. 86)

Not only is this an enthralling drama, but there are multiple messages around the issue of choice, where the viewer can sit outside and possibly pronounce on the folly, or even denounce in the form of 'well what would you expect …' and 'why are characters who are breaking the law shown in such a sympathetic light?' Or perhaps, 'if I was in this situation, what would I do?'

Walter White's choice is located in a context where risk, strategizing, fear and assurance are all reasonable responses regarding the options available, not least how life and death can be paid for: living expenses while someone cannot earn a wage both during the illness and after death, alongside the payment of medical bills. Juxtaposed with this is the school as a backdrop, not least about whether it failed or enabled Jesse, and as the drama unfolds the education of Walter and Skyler White's son, Walter Junior. Drawing on Pierson (2014) a very important point is made by Wagner (2014) that in using his knowledge in response to a set of circumstances, Walter White shows himself to be both a structured neoliberal actor through how the American dream of freedom operates, and a structuring criminal actor through how he learns to make provision for his family. So the teacher from Albuquerque, New Mexico, makes the choice to go into business as an entrepreneurial criminal, and in doing so the focus is on family without community, and is on the self as a cost that must be paid for. The morality of practice is linked to this, but we are also enabled to see values played out in regard to how Walter and Jesse are advised by Saul Goodman as their 'criminal' attorney and accomplice, and how Skyler and Walter Junior handle their lives, aspirations and the consequences of Walter's choices.

Walter White is shaped through *Neoliberalism*, and as such his position is raced, classed and gendered: his predicament is a source of sympathy based on a stark realization for some, and is a source of condemnation for others. He is also located in a neoconservative world of what it means to be a provider, and how this is related to what it means to be a teacher, to be a man, to be a parent. In addition it links to elite interests, where those without the financial worries that Walter White has are enabled to demonstrate their philanthropy, not least when fellow criminal Gustavo Fring operates in plain sight as a respectable business man and charity patron. In sum, when *Breaking Bad* is read through Wacquant's (2009) analysis of the shift from welfare, to workfare, to prisonfare, then we have in front of us the realization of what Harvey

(2005) means when he talks about *Neoliberalism* as 'the financialization of everything' (p. 33). It actually means the individualization of everything, where major changes in public policy are about tax dollars funding incarceration rather than health, accumulating wealth rather than providing paid employment based on appropriate remuneration, and the largesse of giving rather than the anonymous payment of taxes for providing common needs and services. While criminality is to be condemned, there is logic to Walter White's choices.

The use of Walter White's situation as possibly a metaphor and, more likely, as a leitmotif for school leadership could be developed further. However, on the basis that the point has been made, I would like to consider the issue of impossible and unnecessary choices for educational professionals within a privatizing system of education. While there is no doubt that public education needed reform, it is the case that the crisis that was constructed and fabricated to attack, dismantle and replace it is not about reform for and with the public, but for and with corporate interests. Important analysis has been done on this in the United States (Ravitch 2010, 2014; Saltman 2010), where it is not an exaggeration to say that there are now life and death choices for public education, for professionals, for families and for communities. Hence like Walter White, educational professionals have been put in impossible situations, and where the approved of outcome is to become an entrepreneur. Some will break the law (e.g. interventions into examinations in order to manipulate outcomes), and some will sail close to the wind (e.g. selecting evidence for marketing purposes), but most will not, but they may break the settlements that create the conditions in which the law may be broken, or may be changed to be more congenial to particular interests. What this does raise is whether *Knowledge Production* within the field is about enabling educational professionals to handle Walter White situations and/or is about asking more profound questions about the purposes of those situations, and in whose interests those situations operate. After all, corporate elites need Walter Whites if criminalization is to work, and criminals are needed if impossible good and bad choices are to be integral to civil society.

State of the field

School principals are now in high-stakes situations that are similar to those confronted by Walter White: the sourcing of income streams to pay teachers, making teaching jobs redundant, crowd funding for curriculum materials, accessing philanthropic sponsorship for buildings and contents, and marketing the culture instead of focusing on teaching and learning. In order to do this, the profession is being sold *Transformational Leadership*, and its hybrids, as best practice for running the school as a business. Strategy is dealt with elsewhere, and school principals are left with tactics for local delivery (Hartley 2007). Failure is about incentivizing individuals, and enabling them to feel good while knowing that some must fail for all of it to work.

I have been able to reach this stage in the analysis by making the case for an intellectual history that not only examines ideas, but also how they are located in the especial role of elite intellectuals through to ordinary day-to-day intellectual practices within thinking and doing by *knowledge actors*. How this plays out is through the 4 K's of *Knowledge Production*, whereby the *knowledges, knowings, knowers* and *knowledgeabilities* need to be examined within and through a *knowledgeable polity* in regard to the nation state as a place for politics, but also how this is located within and in relation to supranational policy spaces. An intellectual history as a form of *Knowledge Production* has enabled the construction and deployment of a framework that considers: *knowledge traditions, purposes, domains, contexts* and *networks*. Therefore the intellectual history of school leadership that I have constructed and used in this book not only enables the conditions in which practice takes place to be foregrounded but also considers the resources that are used to shape it. The starting point is the person and the community that they are within, and so how *Knowledge Production* takes place within a professional biography matters as it is the site where exchanges, learning and practice take place. *Experience* as a *knowledge tradition* for *situational purposes* enables the professional *in situ* to be the focus, and the search I have undertaken for the interventions into the intellectual activity of the professional has identified a range of *knowledge traditions, purposes* and *domains*. However, while plurality is a feature of the field and it should be site of struggle over the quality and appropriateness of various ideas, uses and claims about change, in reality there is little debate because the solutions have already been identified.

The enduring focus within *Knowledge Production* is to provide certainty and predictability for the professional through scientific intervention into practice. This is the primary *doxa*. Historically, this is located in *positivism* and *behaviourism* through the legacies of Taylorism and the Hawthorne studies, with continued claims for better science in EA and EEIR. The Theory Movement followed by the effectiveness and improvement movement(s) as scientific projects dominate research and professional development in western-style democracies, and as a site for *Knowledge Production* it fed the field with *doxa*-compliant methodologies and outcomes. The challenge to this functional certainty has come from a range of *knowledge actors*, and can be summed up thus:

The reason the science of administration – or of organizations – does not work is stupefyingly simple: the central problems of administrative theory are not scientific at all, but philosophical. That is, the central questions of administration deal not so much with what is, but with what ought to be; they deal with values and morality. (Greenfield 1991, p. 7)

This *values tradition* enabled *realist purposes* to be visible, with concerns about the meanings of change combined with forms of craft knowledge, and so it spoke to the tensions and dilemmas that faced professionals in both everyday problems and longer-term developmental agendas. The relationship between values and injustice has enabled those concerned with the realities of oppression to demonstrate that *philosophical* issues are in fact social and political because of the need to confront the way power works. Hence *critical science* is concerned to not only examine the values issues linked to choices but to ask whose values seem to matter most and why (Blackmore 1999). Consequently, *realism* is linked to *activism*, where change is concerned to shift the locus of power: for the right there is too much power held by the state and privileged groups such as professionals, for the left there is too much power held by corporate interests and privilege groups such as wealth and property owners.

While the challenges from *values* and from the left approach to *critical science* remain strong in a plural field, the endurance of *positivism* and *behaviourism* remains with the emphasis on application, prediction, improvement and effectiveness. This *doxa* is located in claims that the school as an organization is no different from other organizations, and so what has been promoted as effective and efficient decision-making in business could be installed into schools, and could be improved through laboratory-style projects. The counter *doxa* based on *values* begins in a different place and sees education and hence schools as different from a factory or restaurant, and the anti-*doxa* based on *critical science* sees education and hence schools as sites where advantage and disadvantage are constructed, and so schools should be different.

What is currently in play is a form of *Transformational Leadership* that has been produced from the 1990s onwards, a time when science met the market, and the market used the legitimacy of science to enter and replace public education. *Transformational Leadership* seeks legitimacy in this tradition, through what Barber (2007) from the EEIR network calls a 'pseudo science' (p. 79) where elite political power is used to bring about change with measurement studies that proclaim how those who work in, or do business with schools, perceive effective leadership based on charismatic visions for and in relation to followers. The market could buy into this model as it can be easily turned into a product to be branded, sold and resold through upgrades, and it protected existing power structures through how it could enable right-wing transformations in the dismantling of public education in ways that were presented as normal but exciting. The single person in post, professionally known as headteacher or principal, could be reworked as an entrepreneur who could operate in a global market, and so the *transnational leadership package* (Thomson et al. 2014) of easy to adopt and use 'flat pack' templates as professional tools are modern and simple to deliver.

The EEIR and EA networks did the intellectual work for this by producing methodologies and data and ideas, and the EP networks fed off this and fed it with funding and acclaim. Building on Bourdieu (2000), the game in play was attractive to their interests, where capitals in the form of careers, livelihoods and reputations have been staked. This is speedy and risky work, but exciting through the potential for claims to be made for linking transformation with improved student outcomes. Dispositions that are embodied and shared are revealed through what is said and done in public, where acclaim is given to those who are recognized as the repository for the 4Ks by those who are structurally powerful within a *knowledgeable polity*. The increasing dominance of the EP networks, boosted through the interplay between *Neoliberalism–Neoconservatism–Elitism* within and external to the nation state, means that the search for and proclamations about certainty remains, but the ideas, methods and claims are based on an allusion to more science than to robust primary research. The combination of training with close-to-practice consultancy support means that exchange relationships, with 'support' and 'coaching', enables the delivery of how to do it in ways that can speak to the *values tradition*. Hence what English (2003) identifies as 'cookie-cutter' leaders are themselves shaped, and they shape others, but it does not look as grim as this might suggest because the focus on children, the participation of staff in professional matters and the sense of personal responsibility for 'my' school can all be integrated into the parody of the successful entrepreneur. Unlike Walter White, there are good choices to be made in the form of role models that should be emulated, not least those who can do what is necessary and indeed can turn around 'failing schools' (e.g. Goddard 2014; Stubbs 2003). It seems that science is returning to support this through new contributions to *behaviourism*, such as the use of eugenics regarding which children can benefit from education (Ball 2013) and the use of neuroscience regarding how those who do leading and management are enabled to manage the self better (Rose and Abi-Rached 2013). The question for the field is whether such science will be used and popularized in ways that are anti-human and anti-democratic.

There are bad choices to be made, and for Walter White the issue was all about trying to negotiate who the actual enemy is and trying not to get caught. More significantly for neoliberals and neoconservatives, it is making choices to emulate role models that are concerned with democratic forms of transformation that is the real danger, particularly through claims for change that interrupt and destabilize (e.g. Apple and Beane 1999). At best, the forms of *Transformational Leadership* that are travelling the world are located in historical notions of the single person in charge, and how this is legitimated through business and philanthropic role models, enabled through validation data on how those who are led to accept and want to make this situation more workable. Such messages are carried by people who do business, who can intervene in the business of education and who model the charismatic leader that the audience are required to adopt and/or assimilate. The question for the field is whether our *Knowledge Production* and claims can and should be commodified and controlled by those who use and dispose of leadership models rather than work with educational professionals as knowledgeable people who have intellectual work to do.

Field agendas

The intellectual history that I have constructed shows that while there is work that engages with reviewing intellectual resources in the field, on types of leadership (e.g. Gunter et al. 2013; Leithwood et al. 1999; Smyth 1989; York-Barr and Duke 2004), on key areas of research activity (e.g. Eacott 2011a; Oplatka 2010), and on networks (e.g. Burlingame and Harris 1998), it is the case that far too much is engaged with, talked about and written without due respect for the plurality of *Knowledge Production*. A basic study of citations shows that some networked groups are like gated communities where no one is let in or out unless they consecrate and respect particular names and projects, without recognition that it might be different elsewhere. Furthermore, they retain this security by eschewing intellectual work: in trying to prevent the professional from thinking, they have to learn not to think either.

The problems lie within the field, but also external to the field.

Through various reviews in the United States (e.g. Pounder 2000a,b), United Kingdom (e.g. Bush et al. 1999), and across national boundaries (e.g. Reynolds 2014), there are opportunities to see how various epistemic groups identify their purposes and progress made, with engagement with debates that are taking place. This tends to include some historical and contemporary mapping work of projects and contributions, some synthesizing claims about key issues with agenda setting and some interaction with the bigger policy picture regarding how that agenda has been and is shaped by reform and political imperatives. Importantly, who does these reviews, how they come to do them and who is excluded and where the silences are speak to the problematics of a field that does not have a sense of itself as a field. It seems that a field is defined in terms of those who locate within and around a particular way of thinking and doing, rather than through an examination of *Knowledge Production*.

Let me take one example. An enduring issue is how research is interrelated with practice, and hence the questions are about who sets the agenda, and how research is responsive to practitioner requirements. This is often played out in debates about 'theory' as distinct from 'practice', and can be resolved through claims about 'relevance' particularly in regard to 'applied' theory and 'problem solving'. The concerns raised can be about satisfying practitioner demands but at the same time questioning the fads and fashions, and indeed, outlining the need to build a body of evidence over time (Pounder 2000b). In reporting on the AERA Division A Task Force in 2000, various authors take up this issue where quality and utility are seen as in a binary relationship and as *the* problem: first, Ogawa et al. (2000) examine publications, and develop analysis about the coordination of research; second, Tschannen-Moran et al. (2000) examine the work of 'productive and influential scholars', and by examining their reported biographies they found that there are concerns about the composition of the field (not enough women) and the orientation of purposes that divide scholarship from practicality; third, Riehl et al. (2000) examine the separation of knowledge from practice, and go on to make the case for a more robust scholarship that is inclusive of all, particularly through how doctoral programmes enable practitioners to become scholars; and fourth, Anderson and Jones (2000) shift the location of *Knowledge Production* from primarily in universities towards the legitimacy of 'insider' research, on the basis that when practitioners do research they then access and interconnect with the larger-scale projects and analysis produced in the university.

This in-depth analysis of the field is based on research, and *critical* thinking about the field, undertaken by researchers who are positioned in different ontological and epistemological sites. It leads to a set of recommendations that identify the field as a problem: needs better coordination, communication, training, and in doing so, is judging itself on its own terms of improving the effectiveness and efficiency of educational administration (Pounder 2000b). There is a sense of how researchers are produced and need to be better produced (Riehl et al. 2000) and how the field should be inclusive of those who practice (Anderson and Jones 2000), but even with this in-depth analysis there is a sense that the binary of research and practice has only just begun to be surfaced and examined in productive ways, and our intellectual inheritance is an opportunity to take this forward.

There are at least two threads that can contribute to this. The first comes from Paechter (2003), who argues:

> We should focus on conducting good research in the field of education and trust to its utility. We are not always able to predict which areas will

be most fertile for investigation, nor which studies will have most long-term impact. However, I think that anything that tells us more about the world of education (very broadly conceived) will be useful at some point. As long as we ensure that we carry out our work as well as it is possible to do so, with due regard to an underpinning moral imperative, rigour, transparency, connection to theory and research ethics, we will be contributing to knowledge in the field of education. This should be our purpose. (p. 116)

Consequently, we need to have a sense of ourselves as researchers, and in working with professionals we can enable their work and thinking to be equally robust. The second is connected to this point, and lies in how the field is conceptualized, where in Baron's (1969) terms it includes everyone: from children and families through to professors. Anderson and Jones' (2000) analysis enables recognition that the field is not what the professors say it is, and this is a fruitful trajectory for development. Through this book, I have used professional researchers as a label for those who focus primarily on research, and distinct from researching professionals who engage in enquiry about and for practice. Much can be learnt and illuminated by crossing borders that are professional, national and epistemic. One border to be crossed is how children are knowledge producers, through experience and projects, and the raced, classed, gendered and sexualized structures which impact on their agency should be central to field agendas.

From a social science perspective, I find the endurance of the theory–practice binary odd. Following Fay (1975), the shift from positivist to interpretive to critical social science enables travel from the library to the classroom and back again in ways that are productive, where theorizing is normalized. Importantly, school leadership is a field that draws on disciplines and is not a discipline itself, and so the use of empirical, conceptual and methodological insights from sociology, history, economics, political science and psychology is not only enabling of all field members but also can contribute to these disciplines, not least because such an approach is 'box-breaking' (Alvesson and Sandberg 2014, p. 967) through projects that are interdisciplinary, based on partnerships outside of the academy. Perhaps the questions to be asked are who constructs such a divide and in whose interests is it working? A task as field members in higher education, in partnership with field members in other educational organizations such as schools, is to undertake intellectual work where we think through and engage with tough educational matters. In this sense, we would follow English's (2006a) argument that instead of seeking to codify a knowledge base we should recognize a 'knowledge dynamic' where we 'admit to fissures, antimonies, multiplicities and contradictions being part and parcel of growing and vibrant fields of theories and practices' (p. 470).

We have the resources to do that through *philosophical* (e.g. Greenfield and Ribbins 1993; Hodgkinson 1991), humane (e.g. Ribbins 1997; Sugrue 2005) and socially critical traditions (e.g. Bates 1980; Blackmore 2010), and we are not alone in this matter as critical concerns about the state of the field extend beyond education (see Collinson 2014; O'Reilly and Reed 2010).

How agency and structure interplay within our *Knowledge Production* profiles remains an issue. What I want to say here is that research does not take place without due regard to the power structures in which it is located. Anderson and Jones (2000) make the point that a close-to-practice focus can be regarded as second-division research, where professional researchers can seem trapped between the demands for practice and for scholarship. But it is more than this, it is how research agendas are not actually controlled by researchers or practitioners, but by those who are seeking to modernize practitioners as neoliberal 'Walter White' *knowledge actors*, and who need theories of leadership that legitimize this. Therefore, any review of the field in the United States and other sites of *Knowledge Production* needs to embrace the impact of this on leadership (e.g. Anderson 2009; Saltman 2010), and on wider issues of how markets impact on what is worth knowing (e.g. Burch 2009; English 2006a). Furthermore, as such work already acknowledges, there is a need to consider how policy studies as a sociological and political field needs to draw on and think about the relationship between the local, national and global. Even using such terms is problematic because such ways of thinking and fixing produce limited analysis because networking is not only anchored through state institutions but works outside of such boundaries (e.g. Spring 2012).

So what does this mean? It probably means that our reviews and agenda setting need to be more hard hitting (see Fitz 1999; Gorard 2005), with scholarly dispositions where reading needs to go beyond the epistemic or entrepreneurial network that the person is a member of. In relation to our projects, outputs, supervisions and general activity, we need to work for a stronger sense of scholarship and criticality, where assumptions about methodology are open to ongoing challenges (e.g. Seddon 2014). What this actually means is a sense of honesty in regard to the interplay between position taking and positioning. If a professor is a neoliberal or a civic welfarist, then they need to say so, and what this means in relation to what is about to be read or heard. If a consultant has not read or investigated *Knowledge Production* regarding school leadership, then again they need to say what is available and why they are popularizing that particular someone else's work. If a principal is using vision to declare a teacher incompetent, then again they need to be honest about in whose interests this is taking place – the children, or more likely the school owner or sponsor who is demanding better data on school outcomes as an investment matter. Far too many professors in our field are deeply located within powerful corporate interests, and central to our job is to reveal this, and to examine how recognition and misrecognition operates in professional biographies and occupational contexts. This is difficult work, but scholarly leadership is pedagogic with an emphasis on fruitful investigations, not least that people need to read and listen to what troubles them (see Gunter et al. 2014). And, we may need to consider that even with evidence to the contrary, some will not accept 'other' ideas and ways of thinking, and may ontologically and epistemologically not be able to. So this is necessary intellectual but tough work.

Intellectual histories

The field of school leadership is in danger intellectually, and hence practically. For example, the current hybrid of *Transformational Leadership* is 'System Leadership' (Hopkins 2007), which is based on Collins (2001) rather than Apple (2013). In *Breaking Bad* terms, it seems as if Walter White is a model for effective and efficient system leadership, with 'takeovers' and the 'removal' of competitors. The consequences of this is that certain questions are not addressed, not least the debates that are happening about whether leaders, leading and leadership is an appropriate way forward for thinking about schools as organizations (compare Blackmore 1999; Gronn 1996; Lakomski 2005 regarding different positions on this). Asking such questions may enable those who are struggling with the Walter White neoliberal identity and practices to have a wider range of options with a potentially different sense of agency. Research shows that there is evidence of how the profession is, in Bourdieu's (2003) terms, 'firing back', where there are reports that principals are not only speaking up but are also engaging in *Transformative Leadership* through networking and *activism* regarding the learning situation of students (see Gunter 2012a; Shields 2010).

Furedi (2004) helps with the starting point of agenda setting:

> Dumbing down is not an esoteric issue that concerns only academics, artists and intellectuals. The prevailing level of education, culture and intellectual debate is important for the flourishing of a democratic ethos. Intellectuals in different guises play a crucial role in initiating dialogue and engaging the curiosity and passion of the public. Today that engagement is conspicuously feeble. Unsurprisingly, the cultural elites' cynicism towards knowledge and truth has been transmitted to the people through educational and cultural institutions and the media. Apathy and social disengagement are symptoms of a culture that tends to equate debate with

banal exchange of technical opinions. Because all of this really matters, a culture war against the philistines is long overdue. (p. 24)

This 'culture war' does need to begin with the field itself.

Historical work is within the field every day, though it may not be recognized as such, and could even be silenced. The asking of questions can be challenging, not least because there is a lack of knowledge about the recent past, and it is not a feature of professional preparation and training. Indeed, such questions can be regarded as unhelpful or even esoteric, and go against the grain of can do futuring that prevails in the orthodoxy of school leadership. Nevertheless, the field is replete with lies and fabrications about the identified 'crises' in public education, and where the past can be written in ways that are open to dispute. For example, in Brian Simon's 1955 presentation of the evidence and arguments for *The Common Secondary School* he states that generating creativity and a work ethic for *all* children is vital: 'We must provide opportunities and worthwhile objectives, not for the few at the expense of the many, but for the youth of the country as a whole' (Simon 1955, p. 70). However, by 2012, Andrew Adonis was describing the 'comprehensive' school as 'a cancer at the heart of English society' (p. xii). It seems that within a few generations the idea and reality of the common school has become 'toxic' in England with rebranding through specialization, and restructuring through 'independence' from local authority democratic structures. How leaders, leading and leadership is located in this writing of the history of an education system needs careful and forensic analysis, and in many ways it needs to have purposes that are more than standards.

Constructing histories through and with a social and political commitment could be based on Newman's (2007) call to 'rethink "the public"' (p. 27) in ways that shift the 'public imaginary' (p. 43). She argues that such an 'imaginary' is 'transnational' through how political renewal in different nation states are a resource to support the politics of choice beyond borders, not least because it is 'constituted through social and political practice'. There is a need to both understand the corporatization of choice and work for more productive ways of thinking about the public and publicness; and is more challenging than current forms based on consumerism and community (p. 43). This means that the school as a public institution is more than being public through taxation and universal access, but is a site where the idea and practice of the public is thought about, worked for and enacted. This intellectual history of school leadership seems to indicate that not only should history as a resource be rethought for research and practice, but how the public context in which we do this needs to be reimagined. This has implications for *knowledge actors* in a range of organizational sites, but it speaks in particular to schools and the universities as spaces for *Knowledge Production*.

References

Acker, J. (1992). 'Gendering organizational theory'. In A. J. Mills and P. Tancred (eds), *Gendering Organizational Analysis*, 248–60. Newbury Park, CA: Sage.

Addison, B. (2009). 'A feel for the game – a Bourdieuian analysis of principal leadership: A study of Queensland secondary school principals'. *Journal of Educational Administration and History* 41 (4): 327–41.

Adonis, A. (2012). *Education, Education, Education. Reforming England's Schools*. London: Biteback Publishing Ltd.

Ainscow, M., Booth, T., and Dyson, A. (2006). *Improving Schools, Developing Inclusion*. London: Routledge.

Ainscow, M., Dyson, A. Goldrick, S., and West, M. (2012). *Developing Equitable Education Systems*. Abingdon: Routledge.

Ainscow, M. and West, M. (eds) (2006). *Improving Urban Schools, Leadership and Collaboration*. Maidenhead: Oxford University Press.

Allix, N. M. (2000). 'Transformational leadership: Democratic or despotic'. *Educational Management and Administration* 28 (1): 7–20.

Allix, N. and Gronn, P. (2005). '"Leadership" as a manifestation of knowledge'. *Educational Management Administration and Leadership* 33 (2): 181–96.

Alvesson, M. and Sandberg, J. (2014). 'Habitat and Habitus: Boxed in versus box-breaking research'. *Organization Studies* 35 (7): 967–87.

Anderson, G. (2009). *Advocacy Leadership*. New York: Routledge.

Anderson, G. and Jones, F. (2000). 'Knowledge generation in educational administration form the inside out: The promise and perils of site-based administrator research'. *Educational Administration Quarterly* 36 (3): 428–64.

Angus, L. (1989). '"New" leadership and the possibility of educational reform'. In J. Smyth (ed.), *Critical Perspectives on Educational Leadership*, 63–92. London: Falmer Press.

Angus, L. (1993). 'The sociology of school effectiveness'. *British Journal of Sociology of Education* 14 (3): 333–45.

Angus, L. (1994). 'Sociological Analysis and Education Management: The social context of the self-managing school'. *British Journal of Sociology of Education* 15 (1): 79–91.

Anheier, H. K. (2005). 'Introducing the Journal of Civil Society: An editorial statement'. *Journal of Civil Society* 1 (1): 1–3.

Apple, M. W. (2001). *Educating the 'Right' Way*. New York, NY: RoutledgeFalmer.

Apple, M. W. (2006). 'Interrupting the right: On doing critical educational work in conservative times'. In G. Ladson-Billings and W. F. Tate (eds), *Education Research in the Public Interest*, 27–45. New York, NY: Teachers College Press.

Apple, M. W. (2011). 'The politics of compulsory patriotism: On the educational meanings of September 11'. In K. Saltman and D. A. Gabbard (eds), *Education as Enforcement*, second edn, 291–300. New York, NY: Routledge.

Apple, M. W. (2013). *Can Education Change Society?* New York, NY: Routledge.

Apple, M. W., Au, W., and Gandin, L. A. (2009a). 'Mapping critical education'. In M. W. Apple, W. Au, and L. A. Gandin (eds), *The Routledge International Handbook of Critical Education*, 3–19. New York, NY: Routledge.

Apple, M. W., Au, W., and Gandin, L. A. (eds) (2009b). *The Routledge International Handbook of Critical Education*. New York, NY: Routledge.

Apple, M. W. and Beane, J. A. (1999). *Democratic Schools*. Buckingham: Oxford University Press.

Arendt, H. (2009). *The Origins of Totalitarianism* (1958, second edn). Garsinton: Benediction Books.

Arrowsmith, R. (2001). 'A right performance'. In D. Gleeson and C. Husbands (eds), *The Performing School*, 33–43. London: RoutledgeFalmer.

Astle, J. and Ryan, C. (eds) (2008). *Academies and the Future of State Education*. London: CentreForum.

Ball, S. J. (1981). *Beachside Comprehensive: A Case Study of Secondary Schooling*. Cambridge: Cambridge University Press.

Ball, S. J. (1987). *The Micropolitics of the School*. London: Routledge.

Ball, S. J. (1990a). *Politics and Policymaking in Education: Explorations in Policy Sociology*. London: Routledge.

Ball, S. J. (1990b). 'Management as moral technology: A Luddite analysis'. In S. J. Ball (ed.), *Foucault and Education*, 153–66. London: Routledge.

Ball, S. J. (1994). *Education Reform: A Critical and Post-Structural Approach*. Buckingham: Oxford University Press.

Ball, S. J. (1995). 'Intellectuals or technicians? The urgent role of theory in educational studies'. *British Journal of Educational Studies* 43 (3): 255–71.

Ball, S. J. (2003). 'The teacher's soul and the terrors of performativity'. *Journal of Education Policy* 18 (2): 215–28.

Ball, S. J. (2007). *Education PLC*. London: Routledge.

Ball, S. J. (2008a). *The Education Debate*. Bristol: The Policy Press.

Ball, S. J. (2008b). 'New philanthropy, New networks and new governance in education'. *Political Studies* 56 (4): 747–65.

Ball, S. J. (2009). 'Beyond networks? A brief response to "which networks matter in education governance"'. *Political Studies* 57 (3): 688–91.

Ball, S. J. (2010). 'New voices, new knowledges and the new politics of education research: The gathering of the perfect storm?'. *European Educational Research Journal* 9 (2): 124–37.

Ball, S. J. (2012). *Global Education Inc.* London: Routledge.

Ball, S. J. (2013). *Foucault, Power and Education*. New York, NY: Routeldge.

Ball, S. J. and Exley, S. (2010). 'Making policy with "good ideas": Policy networks and the "intellectuals" of New Labour'. *Journal of Education Policy* 25 (2): 151–69.

Ball, S. J. and Junemann, C. (2012). *Networks, New Governance and Education*. Bristol: Policy Press.

Ball, S. J., Maguire, M., and Braun, A., with Hoskins, K. and Perryman, J. (2012). *How Schools Do Policy, Policy Enactments in Secondary Schools*. Abingdon: Routledge.

Balyer, A. (2012). 'Transformational leadership behaviors of school principals: A qualitative research based on teachers' perceptions'. *International Online Journal of Educational Sciences* 4 (3): 581–91.

Barber, M. (1996). *The Learning Game, Arguments for a Learning Revolution*. London: Victor Gollancz.

Barber, M. (1998). 'The dark side of the moon: Imagining an end to failure in urban education'. In L. Stoll and K. Myers (eds), *No Quick Fixes*, 17–33. London: Falmer Press.

Barber, M. (2007). *Instruction to Deliver*. London: Politico's Publishing.

Barber, M., Moffit, A. and Kihn, P. (2011). *Deliverology 101, A Field Guide for Educational Leaders*. London: Sage.

Barker, B. (2005). *Transforming Schools, Illusion or Reality*. Stoke-on-Trent: Trentham Books.

Barker, B. (2010). *The Pendulum Swings*. Stoke-on-Trent: Trentham Books.

Barnard, C. (1938). *The Functions of the Executive*. Cambridge, MA: Harvard University Press.

Barnes, M. and Prior, D. (eds) (2009). *Subversive Citizens*. Bristol: The Policy Press.

Baron, G. (1969). 'The study of educational Administration in England'. In G. Baron and W. Taylor (eds), *Educational Administration and the Social Sciences*, 3–17. London: The Athlone Press.

Baron, G. (1980). 'Research in educational administration in Britain'. *Educational Administration* 8 (1): 1–33.

Baron, G., Cooper, D. H. and Walker, W. G. (eds) (1969). *Educational Administration: International Perspectives*. Chicago: Rand McNally and Company.

Baron, G. and Taylor, W. (eds) (1969). *Educational Administration and the Social Sciences*. London: The Athlone Press.

Bass, B. M. (1985). *Leadership and Performance Beyond Expectations*. New York: Free Press.

Bass, B. M. (1998). *Transformational Leadership: Industrial, Military and Educational Impact*. Mahwah, NJ: Erlbaum.

Bates, R. (1980). 'Educational administration, the sociology of science and the management of knowledge'. *Educational Administration Quarterly* 16 (2): 1–20.

Bates, R. (1989). 'Leadership and the rationalization of society'. In J. Smyth (ed.), *Critical Perspectives on Educational Leadership*, 131–56. London: Falmer Press.

Bates, R. (2006). 'Educational administration and social justice'. *Education, Citizenship and Social Justice* 1 (2): 171–87.

Bates, R. (2008). 'Educational administration and state power: Towards a comparative analysis'. *Journal of Educational Administration and History* 40 (3): 195–264.

Bates, R. (2013). 'Educational administration and the management of knowledge: 1980 revisited'. *Journal of Educational Administration and History* 45 (2): 189–200.

Bates, R. and Eacott, S. (2008). 'Teaching educational leadership and administration in Australia'. *Journal of Educational Administration and History* 40 (2): 149–60.

Bates, Y. (1999). 'A vision for Lilian Baylis'. In H. Tomlinson, H. M. Gunter, and
P. Smith (eds), *Living Headship: Voices, Values and Vision*, 86–95. London:
PCP.

Beachum, F. (2008). 'Towards a transformational theory of social justice'. In
I. Bogotch, F. Beachum, J. Blount, J. Brooks, F. English, and J. Jansen (eds),
Radicalizing Educational Leadership, 39–60. Rotterdam: Sense Publishers.

Becher, T. (1989). *Academic Tribes and Territories*. Buckingham: SRHE and Open
University Press.

Begley, P. T. (1999). 'Introduction'. In P. T. Begley and P. E. Leonard (eds), *The
Values of Educational Administration*, 1–3. London: Falmer Press.

Begley, P. T. and Leonard, P. E. (eds) (1999). *The Values of Educational
Administration*. London: Falmer Press.

Béland, D. (2005). 'Ideas and social policy: An institutionalist perspective'. *Social
Policy and Administration* 39 (1): 1–18.

Belbin, R. M. (1996). *Management Teams: Why They Succeed or Fail*. London:
Butterworth-Heinemann.

Bennett, N. (1995). *Managing Professional Teachers: Middle Management in
Primary and Secondary Schools*. London: Paul Chapman.

Bennett, N., Wise, C., Woods, P. and Harvey, J. (2003). *Distributed Leadership*.
Nottingham: NCSL.

Bennis, W. G. and Nanus, B. (1985). *Leaders: The Strategies for Taking Charge*.
New York, NY: Harper and Row.

Beveridge, W. (1942). *Social Insurance and Allied Services*. Cmd 6404. London:
HMSO.

Bhabha, H. K. (1994). *The Location of Culture*. Abingdon: Routledge.

Bhindi, N. and Duignan, P. (1997). 'Leadership for a new century: Authenticity,
intentionality, spirituality and sensibility'. *Educational Management and
Administration* 26 (2): 117–32.

Biesta, G. (2012). 'Knowledge/democracy: Notes on the political economy of
academic publishing'. *International Journal of Leadership in Education* 15 (4):
407–19.

Bill and Melinda Gates Foundation (undated). *Academy for Urban School
Leadership to Manage Turnaround Efforts in Struggling Chicago
Public Schools*. http://www.gatesfoundation.org/Media-Center/Press-
Releases/2008/01/Academy-for-Urban-School-Leadership-to-Manage-
Turnaround-Efforts-in-Struggling-Chicago-Public-Schools (Accessed 16
February 2015).

Blackler, F. (1995). 'Knowledge, knowledge work and organizations: An overview
and interpretation'. *Organization Studies* 16 (6): 1021–46.

Blackmore, J. (1989). 'Educational leadership: A feminist critique and
reconstruction'. In J. Smyth (ed.), *Critical Perspectives on Educational
Leadership*, 93–129. London: The Falmer Press.

Blackmore, J. (1999). *Troubling Women*. Buckingham: Oxford University Press.

Blackmore, J. (2003). 'Tracking the nomadic life of the educational researcher:
What future for feminist public intellectuals and the performative university?'.
The Australian Educational Researcher 30 (3): 1–24.

Blackmore, J. (2010). 'Disrupting notions of leadership from feminist post-
colonial positions'. *International Journal of Leadership in Education* 13 (1):
1–105.

Blackmore, J. (2011). 'Lost in translation? Emotional intelligence, affective economies, leadership and organizational change'. *Journal of Educational Administration and History* 43 (3): 207–25.

Blackmore J. and Sachs, J. (2007). *Performing and Reforming Leaders: Gender, Educational Restructuring, and Organizational Change*. Albany, NY: State University of New York Press.

Blake, R. R. and Mouton, J. S. (1964). *The Managerial Grid*. Houston, TX: Gulf.

Blase, J. and Anderson, G. (1995). *The Micropolitics of Educational Leadership*. London: Cassell.

Blount, J. (2008). 'History as a way of understanding and motivating'. In I. Bogotch, F. Beachum, J. Blount, J. Brooks, F. English, and J. Jansen (eds), *Radicalizing Educational Leadership*, 17–37. Rotterdam: Sense Publishers.

Bobbitt, P. (2002). *The Shield of Achilles*. London: Penguin Books.

Bogotch, I. E. (2012). 'Who controls our knowledge?'. *International Journal of Leadership in Education* 15 (4): 404–6.

Bogotch, I., Beachum, F., Blount, J., Brooks, J., English, F., and Jansen, J. (2008). *Radicalizing Educational Leadership*. Rotterdam: Sense Publishers.

Bolam, R. (1999). 'Educational administration, leadership and management: Towards a research agenda'. In T. Bush, L. Bell, R. Bolam, R. Glatter (eds), *Educational Management, Redefining Theory, Policy and Practice*, 193–205. London: PCP.

Bottery, M. (1992). *The Ethics of Educational Management*. London: Cassell.

Bottery, M. (2004). *The Challenges of Educational Leadership*. London: PCP.

Bottery, M. (2009). 'An issue with history: A consideration of the impact of sustainable development upon school administration'. *Journal of Educational Administration and History* 41 (4): 343–62.

Bourdieu, P. (1988). *Homo Academicus*. Cambridge: Polity Press in association with Blackwell Publishers, Oxford.

Bourdieu, P. (1989). *The Logic of Practice*. Translated by R. Nice. Cambridge: Polity Press.

Bourdieu, P. (1990). *In Other Words: Essays Towards a Reflexive Sociology*. Translated by Matthew Adamson. Cambridge: Polity Press in association with Blackwell Publishers, Oxford.

Bourdieu, P. (1996). 'Intellectuals and the internationalisation of ideas: An interview with Pierre Bourdieu'. *International Journal of Contemporary Sociology* 33 (2): 237–53.

Bourdieu, P. (2000). *Pascalian Meditations*. Cambridge: Polity Press.

Bourdieu, P. (2003). *Firing Back: Against the Tyranny of the Market 2*. London: Verso.

Boyan, N. J. (ed.) (1988). *Handbook of Research on Educational Administration*. New York: Longman.

Boyson, R. (1975). *The Crisis in Education*. London: The Woburn Press.

Breckman, W. (2014). 'Intellectual history and the interdisciplinary ideal'. In D. M. McMahon and S. Moyn (eds), *Rethinking Modern European Intellectual History*, 275–93. Oxford: Oxford University Press.

Brooks, J. (2008). 'Freedom and justice'. In I. Bogotch, F. Beachum, J. Blount, J. Brooks, F. English, and J. Jansen (eds), *Radicalizing Educational Leadership*, 61–78. Rotterdam: Sense Publishers.

Brooks, J. S. and Miles, M. T. (2008). 'From scientific management to social justice … and back again? Pedagogical shifts in the study and practice of educational leadership'. In A. H. Normore (ed.), *Leadership for Social Justice*, 99–114. Charlotte, NC: IAP.

Buchanan, D. and Huczynski, A. (1997). *Organizational Behaviour, An Introductory Text*. Hemel Hempstead: Prentice Hall Europe.

Burch, P. (2009). *Hidden Markets*. New York: Routledge.

Burlingame, M. and Harris, E. L. (1998). 'Changes in the field of educational administration in the United States from 1967 to 1996 as a revitalization movement'. *Educational Management and Administration* 26 (1): 21–34.

Burns, J. M. (1978). *Leadership*. New York, NY: Harper and Row.

Bush, T. (2007). 'Educational leadership and management: Theory, policy and practice'. *South African Journal of Education* 27 (3): 391–406.

Bush, T. (2011). *Theories of Educational Leadership and Management*. Fourth Edition. London: Sage.

Bush, T., Bell, L., Bolam, R., Glatter, R., and Ribbins, P. (eds) (1999). *Educational Management: Redefining Theory, Policy and Practice*. London: Paul Chapman Publishing.

Busher, H. and Harris, A. with Wise, C. (2000). *Subject Leadership and School Improvement*. London: Paul Chapman.

Caldwell, B. J. (2006). *Re-Imagining Educational Leadership*. London: Sage.

Caldwell, B. J. and Spinks, J. M. (1988). *The Self Managing School*. Lewes: The Falmer Press.

Caldwell, B. J. and Spinks, J. M. (1992). *Leading the Self Managing School*. London: The Falmer Press.

Caldwell, B. J. and Spinks, J. M. (1998). *Beyond the Self Managing School*. London: The Falmer Press.

Callahan, R. A. (1962). *Education and the Cult of Efficiency*. Chicago: University of Chicago Press.

Chapman, C. (2005). *Improving Schools Through External Intervention*. London: Continuum.

Chapman, C., Muijs, D., Reynolds, D., Sammons, P. and Teddlie, C. (eds) (2015). *The Routledge Handbook of Educational Effectiveness and Improvement*. Abingdon: Routledge.

Chubb, J. E. and Moe, T. M. (1990). *Politics, Markets and America's Schools*. Washington, DC: The Brookings Institution.

Clark, P. (1998). *Back from the Brink*. London: Metro Books.

Clarke, C. (2004). *Transforming Secondary Education*. London: DfES.

Clarke, J. and Newman, J. (1997). *The Managerial State*. London: Sage.

Clarke, S. and Wildy, H. (2009a). 'The Europeanisation of educational leadership'. *European Educational Research Journal* 8 (3): 352–475.

Clarke, S. and Wildy, H. (2009b). 'The Europeanisation of educational leadership: Much ado about nothing?'. *European Educational Research Journal* 8 (3): 352–8.

Codd, J. (1989). 'Educational leadership as reflective action'. In J. Smyth (ed.), *Critical Perspectives on Educational Leadership*, 157–78. London: Falmer Press.

Coe, R. (2009). 'School improvement: Reality and illusion'. *British Journal of Educational Studies* 57 (4): 363–79.

Cole, B. and Gunter, H. M. (eds) (2010). *Changing Lives: Women, Inclusion and the PhD*. Stoke on Trent: Trentham Books.

Coleman, J. S., Campbell, E., Hobson, C., McPartland, J., Mood, A., Weinfeld, R., and York, R. (1966). *Equality of Educational Opportunity.* Washington, DC: Government Printing Office.

Coles, M. J. and Southworth, G. (eds) (2005a). *Developing Leadership, Creating the Schools of Tomorrow.* Maidenhead: Oxford University Press.

Coles, M. J. and Southworth, G. (2005b). 'Introduction: Developing leadership – creating the schools of tomorrow'. In M. J. Coles and G. Southworth (eds), *Developing Leadership, Creating the Schools of Tomorrow*, xvii–xxi. Maidenhead: Oxford University Press.

Collins, J. C. (2001). *Good to Great: Why Some Companies Make the Leap ... and Others Don't.* US: Collins Business.

Collinson, D. (2014). 'Dichotomies, dialectics and dilemmas: New directions for critical leadership studies?'. *Leadership* 10 (1): 36–55.

Connell, R. W. (1983). *Which Way Is Up? Essays on Sex, Class and Culture.* Sydney: George Allen & Unwin.

Connell, R. W. (2007). *Southern Theory.* Cambridge: Polity Press.

Court, M. (2003). *Different Approaches to Sharing School Leadership.* Nottingham: NCSL.

Court, M. and O'Neill, J. (2011). '"Tomorrow's Schools" in New Zealand: from social democracy to market managerialism'. *Journal of Educational Administration and History* 43 (2): 119–40.

Courtney, S. J. (2014). 'Inadvertently queer school leadership amongst lesbian, gay and bisexual (LGB) school leaders'. *Organization* 21 (3): 380–96.

Courtney, S. J. and Gunter, H. M. (2015). '"Get off my bus!" School leaders, vision work and the elimination of teachers'. *International Journal of Leadership in Education.* 10.1080/13603124.2014.992476.

Covey, S. R. (2004). *The 7 Habits of Highly Effective People.* London: Simon and Schuster.

Creemers, B., Scheerens, J., and Reynolds, D. (2000). 'Theory development in school effectiveness research'. In C. Teddlie and D. Reynolds (eds), *The Handbook of School Effectiveness Research*, 283–98. New York: Falmer Press.

Crossley, D. (ed.) (2013). *Sustainable School Transformation.* London: Bloomsbury.

Crow, G. and Weindling, D. (2010). 'Learning to be political: New English headteachers' roles'. *Educational Policy* 24 (1): 137–58.

Crowther, F. (1997). 'The William Walker Oration, 1996. Unsung heroes: The leaders in our classrooms'. *Journal of Educational Administration* 35 (1): 5–17.

Culbertson, J. A. (1964). 'The preparation of administrators'. In D. E. Griffiths (ed.), *Behavioural Science and Educational Administration.* The 63rd Yearbook of the National Society for the Study of Education, Part II, Chicago: University of Chicago Press.

Culbertson, J. A. (1969). 'A new initiative in educational administration'. In G. Baron, D. H. Cooper and W. G. Walker (eds), *Educational Administration: International Perspectives.* Chicago: Rand McNally and Company.

Culbertson, J. A. (1983). 'Theory in educational administration: Echoes from critical thinkers'. *Educational Researcher* (December): 15–22.

Culbertson, J. A. (1988). 'A century's quest for a knowledge base'. In N. J. Boyan (ed.), *Handbook of Research on Educational Administration,* 3–26. New York: Longman.

Culbertson, J. A. (1995). *Building Bridges: UCEA's First Two Decades*. University Park, PA: UCEA.

Cutler, V. (1998). 'Highbury Grove – from deconstruction to reconstruction'. In L. Stoll and K. Myers (eds), *No Quick Fixes*, 86–95. London: The Falmer Press.

Czerniawski, G. and Kidd, W. (eds) (2011). *The Handbook of Student Voice*. Bingley: Emerald.

Dantley, M. E. and Tillman, L. C. (2006). 'Social justice and moral transformational leadership'. In C. Marshall and M. Oliva (eds), *Leadership for Social Justice*, 16–30. Boston: Pearson.

Davies, B. (1997). 'Reengineering and its application to education'. *School Leadership and Management* 17 (2): 173–85.

Davies, B. and Davies, B. J. (2005). 'Strategic leadership'. In B. Davies (ed.), *The Essentials of School Leadership*, 10–30. London: Paul Chapman Publishing.

Davies, B., Ellison, L., Osborne, A., and West-Burnham, J. (1990). *Educational Management for the 1990s*. Harlow: Longman.

Davies, B. and West-Burnham, J. (eds) (2003). *Handbook of Educational Leadership and Management*. Harlow: Pearson Education Ltd.

Davies, J. S. (2011). *Challenging Governance Theory*. Bristol: The Policy Press.

Day, C., Harris, A., Hadfield, M., Tolley, H., and Beresford, J. (2000). *Leading Schools in Times of Change*. Buckingham: Oxford University Press.

Day, C., Sammons, P., Hopkins, D., Harris, A., Leithwood, K., Gu, Q., Brown, E., Ahtaridou, E., and Kington, A. (2009). *The Impact of School Leadership on Pupil Outcomes*. London: DCSF/NCSL.

Day, C., Sammons, P., Hopkins, D., Harris, A., Leithwood, K., Gu, Q. and Brown, E. (2010). *10 Strong Claims About Successful School Leadership*. Nottingham: National College for Leadership of Schools and Children's Services.

Dean, M. (2014). 'Rethinking neoliberalism'. *Journal of Sociology* 50 (2): 150–63.

Deem, R. (1996). 'Border territories: A journey through sociology, education and women's studies'. *British Journal of Sociology of Education* 17 (1): 5–19.

DfEE (1997). *Excellence in Schools*. London: DfEE. Cm 3681.

DfEE (1998). *Teachers: Meeting the Challenge of Change*. London: DfEE.

DfES/PwC (2007). *Independent Study into School Leadership*. London: DfES.

Dimitriadis, G. (2012). *Critical Dispositions*. Abingdon: Routledge.

Donmoyer, R. (1999). 'The continuing quest for a knowledge base: 1976-1998'. In J. Murphy and K. Seashore Louis (eds), *Handbook of Research on Educational Administration*, 25–43. San Francisco, CA: Jossey-Bass Publishers.

Donmoyer, R., Imber, M., and Scheurich, J. J. (eds) (1995). *The Knowledge Base in Educational Administration*. Albany, NY: The State University of New York Press.

Dorling, D. (2011). *Injustice: Why Social Inequality Persists*. Bristol: Policy Press.

Du Gay, P. (2005). *The Values of Bureaucracy*. Oxford: Oxford University Press.

Eacott, S. (2011a). *School Leadership and Strategy in Managerialist Times*. Rotterdam: Sense Publishers.

Eacott, S. (2011b). 'Preparing "educational" leaders in managerialist times: An Australian story'. *Journal of Educational Administration and History* 43 (1): 43–59.

Eacott, S. (2013a). 'Special issue, rethinking "leadership" in education: A research agenda'. *Journal of Educational Administration and History* 45 (2): 113–212.

Eacott, S. (2013b). 'Towards a theory of school leadership practice: A Bourdieusian perspective'. *Journal of Educational Administration and History* 45 (2): 174–88.

Earley, P. (2013). *Exploring the School Leadership Landscape.* London: Bloomsbury.

Earley, P., Evans, J., Collarbone, P., Gold, A., and Halpin, D. (2002). *Establishing the Current State of School Leadership in England.* London: DfES.

Edmonds, R. (1979). 'Effective schools for the urban poor'. *Educational Leadership* (October): 15–24.

EMA (1999). 'Special edition: Redefining educational management and leadership'. *Educational Management and Administration* 27 (3): 227–43.

English, F. W. (2003). 'Cookie-cutter leaders for cookie-cutter schools: The teleology of standardization and the de-legitimization of the university in educational leadership preparation'. *Leadership and Policy in Schools* 2 (1): 27–46.

English, F. W. (2006a). 'The unintended consequences of a standardized knowledge base in advancing educational leadership preparation'. *Educational Administration Quarterly* 42 (3): 461–72.

English, F. W. (2006b). 'Understanding Leadership in Education: Life Writing and its Possibilities'. *Journal of Educational Administration and History* 38 (2): 141–54.

English, F. W. (2008). 'Towards a theory of social justice/injustice'. In I. Bogotch, F. Beachum, J. Blount, J. Brooks, F. English, and J. Jansen (2008). *Radicalizing Educational Leadership*, 113–46. Rotterdam: Sense Publishers.

English, F. W. (ed.) (2011). *The Sage Handbook of Educational Leadership: Advances in Theory, Researcvh and Practice.* Thousand Oaks, CA: Sage.

English, F. W., Papa, R., Mullen, C. A., and Creighton, T. (2012). *Educational Leadership at 2050.* Lanham, MA: Rowman & Littlefield Education.

Evans, R. (1999). *The Pedagogic Principal.* Edmonton: Qual Institute Press.

Everard, B. and Morris, G. (1985). *Effective School Management.* London: PCP.

Evers, C. (2003). 'Philosophical reflections on science in educational administration'. *International Studies in Educational Administration* 31 (3): 29–41.

Evers, C. W. and Lakomski, G. (1991). *Knowing Educational Administration.* Oxford: Pergamon.

Evers, C. W. and Lakomski, G. (eds) (1996). *Exploring Educational Administration.* Oxford: Elsevier Science Ltd.

Evers, C. W. and Lakomski, G. (2012). 'Science, Systemcs, and Theoretical Alternatives in Educational Administration: The road less travelled'. *Journal of Educational Administration* 50 (1): 57–75.

Evers, C. W. and Lakomski, G. (2013). 'Methodologocial individualism, educational administration, and leadership'. *Journal of Educational Administration and History* 45 (2): 159–73.

Fay, B. (1975). *Social Theory and Political Practice.* London: George Allen & Unwin Ltd.

Fiedler, F. E., Chemers, M. M., and Mahar, L. (1977). *Improving Leadership Effectiveness: The Leader Match.* New York, NY: John Wiley.

Fielding, M. (2006). 'Leadership, radical student engagement and the necessity of person-centred education'. *International Journal of Leadership in Education* 9 (4): 299–313.

Fielding, M. and Moss, P. (2011). *Radical Education and the Common School.* Abingdon: Routledge.

Fink, D. (2000). *Good Schools/Real Schools: Why Reform Doesn't Last.* New York, NY: Teachers College Press.

Fitz, J. (1999). 'Reflections on the field of educational management'. *Educational Management and Adminstration* 27 (3): 313–21.

Fitzgerald, T. and Gunter, H. M. (2008). 'The state of the field of educational administration'. *Journal of Educational Administration and History* 40 (2): 81–185.

Fitzgerald, T. and Savage, J. (2013). 'Scripting, ritualising and performing leadership: Interrogating recent policy developments in Australia'. *Journal of Educational Administration and History* 45 (2): 126–43.

Fitzgerald, T., White, J., and Gunter, H. M. (2012). *Hard Labour? Academic Work and The Changing Landscape of Higher Education.* Bingley: Emerald.

Fleck, C., Hess, A., and Lyon, E. S. (2009). 'Introduction. Intellectuals and their publics: Perspectives from the social sciences'. In C. Fleck, A. Hess, and E. S. Lyon (eds), *Intellectuals and their Publics: Perspectives from the Social Sciences*, 1–16. Farnham: Ashgate Publishing Limited.

Flinders, M. and Wood, M. (2014). 'Special Issue: Depoliticisation, governance and the state'. *Policy & Politics* 42 (2): 135–311.

Foster, W. (1986). *Paradigms and Promises.* Amherst, NY: Prometheus Books.

Foster, W. (1989). 'Towards a critical practice of leadership'. In J. Smyth (ed.), *Critical Perspectives on Educational Leadership*, 39–62. London: Falmer Press.

Fraser, N. (2014). 'Can society be commodities all the way down? Post-Polyian reflections on capitalist crisis'. *Economy and Society.* DOI 10.1080/03085147.2014.898822

Freeman, R. and Sturdy, S. (2014a). 'Introduction: Knowledge in policy – embodied, inscribed, enacted'. In R. Freeman and S. Sturdy (eds), *Knowledge in Policy, Embodied, Inscribed, Enacted*, 1–17. Bristol: Policy Press.

Freeman, R. and Sturdy, S. (2014b). 'Knowledge and policy in research and practice'. In R. Freeman and S. Sturdy (eds), *Knowledge in Policy, Embodied, Inscribed, Enacted*, 201–18. Bristol: Policy Press.

Friedman, M. (1962). *Capitalism and Freedom.* Chicago, IL: University of Chicago Press.

Fullan, M. with Stiegelbauer, S. (1991). *The new meaning of educational change.* London: Cassell.

Fullan, M. (1992). *What's worth fighting for in headship?* Buckingham: Open University Press.

Fullan, M. (2001). *Leading in a Culture of Change.* San Francisco, CA: Jossey-Bass Publishers.

Fuller, S. (2005). *The Intellectual.* Cambridge: Icon Books Ltd.

Furedi, F. (2004). *Where Have All the Intellectuals Gone?* London: Continuum.

Gandin, L. A. and Apple, M. (2003). 'Educating the state, democratizing knowledge: The citizen school project in Porte Alegre, Brazil'. In M. W. Apple, P. Aasen, M. Kim Cho, L. A. Gandin, A. Oliver, Y.-K. Sung, H. Tavares, and T.-H. Wong (eds), *The State and the Politics of Knowledge*, 193–219. New York: RoutledgeFalmer.

Geijsel, F., Sleegers, P., Leithwood, K., and Jantzi, D. (2003). 'Transformational leadership effects on teachers' commitment and effort toward school reform'. *Journal of Educational Administration* 41 (3): 228–56.

Gewirtz, S. (2002). *The Managerial School*. London: Routledge.

Gewirtz, S. and Ball, S. J. (2000). 'From "welfarism" to "new managerialism":
Shifting discourses of school headship in the education marketplace'.
Discourse: Studies in the Cultural Politics of Education 21 (3): 253–68.

Gewirtz, S., Ball, S. J., and Bowe, R. (1993). 'Values and Ethics in the Education
Market Place: The case of Northwark Park'. *International Studies in Sociology
of Education* 3 (2): 233–54.

Gibbons, M., Limoges, C., Nowotny, H., Schwartzman, S., Scott, P., and
Trow, M. (1994). *The New Production of Knowledge*. London: Sage.

Gillies, D. (2014). *Educational Leadership and Michel Foucault*. Abingdon:
Routledge.

Giuliani, R. W. with Kurson, K. (2002). *Leadership*. London: Time Warner
Paperbacks.

Glatter, R. (1979). 'Education "policy" and "management": One field or two?'.
In T. Bush, R. Glatter, J. Goodey, and C. Riches (eds), *Approaches to School
Management*, 26–37. London: Harper Educational Series.

Glatter, R. (2011). 'Joining up the dots: Academies and system coherence'.
In H. M. Gunter (ed.), *The State and Education Policy: The Academies
Programme*, 159–70. London: Bloomsbury.

Goddard, V. (2014). *The Best Job in the World*. Carmarthen: Independent Thinking
Press.

Gold, A., Evans, J., Earley, P., Halpin, D., and Collarbone, P. (2003). 'Principled
Principals? Values-Driven Leadership: Evidence from ten case studies of
"outstanding" school leaders'. *Educational Management and Administration*
31 (2): 127–38.

Goldberg, J. (2003). *The Neoconservative Invention*. National Review Online.
http://www.nationalreview.com/articles/206955/neoconservative-invention/
jonah-goldberg (Accessed 10 February 2014).

Goleman, D. (1996). *Emotional Intelligence: Why It Can Matter More Than IQ*.
London: Bloomsbury.

Goodin, R. E. (1988). *Reasons for Welfare: The Political Theory of the Welfare
State*. Princeton, NJ: Princeton University Press.

Goodwin, M. (2009). 'Which Networks Matter in Education Governance? A
reply to Ball's "New Philanthropy, New Networks and New Governance in
Eduation".' *Political Studies* 57 (3): 680–7.

Gorard, S. (2005). 'Current contexts for research in educational leadership and
management'. *Educational Management Administration and Leadership*
33 (2): 155–64.

Gorard, S. (2010). 'Serious doubts about school effectiveness'. *British Educational
Research Journal* 36 (5): 645–766.

Gorard, S. (2011). 'Doubts about school effectiveness exacerbated – by attempted
justification'. *Research Intelligence*. Issue 114 (Spring): 26.

Gorur, R. (2014). 'Producing calculable worlds: Education at a glance'. *Discourse:
Studies in the Cultural Politics of Education* 36 (4): 578–89.

Grace, G. (1995). *School Leadership: Beyond Education Management*. London:
The Falmer Press.

Gramsci, A. (1971). *Selections from the Prison Notebooks*. Edited and Translated
by Q. Hoare and G. Nowell Smith. London: Lawrence and Wishart.

Gray, J. (2010). 'The nanny diaries'. *New Statesman* (11 January 2010): 52–3.

Gray, M. with McMahon, A. (1997). 'Mary Gray in conversation with Agnes McMahon'. In P. Ribbins (ed.), *Leaders and Leadership in the School, College and University*, 23–37. London: Cassell.

Gray, S. P. and Streshly, W. A. (2008). *From Good Schools to Great Schools*. Thousand Oaks, CA: Corwin Press.

Greenfield, T. B. (1978). 'Where does self belong in the study of organisation? Response to a Symposium'. *Educational Administration* 6 (1): 81–101.

Greenfield, T. B. (1988). 'The decline and fall of science in educational administration'. In A. Westoby (ed.), *Culture and Power in Educational Organisations*, 115–41. Milton Keynes: Oxford University Press.

Greenfield, T. B. (1991). 'Foreward'. In C. Hodgkinson (ed.), *Educational Leadership: The Moral Art*, 3–9. Albany, NY: State University of New York Press.

Greenfield, T. and Ribbins, P. (eds) (1993). *Greenfield on Educational Administration*. London: Routledge.

Grek, S. (2013). 'Expert moves: International comparative testing and the rise of expertocracy'. *Journal of Education Policy* 28 (5): 695–709.

Griffiths, D. E. (1958). 'Administration as Decision-making'. In A. W. Halpin (ed.), *Administrative Theory in Education*. London: Macmillan.

Griffiths, D. E. (ed.) (1964). '*Behavioural Science and Educational Administration*'. The 63rd Yearbook of the National Society for the Study of Education, Part II, Chicago: University of Chicago Press.

Griffiths, D. E. (1969). 'Theory in educational administration: 1966'. In G. Baron, D. H. Cooper, and W. G. Walker (eds), *Educational Administration: International Perspectives*. Chicago: Rand McNally and Company.

Griffiths, D. E. (1979). 'Intellectual turmoil in educational administration'. *Educational Administration Quarterly* 15 (3): 43–65.

Griffiths, M. (1998). *Educational Research for Social Justice*. Buckingham: Open University Press.

Gronn, P. (1985). 'After T. B. Greenfield, With Educational Administration'. *Educational Management and Administration* 13: 55–61.

Gronn, P. (1996). 'From Transactions to Transformations'. *Educational Management and Administration* 24 (1): 7–30.

Gronn, P. (1999). *The Making of Educational Leaders*. London: Cassell.

Gronn, P. (2000). 'Distributed properties: A new architecture for leadership'. *Educational Management and Administration* 28 (3): 319–38.

Gronn, P. (2003a). *Leadership: Who needs it?* Keynote addess to ESRC seminar series "Challenging the orthodoxy of school leadership: Towards a new theoretical perspective". University of Birmingham, February 2003.

Gronn, P. (2003b). *The New Work of Educational Leaders*. London: PCP.

Gronn, P. (2009). 'Hybrid Leadership'. In K. Leithwood, B. Mascall, and T. Strauss (eds), *Distributed Leadership According to the Evidence*, 17–40. New York: Routledge.

Gronn, P. (2010). 'Leadership: Its genealogy, configuration and trajectory'. *Journal of Educational Administration and History* 42 (4): 405–35.

Grubb, W. N. and Flessa, J. J. (2006). 'A job too big for one: Principals and other non-traditional approaches to school leadership'. *Educational Administration Quarterly* 42 (4): 518–50.

Grundmann, R. and Stehr, N. (2012). *The Power of Scientific Knowledge*. Cambridge: Cambridge University Press.

Gunter, H. M. (1997). *Rethinking Education: The Consequences of Jurassic Management*. London: Cassell.

Gunter, H. M. (1999). *An Intellectual History of the Field of Education Management from 1960*. Unpublished PhD, Keele University.

Gunter, H. M. (2001). *Leaders and Leadership in Education*. London: Paul Chapman.

Gunter, H. M. (2004). 'Labels and Labelling in the field of educational leadership'. *Discourse* 25 (1): 21–42.

Gunter, H. M. (2005a). 'Conceptualising research in educational leadership'. *Educational Management, Administration and Leadership* 33 (2): 165–80.

Gunter, H. M. (2005b). *Leading Teachers*. London: Continuum.

Gunter, H. M. (2010). 'Dusting off my doctorate'. In B. Cole and H. M. Gunter (eds), *Changing Lives: Women, Inclusion and the PhD*, 81–97. Stoke on Trent: Trentham Books.

Gunter, H. M. (ed.) (2011). *The State and Education Policy: The Academies Programme*. London: Continuum.

Gunter, H. M. (2012a). *Leadership and the Reform of Education*. Bristol: The Policy Press.

Gunter, H. M. (2012b). 'The field of educational administration'. *British Journal of Educational Studies* 60 (4): 337–56.

Gunter, H. M. (2012c). 'Intellectual work and knowledge production'. In T. Fitzgerald, J. White, and H. M. Gunter (eds), *Hard Labour? Academic Work and the Changing Landscape of Higher Education*, 23–40. Bingley: Emerald.

Gunter, H. M. (2013a). 'On not researching school leadership: The contribution of S. J. Ball'. *London Review of Education* 11 (3): 218–28.

Gunter, H. M. (2013b). '*BELMAS: Perspectives on Origins and Development*'. Essay in celebration of the fortieth anniversary of the British Educational Leadership Management and Administration Society. http://www.belmas.org.uk/About/BELMAS-History

Gunter, H. M. (2014). *Educational Leadership and Hannah Arendt*. Abingdon: Routledge.

Gunter, H. M. and Fitzgerald, T. (2011). 'The pendulum swings – but where? Part I'. *Journal of Educational Administration and History* 43 (4): 283–362.

Gunter, H. M. and Fitzgerald, T. (2012). 'The pendulum swings – but where? Part II'. *Journal of Educational Administration and History* 44 (1): 1–88.

Gunter, H. M. and Fitzgerald, T. (2013a). 'Editorial: New Public Management and the modernisation of education 1'. *Journal of Educational Administration and History* 45 (3): 213–19.

Gunter, H. M. and Fitzgerald, T. (2013b). 'Editorial: New Public Management and the modernisation of education 2'. *Journal of Educational Administration and History* 45 (4): 303–5.

Gunter, H. M. and Fitzgerald, T. (2014). 'Educational Administration and the Social Sciences: Reflecting on Baron and Taylor after 45 years'. *Journal of Educational Administration and History* 46 (3): 235–366.

Gunter, H. M. and Forrester, G. (2008). *Knowledge Production in Educational Leadership Project*. Final Report to the ESRC. RES-000-23-1192.

Gunter, H. M. and Forrester, G. (2009). 'Education reform and school leadership'. In S. Brookes and K. Grint (eds), *The Public Sector Leadership Challenge*, 54–69. London: Palgrave.

Gunter, H. M., Grimaldi, E., Hall, D., and Serpieri, R. (eds) (2016). *New Public Management and the Reform of Education: European Lessons for Policy and Practice*. London: Routledge.

Gunter, H. M. and Hall, D. (2013). 'Public trust and education'. In S. Llewellyn, S. Brookes, and A. Mahon (eds), *Trust and Confidence in Government and Public Services*, 204–20. Abingdon: Routledge.

Gunter, H. M., Hall, D., and Apple, M. (eds) (2016). *Corporate Elites and the Reform of Public Education*. Bristol: Policy Press.

Gunter, H. M., Hall, D., and Bragg, J. (2013). 'Distributed leadership: A study in knowledge production'. *Educational Leadership, Management and Administration* 41 (5): 556–81.

Gunter, H. M., Hall, D., and Mills, C. (2014b). 'Consultants, consultancy and consultocracy in education policymaking in England'. *Journal of Education Policy*. 10.1080/02680939.2014.963163

Gunter, H. M. and McGinity, R. (2014). 'The politics of the academies programme: Natality and plurality in education policymaking'. *Research Papers in Education* 29 (3): 300–14.

Gunter, H. M. and Mills, C. (2016). *Consultants and Consultancy: The Case of Education*. Cham, Switzerland: Springer.

Gunter, H. M. and Ribbins, P. (2002). 'Leadership studies in education: Towards a map of the field'. *Educational Management and Administration* 30 (4): 387–416.

Gunter, H. M. and Ribbins, P. (2003a). 'The field of educational leadership: Studying maps and mapping studies'. *British Journal of Educational Studies* 51 (3): 254–81.

Gunter, H. M. and Ribbins, P. (2003b). Challenging orthodoxy in school leadership studies: Knowers, knowing and knowledge? *School Leadership and Management*, 23 (2), 129–46.

Gunter, H. M. and Thomson, P. (2010). 'Life on Mars: Headteachers before the National College'. *Journal of Educational Administration and History* 42 (3): 203–22.

Gunter, H. M. and Willmott, R. (2001). 'Biting the bullet'. *Management in Education* 15 (5): 35–7.

Hall, S. (2011). 'The neoliberal revolution'. *Cultural Studies* 25 (6): 705–28.

Hall, V. (1996). *Dancing on the Ceiling: A Study of Women Managers in Education*. London: Paul Chapman Publishing.

Hallinger, P. (2003). 'Leading educational change: Reflections on the practice of instructional and transformational leadership'. *Cambridge Journal of Education* 33 (3): 329–51.

Hallinger, P. (2013). 'Reviewing reviews of research in educational leadership: an empirical Assessment'. *Educational Administration Quarterly*. DOI: 10.1177/0013161X13506594.

Hallinger, P. and Chen, J. (2015). 'Review of research on educational leadership and management in Asia: A comparative analysis of research topics and methods, 1995–2012'. *Educational Management Administration and Leadership* 43 (1): 5–27.

Hallinger, P. and Heck, R. H. (1998). 'Exploring the principal's contribution to school effectiveness: 1980-1995'. *School Effectiveness and School Improvement* 9 (2): 157–91.

Halpin, A. W. (ed.) (1958). *Administrative Theory in Education*. London: Macmillan.

Halpin, A. W. (1966). *Theory and Research in Administration*. New York: The Macmillan Company.

Handy, C. and Aitken, R. (1990). *Understanding Schools as Organisations*. London: Penguin.

Harber, C. and Davies, L. (2006). *School Management and Effectiveness in Developing Countries: The Post-Bureaucratic School*. London: Continuum.

Hargreaves, A. (1994). *Changing Teachers, Changing Times*. London: Cassell.

Hargreaves, A. (1997). 'Rethinking educational change'. In M. Fullan (ed.), *The Challenge of School Change*, 3–32. Arlington Heights, IL: IRI/Skylight Training and Publishing Inc.

Hargreaves, A. and Fink, D. (2006). *Sustainable Leadership*. San Francisco, CA: Jossey-Bass Publishers.

Hargreaves, D. H. and Hopkins, D. (1991). *The Empowered School: The Management and Practice of Development Planning*. London: Cassell.

Harris, A. (2001). 'Department improvement and school improvement: A missing link?'. *British Educational Research Journal* 27 (4): 477–86.

Harris, A. (2005a). 'Leading from the Chalk-face: An overview of school leadership'. *Leadership* 1 (1): 73–87.

Harris, A. (2005b). *Crossing Boundaries and Breaking Barriers, Distributing Leadership in Schools*. London: Specialist Schools Trust.

Harris, A. (2008). *Distributed School Leadership*. London: Routledge.

Harris, A. (2014). 'Still making a difference: Reflections on the field'. *School Effectiveness and School Improvement: An International Journal of Research, Policy and Practice* 25 (2): 193–4.

Harris, A. and Bennett, N. (eds) (2001). *School Effectiveness and School Improvement, Alternative Perspectives*. London: Continuum.

Harris, A. and Chapman, C. (2002). *Effective Leadership in Schools Facing Challenging Circumstances*. Nottingham: NCSL.

Harris, A., Day, C., Hadfield, M., Hopkins, D., Hargreaves, A., and Chapman, C. (2003). *Effective Leadership for School Improvement*. London: RoutledgeFalmer.

Harris, A., James, S., Gunraj, J., Clarke, P., and Harris, B. (2006). *Improving Schools in Exceptionally Challenging Circumstances*. London: Continuum.

Harris, A. and Lambert, L. (2003). *Building Leadership Capacity for School Improvement*. Maidenhead: Oxford University Press.

Harris, A. and Muijs, D. (2003). *Teacher Leadership: Principals and practice*. Nottingham: NCSL.

Harris, B. (2007). *Supporting the Emotional Work of School Leaders*. London: Sage.

Hart, A. W. (1993). *Principal Succession: Establishing Leadership in Schools*. New York: State University of New York Press.

Hartley, D. (1997). 'The new managerialism in education: A mission impossible?'. *Cambridge Journal of Education* 27 (1): 47–58.

Hartley, D. (1998). 'In search of structure, theory and practice in the management of education'. *Journal of Education Policy* 12 (1): 153–62.

Hartley, D. (2004). 'Management, leadership and the emotional order of the school'. *Journal of Education Policy* 19 (5): 583–94.

Hartley, D. (2007). 'The emergence of distributed leadership in education; why now?'. *British Journal of Educational Studies* 55 (2): 202–14.

Hartley, D. (2010). 'Marketing and the "re-enchantment" of school management'. *British Journal of Sociology of Education* 20 (3): 309–23.

Harvey, D. (2005). *The New Imperialism*. Oxford: Oxford University Press.

Harvey, D. (2007). *A Brief History of Neoliberalism*. Oxford: Oxford University Press.

Hatcher, R. (2001). 'Getting down to business: Schooling in the globalised economy'. *Education and Social Justice* 3 (2): 45–59.

Hatcher, R. (2005). 'The distribution of leadership and power in schools'. *British Journal of Sociology of Education* 26 (2): 253–67.

Hay, C. (2014). 'Depoliticisation as a process, governance as practice: What did the "first wave" get wrong and do we need a "second wave" to put it right?'. *Policy & Politics* 42 (2): 293–311.

Hayek, F. A. (1944). *The Road to Serfdom*. London: Routledge and Kegan Paul.

Herzberg, F. (1992). *Motivation to Work*. Piscataway, NJ: Transaction Publishers.

Hill, R. (2006). *Leadership that Lasts, Sustainable School Leadership in the 21st Century*. London: ASCL, CfBT, Harcourt.

Hind, D. (2010). *The Return of the Public*. London: Verso.

Hirschman, A. O. (1970). *Exit, Voice, and Loyalty: Responses to the Decline in Firms, Organizations and States*. Cambridge, MA: Harvard University Press.

Hodgkinson, C. (1978). *Towards a Philosophy of Administration*. Oxford: Basil Blackwell.

Hodgkinson, C. (1983). *The Philosophy of Leadership*. Oxford: Basil Blackwell.

Hodgkinson, C. (1993). 'Foreword'. In T. Greenfield and P. Ribbins (eds), *Greenfield on Educational Administration*, x–xvii. London: Routledge.

Hodgkinson, C. (1991). *Educational Leadership: The Moral Art*. Albany, NY: State University of New York Press.

Hoffman, L. P. (2009). 'Educational leadership and social activism: A call for action'. *Journal of Educational Administration and History* 41 (4): 391–410.

Hopkins, D. (ed.) (1987). *Improving the Quality of Schooling*. Lewes: Falmer.

Hopkins, D. (2001). *School Improvement for Real*. London: RoutledgeFalmer.

Hopkins, D. (2007). *Every School a Great School*. Maidenhead: Oxord University Press.

Hopkins, D., Ainscow, M., and West, M. (1994). *School Improvement in an Era of Change*. London: Cassell.

Hopkins, D. (1996). *Improving the Quality of Education for All*. London: David Fulton.

Hopkins, D., Stringfield, S., Harris, A., Stoll, L., and Mackay, T. (2014). 'School and system impovement: A narrative state-of-the-art review'. *School Effectiveness and School Improvement* 25 (2): 257–81.

Hoy, W. K. (2012). 'School characteristics that make a difference for the achievement of students: A 40 year odyssey'. *Journal of Educational Administration* 50 (1): 76–97.

Hoy, W. K. and Miskel, C. G. with Tarter, C. J. (2013). *Educational Administration, Theory, Research and Practice*. Nineth Edition. New York, NY: McGraw-Hill.

Hoyle, E. (1982). 'Micropolitics of educational organisations'. *Educational Management and Administration* 10 (2): 87–98.

Hoyle, E. (1999). 'The two faces of micropolitics'. *School Leadership and Management* 19 (2): 213–22.

Hoyle, E. and Wallace, M. (2005). *Educational Leadership: Ambiguity, Professionals and Managerialism*. London: Sage.

Hughes, M., Ribbins, P., and Thomas, H. (1985). *Managing Education: The System and The Institution*. Eastbourne: Holt, Rinehart and Winston.

Hyung Park, S. (1999). 'The development of Richard Bates' critical theory in educational administration'. *Journal of Educational Administration* 37 (4): 367–88.

Jackson, D. S. (2000). 'The school improvement journey: Perspectives on leadership'. *School Leadership and Management* 20 (1): 61–78.

Jansen, J. (2008). 'The challenge of the ordinary'. In I. Bogotch, F. Beachum, J. Blount, J. Brooks, F. English, and J. Jansen (eds), *Radicalizing Educational Leadership*, 147–55. Rotterdam: Sense Publishers.

Jean-Marie, G. and Normore, A. H. (2008). 'A repository of hope for social justice: Black women leaders at historically black colleges and universities'. In A. H. Normore (ed.), *Leadership for Social Justice*, 3–35. Charlotte, NC: IAP.

Jessop, B. (2014). 'A specter is haunting Europe: A neoliberal phantasmagoria'. *Critical Policy Studies* 8 (3): 352–5.

John, D. (1980). *Leadership in Schools*. London: Heinemann Educational Books.

Judt, T. (2010). *Ill Fares the Land*. New York: The Penguin Press.

Karagiorgi, Y. (2011). 'On democracy and leadership: From rhetoric to reality'. *International Journal of Leadership in Education* 14 (3): 369–84.

Kelley, D. R. (2002). *The Descent of Ideas: The History of Intellectual History*. Aldershot: Ashgate Publishing Limited.

Kerr, S. and Jermier, J. M. (1978). 'Substitutes for leadership: Their meaning and measurement'. *Organizational Behavior and Human Performance* 22: 375–403.

Kettle, M. (2013). *Thatcher's Funeral: An Exercise in Downton Abbey Politics*. http://www.theguardian.com/commentisfree/2013/apr/17/thatcher-funeral-downton-abbey-politics-bluff (Accessed 14 February 2014).

Kildal, N. and Kuhnle, S. (2005). 'The Nordic welfare model and the idea of universalism'. In N. Kildal and S. Kulnle (eds), *Normative Foundation sof the Welfare State: The Nordic Experience*, 13–33. Abingdon: Routledge.

Koyama, J. (2010). *Making Failure Pay: For-profit Tutoring, High-stakes Testing, and Public Schools*. Chicago, IL: University of Chicago Press.

Kuhn, T. (1975). *The Structure of Scientific Revolutions* (Sixth Impression). London: The University of Chicago Press.

Kurzman, C. and Owens, L. (2002). 'The sociology of intelletuals'. *Annual Review of Sociology* 28: 63–90.

Lakomski, G. (2005). *Managing Without Leadership*. Amsterdam: Elsevier.

Lane, T. (1996). 'Patterns of thinking in educational administration'. *Journal of Educational Administration* 33 (1): 63–78.

Lawn, M. and Grek, S. (2012). *Europeanizing Education: Governing a New Policy Space*. Oxford: Symposium Books Ltd.

Leithwood, K., Begley, P. T., and Cousins, J. B. (1994). *Developing Expert Leadership for Future Schools*. London: Falmer Press.

Leithwood, K., Day, C., Sammons, P., Harris, A., and Hopkins, D. (2006). *Seven Strong Claims About Successful School Leadership*. Nottingham: NCSL.

Leithwood, K. and Duke, D. L. (1999). 'A century's quest to understand school leadership'. In J. Murphy and K. Seashore Louis (eds), *Handbook of Research on Educational Administration*, 45–71. San Francisco, CA: Jossey-Bass Publishers.

Leithwood, K., Jantzi, D., and Steinbach, R. (1999). *Changing Leadership for Changing Times*. Buckingham: Oxford University Press.

Leithwood, K. and Levin, B. (2005). *Assessing School Leader and Leadership Programme Effects on Pupil Learning*. London: DfES.

Leithwood, K., Mascall, B., and Strauss, T. (eds) (2009). *Distributed Leadership According to the Evidence*. New York: Routledge.

Leithwood, K. and Riehl, C. (2003). *What We Know About Successful School Leadership*. Nottingham: NCSL.

Leithwood, K., Seashore Louis, K., Anderson, S., and Wahlstrom, K. (2004). *How Leadership Influences Student Learning*. New York, NY: The Wallace Foundation.

Leithwood, K. and Sleegers, P. (2006). 'Transformational school leadership: introduction'. *School Effectiveness and School Improvement* 17 (2): 143–4.

Lemert. C. C. (ed.) (1991). *Intellectuals and Politics: Social Theory in a Changing World*. Newbury Park, CA: Sage Publications Inc.

Leonard, P. (2008). 'Ethics, values and social justice leadership: Embarking on a moral quest for authenticity'. In A. H. Normore (ed.), *Leadership for Social Justice*, 243–56. Charlotte, NC: IAP.

Levin, B. (2008). *How to Change 5000 Schools: A Practical and Positive Approach for Leading Change at Every Level*. Cambridge, MA: Harvard Educational Publishing Group.

Lightfoot, J. D. (2008). 'Separate is inherently unequal: Rethinking commonly held wisdom'. In A. H. Normore (ed.), *Leadership for Social Justice*, 37–59. Charlotte, NC: IAP.

Likert, R. and Likert, J. G. (1976). *New Ways of Managing Conflict*. New York, NY: McGraw- Hill.

Lindle, J. C. (1999). 'What can the study of micropolitics contribute to the practice of leadership in reforming schools?'. *School Leadership and Management* 19 (2): 171–8.

Lingard, B., Hayes, D., Mills, M., and Christie, P. (2003). *Leading Learning*. Maidenhead: Oxford University Press.

López, G. R. and Vàzquez, V. A. (2008). '"They don't speak English": Interrogating (racist) ideologies and perceptions of school personnel in a midwestern state'. In A. H. Normore (ed.), *Leadership for Social Justice*, 75–96. Charlotte, NC: IAP.

Lortie, D. C. (2009). *School Principal, Managing in Public*. Chicago: The University of Chicago Press.

Lumby, J. and Coleman, M. (2007). *Leadership and Diversity: Challenging Theory and Practice in Education*. London: Sage.

Lumby, J., Crow, G., and Pashiardis, P. (eds) (2008). *International Handbook of the Preparation and Development of School Leaders*. New York: Routledge.

Lumby, J., Foskett, N., and Fidler, B. (2005). 'Special edition: Researching leadership – A review of progress'. *Educational Management, Administration and Leadership* 33 (2): 135–253.

Lyon, E. S. (2009). 'What influence? Public intellectuals, the state and civil society'. In C. Flick, A. Hess, and E. S. Lyon (eds), *Intellectuals and their Publics: Perspectives from the Social Sciences*, 69–87. Farnham: Ashgate Publishing Limited.

MacBeath, J. (ed.) (1998). *Effective School Leadership, Responding to Change*. London: PCP.

MacBeath, J. and Mortimore, P. (eds) (2001). *Improving School Effectiveness*. Buckingham: Oxford University Press.

MacBeath, J. and McGlynn, A. (2002). *Self-Evaluation: What's in it for Schools?* London: RoutledgeFalmer.

MacGilchrist, B., Mortimore, P., Savage, J., and Beresford, C. (1995). *Planning Matters*. London: Paul Chapman Publishing.

MacGilchrist, B., Myers, K., and Reed, J. (1997). *The Intelligent School*. London: Paul Chapman Publishing.

Maclean, I. (1990). 'Responsibility and the act of interpretation: The case of law'. In I. Maclean, A., Montefiore and P. Winch (eds), *The Political Responsibility of Intellectuals*. Cambridge: Cambridge University Press.

Maclean, I., Montefiore, A., and Winch, P. (eds) (1990). *The Political Responsibility of Intellectuals*. Cambridge: Cambridge University Press.

Major, J. (1993). *Mr Major's Speech to 1993 Conservative Party Conference*. http://www.johnmajor.co.uk/page1096.html (Accessed 10 February 2014).

Mannheim, K. (1954 [1936]). *Ideology and Utopia*. London: Routledge and Kegan Paul Ltd.

Marquand, D. (2004). *Decline of the Public*. Cambridge: Polity Press.

Marshall, C. and Oliva, M. (eds) (2006a). *Leadership for Social Justice*. Boston, MA: Pearson.

Marshall, C. and Oliva, M. (2006b). 'Building the capacities of social justice leaders'. In C. Marshall and M. Oliva (eds), *Leadership for Social Justice*, 1–15. Boston, MA: Pearson.

Martin, W. C. (1987). 'The role of the intellectual in revolutionary institutions'. In R. P. Mohan (ed.), *The Mythmakers: Intellectuals and the Intelligentsia in Perspective* Westport. Connectict: Greenwood Press Inc.

Martindale, D. (1987). 'The sociology of intellectual creativity'. In R. P. Mohan (ed.), *The Mythmakers: Intellectuals and the Intelligentsia in Perspective*. Westport, Connectict: Greenwood Press Inc.

Marx, K. (2009). *The Eighteenth Brumaire of Louis Bonaparte*. Rockville, MD: Serenity Publishers.

Mawhinney, H. G. (1999). 'Reappraisal: The problems and prospects of studying the micropolitics of leadership in reforming schools'. *School Leadership and Management* 19 (2): 159–70.

Mayo, E. (1933). *The Human Problems of an Industrial Civilization*. Boston: Harvard Business School.

McGinity, R. and Gunter, H. M. (2012). 'Living improvement 2: A case study of a secondary school in England'. *Improving Schools* 15 (3): 228–44.

McMahon, D. M. and Moyn, S. (eds) (2014). *Rethinking Modern European Intellectual History*. Oxford: Oxford University Press.

McNulty, P. (2005). *Extreme Headship: A Case Study in Educational Leadership and School Improvement*. Oxford: Trafford Publishing.

Mertz, N. T. (ed.) (2009). *Breaking Into the All-Male Club, Female Professors of Educational Administration*. Albany, NY: State University of New York.

Mills, C. W. (1959). *The Sociological Imagination*. Harmondsworth: Penguin.

Mills, M. (1997). 'Towards a disruptive pedagogy: Creating spaces for student and teacher resistance to social injustice'. *International Studies in Sociology of Education* 7 (1): 35–55.

Mitchell, D. E. (ed.) (2006). *New Foundations for Knowledge in Educational Administration, Policy and Politics*. Mahwah, NJ: Lawrence Erlbaum Associates Inc., Publishers.

Mitra, D. L. (2008). 'Student voice or empowerment? Examining the role of
    school-based youth-adult partnerships as an avenue toward focusing on
    social justice'. In A. H. Normore (ed.), *Leadership for Social Justice*, 195–214.
    Charlotte, NC: IAP.

Mitra, D., Serriere, S., and Stoicovy, D. (2012). 'The role of leaders in enabling
    student voice'. *Management in Education* 26 (3): 104–12.

Møller, J. (2009). 'Approaches to school leadership in Scandanavia'. *Journal of
    Educational Administration and History* 41 (2): 165–77.

Møller, J., Vedøy, G., Presthus, A. M., and Skedsmo, G. (2009). 'Fostering
    learning and sustained improvement: The influence of principalship'. *European
    Educational Research Journal* 8 (3): 359–71.

Molnar, T. (1961). *The Decline of the Intellectual.* Cleveland, Ohio: Meridan Books/
    The World Publishing Company.

Montefiore, A. (1990). 'The political responsibility of intellectuals'. In I. Maclean,
    A. Montefiore, and P. Winch (eds), *The Political Responsibility of Intellectuals.*
    Cambridge: Cambridge University Press.

Moore, R. (2007). *Sociology of Knowledge and Education.* London: Continuum.

Moos, L. (2009). 'Hard and soft governance: The journey from transnational
    agencies to school leadership'. *European Educational Research Journal* 8 (3):
    397–406.

Moos, L. and Dempster, N. (1998). 'Some comparative learnings from the study'.
    In J. MacBeath (ed.), *Effective School Leadership: Responding to Change*,
    98–111. London: PCP.

Morley, L. and Rassool, N. (1999). *School Effectiveness, Fracturing the Discourse.*
    London: Falmer Press.

Moss, G. (2013). 'Research, policy and knowledge flows in education: What
    counts in knowledge mobilisation?'. *Contemporary Social Science* 8 (3):
    237–48.

Mourshed, M., Chijoke, C., and Barber, M. (2010). *How the World's Most
    Improved School Systems Keep Getting Better.* London: McKinsey

Muijs, D. (2011). 'Leadership and organisational performance: From research
    to prescription'. *International Journal of Educational Management* 25 (1):
    45–60.

Muijs, D. (2012). 'Methodological change in educational effectiveness research'.
    In C. Chapman, P. Armstrong, A. Harris, D. Muijs, D. Reynolds, and
    P. Sammons (eds), *School Effectiveness and Improvement Research, Policy
    and Practice. Challenging the Orthodoxy?*, 58–66. Abingdon: Routledge.

Muijs, D., Kelly, T., Sammons, P., Reynolds, D., and Chapman, C. (2011). 'The
    value of educational effectiveness research – A response to recent criticism'.
    Research Intelligence. Spring 2011 (114): 24–5.

Muijs, D., Kyriakides, L., van der Werf, G., Creemers, B., Timperley, H., and Earl,
    L. (2014). 'State of the art – teacher effectiveness and professional learning'.
    School Effectiveness and School Improvement 25 (2): 231–56.

Mulford, B. (2012). 'Tinkering towards Utopia: Trying to make sense of my
    contribution to the field'. *Journal of Educational Administration* 50 (1):
    98–124.

Mulford, B. and Silins, H. (2011). 'Revised models and conceptualisation of
    successful school principalship that improves student outcomes'. *International
    Journal of Educational Management* 25 (1): 61–82.

Murphy, J. and Seashore Louis, K. (eds) (1999). *Handbook of Research on Educational Administration*. San Francisco, CA: Jossey-Bass Publishers.

Myers, I. B. and Myers, P. B. (1995). *Gifts Differing: Understanding Personality Type*. Mountain View, CA: Davies-Black Publishing.

Neave, G. (1988). 'On the cultivation of quality, efficiency and enterprise: An overview of recent trends in higher education in Western Europe, 1986-1988'. *European Journal of Education* 23 (1/2): 7–23

Newman, J. (2007). 'Rethinking "the public" in troubled times'. *Public Policy and Administration* 22 (1): 27–47.

Newman, J. and Clarke, J. (2009). *Publics, Politics and Power*. London: Sage.

Nguni, S., Sleegers, P. J. C., and Denessen, E. (2006). 'Transformational and transactional leadership effects on teachers' job satisfaction, organizational commitment, and organizational citizenship behavior in primary shcools: The Tanzanian Case'. *School Effectiveness and School Improvement* 17 (2): 145–77.

Niesche, R. (2013). 'Foucault, counter-conduct and school leadership as a form of political subjectivity'. *Journal of Educational Administration and History* 45 (2): 144–58.

Niesche, R. (2014). *Deconstructing Educational Leadership. Derrida and Lyotard*. Abingdon: Routledge.

Normore, A. H. (ed.) (2008). *Leadership for Social Justice*. Charlotte, NC: IAP.

Normore, A. H. and Blanco, R. I. (2008). 'Leadership for social justice and Morality: Collaborative partnerships, school-linked services and the plight of the poor'. In A. H. Normore (ed.), *Leadership for Social Justice*, 215–40. Charlotte, NC: IAP.

Northouse, P. G. (2010). *Leadership, Theory and Practice*. Fifth Edition. Thousand Oaks, CA: Sage.

O'Hair, M. J. and Reitzug, U. C. (2008). 'A neglected dimension of social justice: A model for science education in rural schools'. In A. H. Normore (ed.), *Leadership for Social Justice*, 151–67. Charlotte, NC: IAP.

O'Reilly, D. and Reed, M. (2010). '"Leaderism": An evolution of managerialism in UK public service reform'. *Public Administration* 88 (4): 960–78.

OECD (2008). *Improving School Leadership Policy and Practice*. Paris: OECD.

OECD (2013). *Leadership for 21st Century Learning*. Paris: OECD Publishing.

Ogawa, R. T., Goldring, E. B., and Conley, S. (2000). 'Organizing the field to improve research on educational administration'. *Educational Administration Quarterly* 36 (3): 340–57.

Olmedo, A. (2014). 'From England with love ... ARK, heterarchies and global "philanthropic governance"'. *Journal of Education Policy* 29 (5): 575–97.

Oplatka, I. (2009). 'The field of educational administration: A historical overview of scholarly attempts to recognize epistemological identities, meanings and boundaries from the 1960s onwards'. *Journal of Educational Administration* 47 (1): 8–35.

Oplatka, I. (2010). *The Legacy of Educational Administration, A Historical Analysis of an Academic Field*. Frankfurt am Main: Peter Lang.

Oplatka, I. (2012). 'Fifty years of publication: Pondering the legacies of the *Journal of Educational Administration*'. *Journal of Educational Administration* 50 (1): 34–56.

Osborne, D. and Gaebler, T. (1993). *Reinventing Government*. New York: A Plume Book, Penguin.

Ozga, J. (1992). 'Review essay: Education management'. *British Journal of Sociology of Education* 13 (2): 279–80.

Ozga, J. (2009). 'Governing education thorugh data in England: From regulation to self-evaluation'. *Journal of Education Policy* 24 (2): 149–62.

Paechter, C. (2001). 'Schooling and the ownership of knowledge'. In C. Paechter, M. Preedy, D. Scott, and J. Soler (eds), *Knowledge, Power and Learning*, 167–80. London: Paul Chapman.

Parker, I., and Thomas, R. (2011). 'What is a critical journal?'. *Organization* 18 (4): 419–27.

Parry, G. (1976). *Political Elites*. London: George Allen & Unwin.

Pascal, C. and Ribbins, P. (1998). *Understanding Primary Headteachers*. London: Cassell.

Pearton, M. (1982). *The Knowledgeable State, Diplomacy, War and Technology since 1830*. London: Burnett Books.

Pels, D. (1995). 'Knowledge politics and anti-politics: Toward a critical appraisal of Bourdieu's concept of intellectual autonomy'. *Theory and Society* 24 (1): 79–104.

Peters, T. and Waterman, R. (1982). *In Search of Excellence*. Glasgow: Harper/Collins.

Pierson, D. P. (ed.) (2014). *Breaking Bad: Critical Essays on the Contexts, Politics, Style and Reception of the Television Series*. Lanham, MD: Lexington Books.

Pont, B., Nusche D., and Moorman H. (2008a). *Improving School Leadership, Volume 1: Policy and Practice*. OECD: Paris.

Pont, B., Nusche D., and Hopkins D. (eds) (2008b). *Improving School Leadership, Volume 2: Case Studies on System Leadership*. OECD: Paris.

Pounder, D. G. (2000a). 'Introduction to the special issue'. *Educational Administration Quarterly* 36 (3): 336–9.

Pounder, D. G. (2000b). 'A Discussion of the task force's collective findings'. *Educational Administration Quarterly* 36 (3): 465–73.

Radaelli, C. M. (1995). 'The role of knowledge in the policy process'. *Journal of European Public Policy* 2 (2): 159–83.

Raffo, C. and Gunter, H. M. (2008). 'Leading schools to promote social inclusion: Developing a conceptual framework for analysing research, policy and practice'. *Journal of Education Policy* 23 (4): 363–80.

Ramsay, W. and Clark, E. E. (1990). *New Ideas for Effective School Improvement*. Basingstoke: The Falmer Press.

Rapp, D. (2002). 'Commentary, on lies, secrets, and silence: A plea to educational leaders'. *International Journal of Leadership in Education* 5 (2): 175–85.

Rasiel, E. M. and Friga, P. N. (2001). *The McKinsey Way*. New York: McGraw-Hill.

Ravitch, D. (2010). *The Death and Life of the Great American School System*. New York: Basic Books.

Ravitch, D. (2014). *Reign of Error: The Hoax of the Privatization Movement and the Danger to America's Public Schools*. New York, NY: Alfred A. Knopf.

Rawolle, S., Wilkinson, J., and Hardy, I. (2010). 'Special Issue: Policy and leadership as practice: Foregrounding practice in educational research'. *Critical Studies in Education* 51 (1): 1–111.

Reckhow, S. and Snyder, J. W. (2014). 'The Expanding Role of Philanthropy in Education Polities'. *Educational Resarcher* 43 (4): 186–95.

Reynolds, D. (2012). 'Thinking the unthinkable? The future of school effectiveness and school improvement to be realised through closer relationships with educational policies and policy makers'. In C. Chapman, P. Armstrong,

A. Harris, D. Muijs, D. Reynolds, and P. Sammons, (eds), *School Effectiveness and Improvement Research, Policy and Practice. Challenging the Orthodoxy?*, 205–20. Abingdon: Routledge.

Reynolds, D. (2014). 'Editorial'. *School Effectiveness and School Improvement: An International Journal of Research, Policy and Practice* 25 (2): 195–6.

Reynolds, D., Sammons, P., de Fraine, B., van Damme, J., Townsend, T., Teddlie, C., and Stringfield, S. (2014). 'Educational Effectiveness Research (EER): A state-of-the-art review'. *School Effectiveness and School Improvement: An International Journal of Research, Policy and Practice* 25 (2): 197–230.

Reynolds, D., Sammons, P., Stoll, L., Barber, M., and Hillman, J. (1996). 'School effectiveness and school improvement in the United Kingdom'. *School Effectiveness and School Improvement* 7 (2): 133–58.

Reynolds, D. and Teddlie, C. (2001). 'Reflections on the critics, and beyond them'. *School Effectiveness and School Improvement* 12 (1): 99–113.

Ribbins, P. (ed.) (1997a). *Leaders and Leadership in the School, College and University.* London: Cassell.

Ribbins, P. (1997b). 'A prelude'. In P. Ribbins (ed.), *Leaders and Leadership in the School, College and University*, 3–20. London: Cassell.

Ribbins, P. (1999). 'Foreword'. In P. T. Begley and P. E. Leonard (eds), *The Values of Educational Administration*, ix–xvii. London: Falmer Press.

Ribbins, P. (2003). 'Through the looking-glass with Christopher Hodgkinson: Letters and lessons on life and leadership from Arcadia West'. In E. A. Samier (ed.), *Ethical Foundations for Educational Administration: Essays in Honour of Christopher Hodgkinson*, 3–28. London: RoutledgeFalmer.

Ribbins, P. (2006a). 'Administration and leadership in education: A case for history?'. *Journal of Educational Administration and History* 38 (2): 113–218.

Ribbins, P. (2006b). 'Aesthetics and art. Their place in the theory and practice of leadership in education'. In E. A. Samier and R. Bates (eds), *Aesthetic Dimensions of Educational Administration and Leadership*, 175–90. Abingdon: Routledge.

Ribbins, P. and Gunter, H. M. (2002). 'Mapping leadership studies in education: Towards a typology of knowledge domains'. *Educational Management and Administration* 30 (4): 359–86.

Ribbins, P. and Marland, M. (1994). *Headship Matters.* Harlow: Longman.

Ribbins, P. and Sherratt, B. (1999). 'Managing the secondary school in the 1990s: A new view of Headship'. In M. Strain, B. Dennison, J. Ouston, and V. Hall (eds), *Policy, Leadership and Professional Knowledge in Education*, 183–94. London: PCP.

Richmon, M. J. (2004). 'Values in educational administration: Them's fighting words!'. *International Journal of Leadership in Education* 7 (4): 339–56.

Riehl, C., Larson, C. L., Short, P. M., and Reitzug, U. C. (2000). 'Reconceptualizing research and scholarship in educational administration: Learning to know, knowing to do, doing to learn'. *Educational Administration Quarterly* 36 (3): 391–427.

Riley, K. (2013). *Leadership of Place. Stories from Schools in the US, UK and South Africa.* London: Bloomsbury.

Rizvi, F. (1989). 'In defence of organizational democracy'. In J. Smyth (ed.), *Critical Perspectives on Educational Leadership*, 205–34. London: Falmer Press.

Robertson, J. (2008). *Coaching Educational Leadership.* London: Sage.

Robinson, N. (2013). Are we all Thatcherites now? http://www.bbc.co.uk/news/uk-politics-22180611 (Accessed 6 February 2014).

Robinson, V. M. J. (2007). *School Leadership and Student Outcomes: Indentifying What Works and Why*. Melbourne: ACEL.

Robinson, V. M., Lloyd, C. A., and Rowe, K. J. (2008). 'The impact of leadership on student outcomes: An analysis of the differential effects of leadership types'. *Educational Administration Quarterly* 44(5): 635–74.

Rose, G. W. (1977). 'An emerging field of study'. *Review of Education, Pedagogy and Cultural Studies* 3 (4): 303–12.

Rose, N. and Abi-Rached, J. M. (2013). *Neuro: The New Brain Sciences and the Management of the Mind*. Princeton, NJ: Princeton University Press.

Ross Thomas, A. (2012). 'Succeed or else! Reflections on the 50th Anniversary of the *Journal of Educational Administration*'. *Journal of Educational Administration* 50 (1): 12–33.

Rousmaniere, K. (2009a). 'Special issue, historical perspectives on the principalship'. *Journal of Educational Administration and History* 41 (3): 215–300.

Rousmaniere, K. (2009b). 'Historical perspectives on the principalship'. *Journal of Educational Administration and History* 41 (3): 215–21.

Rowan, B. (2002). 'The ecology of school improvement: Notes on the school improvement industry in the United States'. *Journal of Educational Change* 3 (3–4): 283–14.

Rudduck, J. and Flutter, J. (2004). *How to Improve Your School*. London: Continuum.

Rusch, E. A. and Marshall, C. (2006). 'Gender filters and leadership: Plotting a course to equity'. *International Journal of Leadership in Education* 9 (3): 229–50.

Rutter, M., Maughan, B., Mortimore, P., Ouston, J. with Smith, A. (1979). *Fifteen Thousand Hours: Secondary Schools and their Effects on Children*. Cambridge, MA: Harvard University Press.

Ryan, J. (2010). 'Promoting social justice in schools: Principals' political strategies'. *International Journal of Leadership in Education* 13 (4): 357–76.

Saint-Martin, D. (2001). 'How the reinventing government movement in public administration was exported from the US to other countries'. *International Journal of Public Administration* 24 (6): 573–604.

Sallis, E. (1993). *Total Quality Management in Education*. London: Routledge.

Saltman, K. J. (2010). *The Gift of Education*. New York: Palgrave MacMillan.

Saltman, K. and Gabbard, D. A. (eds) (2011). *Education as Enforcement*. Second Edition. New York: Routledge.

Samier, E. A. (ed.) (2003). *Ethical Foundations for Educational Administration. Essays in Honour of Christopher Hodgkinson*. London: RoutledgeFalmer.

Samier, E. A. (2006). 'Educational administration as a historical discipline: An *Apologia Pro Vita Historia*'. *Journal of Educational Administration and History* 38 (2): 125–39.

Samier, E. A. (2008). 'The problem of passive evil in educational administration: Moral implications of doing nothing'. *International Studies in Educational Administration* 36 (1): 2–21.

Samier, E. A. and Bates, R. (eds) (2006). *Aesthetic Dimensions of Educational Administration and Leadership*. London: Routledge.

Samier, E. A. and Schmidt, M. (eds) (2010). *Trust and Betrayal in Educational Administration and Leadership*. New York, NY: Routledge.

Sammons, P., Hillman, J., and Mortimore, P. (1995). *Key Characteristics of Effective Schools: A Review of School Effectiveness Research*. London: OfSTED.

Sammons, P. (1999). *School Effectiveness: Coming of Age in the Twenty First Century*. Lisse: Swets and Zeitlinger.

Sammons, P., Chapman, C., Muijs, D., Day, C., Gu, Q., Harris, A., Kelly, A., and Reynolds, D. (2010). 'Evidence shows we can effect change'. *Times Educational Supplement*, 12 March 2010. www.tes.co.uk/article. aspx?storycode=6038668 (Accessed 25 June 2010).

Sammons, P., Hillman, J., and Mortimore, P. (1997). 'Key characteristics of effective schools: A review of school effectiveness research'. In J. White and M. Barber (eds), *Perspectives on School Effectiveness and School Improvement*, 77–124. London: Institute of Education Bedford Way Papers.

Sammons, P., Thomas, S., and Mortimore, P. (1997). *Forging Links, Effective Schools and Effective Departments*. London: Paul Chapman Publishing.

San Antonio, D. M. (2008). 'Creating better schools through democratic school leadership'. *International Journal of Leadership in Education* 11 (1): 43–62.

Sandler, M. R. (2010). *Social Entrepreneurship in Education*. Lanham, MA: Rowman and Littlefield Education.

Sapre, P. M. (2000). 'Realizing the potential of management and leadership: Towards a synthesis of Western and indigenous perspectives in the modernisation of non-Western countries'. *International Journal of Leadership in Education* 3 (3): 293–305.

Scheerens, J. (1992). *Effective Schooling*. London: Cassell.

Scheerens, J. (2014). 'School, teaching, and system effectiveness: Some comments on three state-of-the-art reviews'. *School Effectiveness and School Improvement* 25 (2): 282–90.

Scheerens, J., Bosker, R. J., and Creemers, B. P. M. (2001). 'Time for Self-criticism: On the viability of school effectiveness research'. *School Effectiveness and School Improvement* 12 (1): 131–57.

Scherrer, C. (2014). 'Neoliberalism's resilience: A matter of class'. *Critical Policy Studies*. DOI 10.1080/19460171.2014.944366.

Schwandt, T. A. (2007). 'First words'. In B. Somekh and T. A. Schwandt (eds), *Knowledge Production, Research Work in Interesting Times*, 1–5. London: Routledge.

Scott, J. C. (1998). *Seeing Like a State*. New Haven, Con: Yale University Press.

Seddon, T. (2014). 'Renewing sociology of education? Knowledge spaces, situated enactments and sociological practice in a world on the move'. *European Educational Research Journal* 13 (1): 9–25.

Senge, P. (2006). *The Fifth Discipline: The Art and Practice of the Learning Organization*. London: Random House.

Senge, P., Cambran-McCabe, N., Lucas, T., Smith,B., Dutton, J. and Kleiner, A. (2012). *Schools that Learn: A Fifth Discipline Fieldbook for Educators, Parents and Everyone Who Cares About Education*. London: Nicholas Brealey Publishing.

Sergiovanni, T. J. (2001). *Leadership*. London: RoutledgeFalmer.

Shakeshaft, C. (1989). 'The gender gap in research in educational administration'. *Educational Administration Quarterly* 25 (4): 324–37.

Shapiro, J. P. (2008). 'Ethics and social justice within the New DEEL: Addressing the paradox of control/democracy'. In A. H. Normore (ed.), *Leadership for Social Justice*, 287–301. Charlotte, NC: IAP.

Shields, C. M. (1999). 'Learning from students about representation, identity, and community'. *Educational Administration Quarterly* 35 (1): 106–29.

Shields, C. M. (2004). 'Dialogic leadership for social justice: Overcoming pathologies of silence'. *Educational Administration Quarterly* 40 (1): 109–32.

Shields, C. M. (2010). 'Transformative leadership: Working for equity in diverse contexts'. *Educational Administration Quarterly* 46 (4): 558–89.

Shoho, A. R., Barnett, B. G., and Tooms, A. K. (eds) (2010). *The Challenges for New Principals in the Twenty-First Century*. Charlotte, NC: IAP.

Silins, H. and Mulford, B. (2002). 'Leadership and school results'. In K. Leithwood and P. Hallinger (eds), *Second International Handbook of Educational Leadership and Administration*, 561–612. Norwell, MA: Kluwer Academic Publishers.

Silver, H. (1990). *Education, Change and the Policy Process*. Lewes: The Falmer Press.

Simon, B. (1955). *The Common Secondary School*. London: Lawrence and Wishart.

Simon, H. A. (1945). *Administrative Behavior: A Study of Decision-Making Processes in Administrative Organization*. New York: Macmillan.

Skeggs, B. (1997). *Formations of Class and Gender*. London: Sage.

Slee, R. and Weiner, G. with Tomlinson, S. (eds) (1998). *School Effectiveness for Whom?* London: Falmer Press.

Slee, R. and Weiner, G. (2001). 'Education reform and reconstruction as a challenge to research genres: Reconsidering school effectiveness research and inclusive schooling'. *School Effectiveness and School Improvement* 12 (1): 83–98.

Smith, L. (2012). *Decolonising Methodologies*. London: Zed Books.

Smith, M. (2002). 'The school leadership initiative: An ethically flawed project?'. *Journal of Philosophy of Education* 36 (1): 21–39.

Smyth, J. (ed.) (1989a). *Critical Perspectives on Educational Leadership*. London: Falmer Press.

Smyth, J. (1989b). 'Preface'. In J. Smyth (ed.), *Critical Perspectives on Educational Leadership*, 1–8. London: Falmer Press.

Smyth, J. (1989c). 'A "Pedagogical" and "Educative" view of leadership'. In J. Smyth (ed.), *Critical Perspectives on Educational Leadership*, 157–204. London: Falmer Press.

Smyth, J. (ed.) (1993a). *A Socially Critical View of the Self Managing School*. London: The Falmer Press.

Smyth, J. (1993b). 'Introduction'. In J. Smyth (ed.), *A Socially Critical View of the Self Managing School*, 1–9. London: The Falmer Press.

Smyth, J. (ed.) (1995). *Academic Work: The Changing Labour Process in Higher Education*. Buckingham: Open University Press.

Smyth, J. (2006a). 'Educational leadership that fosters "student voice"'. *International Journal of Leadership in Education* 9 (4): 279–84.

Smyth, J. (2006b). '"When students have power": Student engagement, student voice, and the possibilities for school reform around "dropping out" of school'. *International Journal of Leadership in Education* 9 (4): 285–98.

Smyth, J. (2011a). 'The *disaster* of the "self-managing school" – genesis, trajectory, undisclosed agenda, and effects'. *Journal of Educational Administration and History* 43 (2): 95–117.

Smyth, J. (2011b). *Critical Pedagogy for Social Justice*. New York: Continuum.

Smyth, J. (2012). 'Editorial. Policy activism: An animating idea with/or young people'. *Journal of Educational Administration and History* 44 (3): 179–86.

Smyth, J., Angus, L., Down, B., and McInerney, P. (2008). *Critically Engaged Learning, Connecting to Young Lives*. New York: Peter Lang.

Smyth, J., Down, B., McInerney, P., and Hattam, R. (2014). *Doing Critical Educational Research*. New York: Peter Lang.

Smyth, J. and Hattam, R., with Cannon, J., Edwards, J., Wilson, N., and Wurst, S. (2004). *'Dropping Out', Drifting Off, Being Excluded*. New York, NY: Peter Lang.

Southworth, G. (1995). *Looking into Primary Headship*. London: The Falmer Press.

Southworth, G. (1999). 'Primary school leadership in England: Policy, practice and theory'. *School Leadership and Management* 19 (1): 49–65.

Southworth, G. (2002). 'Instructional leadership in schools: Reflections and empirical evidence'. *School Leadership and Management* 22 (1): 73–91.

Southworth, G. (2005). 'Overview and conclusions'. In M. J. Coles and G. Southworth (eds), *Developing Leadership, Creating the Schools of Tomorrow*, 158–73. Maidenhead: Oxford University Press.

Spillane, J. P. (2006). *Distributed Leadership*. San Francisco, CA: Jossey-Bass Publishers.

Spillane, J. P. and Diamond, J. B. (eds) (2007). *Distributed Leadership in Practice*. New York: Teachers College Press.

Spring, J. (2012). *Education Neworks. Power, Wealth, Cyberspace, and the Digital Mind*. New York, NY: Routledge.

Stanley, L. and Wise, S. (2002). *Breaking Out Again*. London: Routledge.

Starratt, R. J. (2003). *Centering Educational Administration*. Mahwah, NJ: Lawrence Erlbaum Associates, Publishers.

Steadman, C. (2001). *Dust*. Manchester: Manchester University Press.

Stevenson, H. and Tooms, A. (2010). 'Connecting "up there" with "down here"; thoughts on globalization, neo-liberalism and leadership praxis'. In A. H. Normore (ed.), *Global Perspectives on Educational Leadership Reform: The Development and Preparation of Leaders of Learning and Learners of Leadership*, 3–21. Bingley: Emerald.

Stewart, J. (2006). 'Transformational leadership: An evolving concept examined through the works of Burns, Bass, Avolio, and Leithwood'. *Canadian Journal of Educational Administration and Policy* 54 (June): 1–24.

Stogdill, R. M. (1974). *Handbook of Leadership: A Survey of Theory and Research*. New York, NY: Free Press.

Stoll, L. and Fink, D. (1996). *Changing Our Schools: Linking School Effectiveness and School Improvement*. Buckingham: Open University Press.

Stoll, L. and Mortimore, P. (1997). 'School effectiveness and school improvement'. In J. White and M. Barber (eds), *Perspectives on School Effectiveness and School Improvement*, 9–24. London: Institute of Education Bedford Way Papers.

Stoll, L. and Myers, K. (eds) (1998a). *No Quick Fixes*. London: The Falmer Press.

Stoll, L. and Myers, K. (1998b). 'No quick fixes: An introduction'. In L. Stoll and K. Myers (eds), *No Quick Fixes*, 1–16. London: The Falmer Press.

Storey, V. A. and Beeman, T. E. (2008). 'A New DEEL for an old problem: Social justice at the core'. In A. H. Normore (ed.), *Leadership for Social Justice*, 267–85. Charlotte, NC: IAP.

Stubbs, M. (2003). *A Head of the Class*. London: John Murray.

Sugrue, C. (ed.) (2005). *Passionate Principalship, Learning from the Life Histories of School Leaders*. Abingdon: RoutledgeFalmer.

Sugrue, C. (2009). 'From heroes and heroines to hermaphrodites: Emasculation or emancipation of school leaders and leadership?'. *School Leadership and Management* 29 (4): 353–71.

Sungaila, H. (2008). 'The history of education and the study of educational administration'. *Journal of Educational Administration and History* 40 (1): 41–5.

Swail, W. S. (ed.) (2012). *Finding Superman: Debating the Future of Public Education in America*. New York, NY: Teachers College Press.

Taylor, C. (2009). *A Good School for Every Child*. London: Routledge.

Taylor, C. and Ryan, C. (2005). *Excellence in Education: The Making of Great Schools*. London: David Fulton Publishers Ltd.

Taylor, F. W. (1911). *Principles of Scientific Management*. New York: Harper.

Teddlie, C. and Reynolds, D. (eds) (2000). *The International Handbook of School Effectiveness Research*. New York: Falmer Press.

Teddlie, C. and Reynolds, D. (2001). 'Countering the critics: Responses to recent criticisms of school effectiveness research'. *School Effectiveness and School Improvement* 12 (1): 41–82.

The Future Leaders Charitable Trust (2014). *Webpages*. http://www.future-leaders.org.uk (Accessed 21 September 2014).

Thompson, K., with Davies, B., and Ellison, L. (2004). *Can Private Companies Successfully Turn Around a Failing School?* Nottingham: NCSL.

Thomson, P. (2001). 'How principals lose "face": A disciplinary tale of educational administration and modern managerialism'. *Discourse: Studies in the Cultural Politics of Education* 22 (1): 5–22.

Thomson, P. (2004). 'Severed heads and compliant bodies? A speculation about principal identities'. *Discourse: Studies in the Cultural Politics of Education* 25 (1): 43–59.

Thomson, P. (2005). 'Bringing Bourdieu to policy sociology: Codification, misrecognition and exchange value in the UK context'. *Journal of Education Policy* 20 (6): 741–58.

Thomson, P. (2007). 'Leading schools in high poverty neighbourhoods: The National College for school leadership and beyond'. In T. W. Pink and G. W. Noblit (eds), *The International Handbook of Urban Education*, 1049–78. Dordrecht: Springer.

Thomson, P. (2008). 'Headteacher critique and resistance: A challenge for policy, and for leadership/management scholars'. *Journal of Educational Administration and History* 40 (2): 85–100.

Thomson, P. (2009). *School Leadership, Heads on the Block?* London: Routledge.

Thomson, P. (2010a). 'Headteacher autonomy: A sketch of a Bourdieuian field analysis of position and practice'. *Critical Studies in Education* 51 (1): 5–20.

Thomson, P. (2010b). 'A critical pedagogy of global place: Regeneration in and as action'. In C. Raffo, A. Dyson, H. Gunter, D. Hall, L. Jones, and A. Kalambouka (eds), *Education and Poverty in Affluent Countries*, 124–34. New York: Routledge.

Thomson, P. and Blackmore, J. (2006). 'Beyond the power of one: Redesigning the work of school principals'. *Journal of Educational Change* 7: 161–77.

Thomson, P., Blackmore, J., and Gunter, H. M. (2014). 'Series foreword'. In H. M. Gunter (ed.), *Educational Leadership and Hannah Arendt*, vi–xii. London: Routledge.

Thomson, P. and Gunter, H. M. (2006). 'From "consulting pupils" to "pupils as researchers": A situated case narrative'. *British Educational Research Journal* 32 (6): 839–56.

Thomson, P. and Gunter, H. M. (2011). 'Inside, outside, upside down: The fluidity of academic researcher "identity" in working with/in school'. *International Journal of Research and Method in Education* 34 (1): 17–30.

Thrift, N. (2005). *Knowing Capitalism*. London: Sage.

Thrupp, M. (1999). *Schools Making a Difference: Let's be Realitic!* Buckingham: Oxford University Press.

Thrupp, M. (2001). 'Sociological and political concerns about school effectiveness research: Time for a new agenda'. *School Effectiveness and School Improvement* 12 (1): 7–40.

Thrupp, M. (2005). *School Improvement, An Unofficial Approach*. London: Continuum.

Thrupp, M. and Willmott, R. (2003). *Education Management in Managerialist Times*. Maidenhead: Oxford University Press.

Tomlinson, H., Gunter, H., and Smith, P. (eds) (1999). *Living Headship, Voices, Values and Vision*. London: PCP.

Tooley, J. (1995). 'Markets or democracy for education? A reply to Stewart Ranson'. *British Journal of Educational Studies* 43 (1): 21–34.

Tooley, J. (1996). *Education Without the State*. London: IEA.

Tooley, J. (2000). *Reclaiming Education*. London: Continuum.

Tooley, J. (2009). *The Beautiful Tree*. Washington, DC: Cate Institute

Tooley, J. (2012). *From Village School to Global Brand*. London: Profile Books.

Tooley, J. and Howes, A. (1999). *Seven Habits of Highly Effective Schools*. London: CTC Trust.

Tooms, A. and Alston, J. A. (2008). '(OUT)siders at the gates: Administrative aspirants' attitudes towards the gay community'. In: A. H. Normore (ed.), *Leadership for Social Justice*, 61–74. Charlotte, NC: IAP.

Townsend, T. (2001). 'Satan or Saviour? An analysis of two decades of school effectiveness research'. *School Effectiveness and School Improvement* 12 (1): 115–29.

Tschannen-Moran, M., Firestone, W. A., Hoy, W., and Moore Johnson, S. (2000). 'The write stuff: A study of productive scholars in educational administration'. *Educational Administration Quarterly* 36 (3): 358–90.

Usher, R. (2001). 'Telling a story about research and research as story telling: Postmodern approaches to social research'. In C. Paechter, M. Preedy, D. Scott, and J. Soler (eds), *Knowledge, Power and Learning*, 47–55. London: Paul Chapman.

Vincent, C., Martin, J., and Ranson, S. (2000). *Little Polities: Schooling, Governance and Parental Participation*. Final Report to the ESRC, R000237123.

Wacquant, L. (1989). 'Towards a reflexive sociology: A workshop with Pierre Bourdieu'. *Sociological Theory* 7.

Wacquant, L. (2009). *Punishing the Poor*. Durham, NC: Duke University Press.

Wagner, E. (2014). 'Cooking for capitalism'. *New Statesman* (19 December 2014): 86–9.

Waite, D. (2012). 'Who controls our knowledge?'. *International Journal of Leadership in Education* 15 (4): 505–8.

Walker, W. G. (1969). 'Trends and Issues in the preparation of educational administrators'. In G. Baron, D. H. Cooper, and W. G. Walker (eds), *Educational Administration: International Perspectives.* Chicago: Rand McNally and Company.

Walker, W. G. (1984). 'Administrative narcissism and the tyranny of isolation: Its decline and fall, 1954–84'. *Educational Administration Quarterly* 20 (4): 6–23.

Ward, S. C. (2012). *Neoliberalism and the Global Restructuring of Knowledge in Education.* New York: Routledge.

Watkins, P. (1989). 'Leadership, power and symbols in educational administration'. In J. Smyth (ed.), *Critical Perspectives on Educational Leadership,* 9–37. London: Falmer Press.

Weindling, D. (1999). 'Stages of headship'. In T. Bush, L. Bell, L. Bolam, R. Glatter, and P. Ribbins (eds), *Educational Management,* 90–101. London: PCP.

West, M. (1999). 'Leadership and all that ... The need to increase the micropolitical awareness and skills of school leaders'. *School Leadership and Management* 19 (2): 189–95.

White, M. (2013). 'Boris the clever cornflake gets his IQ in a twist'. http://www.theguardian.com/politics/2013/nov/28/boris-johnson-iq-intelligence-gordon-gekko (Accessed 14 February 2014).

Wilkins, R. (2014). *Education in the Balance.* London: Bloomsbury.

Wilkinson, J. and Kemmis, S. (2014). 'Practice theory: Viewing leadership as leading'. *Educational Philosophy and Theory* 47 (4): 342–58.

Wilkinson, R. and Pickett, K. (2009). *The Spirit Level.* London: Allen Lane.

Willmott, R. (1999). 'School effectiveness research: An ideological commitment?'. *Journal of Philosophy of Education* 33 (2): 253–68.

Willower, D. J. (1980). 'Contemporary issues in theory in educational administration'. *Educational Administration Quarterly* 16 (3): 1–25.

Willower, D. J. (1998). 'Work on values in educational administration: Some observations'. *Leading and Managing* 4 (4): 232–42.

Willower, D. J. and Forsyth, P. B. (1999). 'A brief history of scholarship in educational administraiton'. In J. Murphy and K. Seashore Louis (eds), *Handbook of Research on Educational Administration,* 1–23. San Francisco, CA: Jossey-Bass Publishers.

Winkley, D. with Pascal, C. (1998). 'Developing a radical agenda'. In C. Pascal and P. Ribbins (eds), *Understanding Primary Headteachers,* 230–51. London: Cassell.

Winkley, D. (2002). *Handsworth Revolution, The Odyssey of a School.* London: Giles de la Mare Publishers Limited.

Wintour, P. (2013). *Genetics Outweighs Teaching, Gove Adviser Tells his Boss.* http://www.theguardian.com/politics/2013/oct/11/genetics-teaching-gove-adviser (Accessed 14 February 2014).

Wohlstetter, P., Malloy, C. L., Chau, D., and Polhemus, J. L. (2003). 'Improving schools through networks: A new approach to urban school reform'. *Educational Policy* 17 (4): 399–430.

Wolcott, H. F. (1973). *The Man in the Principal's Office.* New York: Holt, Rinehart and Winston, Inc.

Wood, M. and Flinders, M. (2014). 'Rethinking depoliticisation: Beyond the governmental'. *Policy & Politics* 42 (2): 151–70.

Woods, P. A. (2005), *Democratic Leadership in Education.* London: PCP.

Wright, N. (2001), 'Leadership, "bastard leadership" and managerialism'. *Educational Management and Administration* 29 (3): 275–90.

Wright, N. (2003), 'Principled "bastard" leadership? A rejoinder to Gold, Evans, Earley, Halpin and Collarbone'. *Educational Management and Administration* 31 (2): 139–43.

Wrigley, T. (2004). '"School effectiveness": The problem of reductionism'. *British Educational Research Journal* 30 (2): 227–44.

Wrigley, T. (2013). 'Rethinking school effectiveness and improvement: A question of paradigms'. *Discourse: Studies in the Cultural Politics of Education* 34 (1): 31–47.

Wrigley, T., Thomson, P., and Lingard, B. (eds) (2012). *Changing Schools, Alternative Ways to Make a World of Difference*. Abingdon: Routledge.

Yellup, A. (2013). 'Making sure every person matters'. In D. Crossley (ed.), *Sustainable School Transformation*, 253–76. London: Bloomsbury.

York-Barr, J. and Duke, K. (2004). 'What do we know about teacher leadership? Findings from two decades of scholarship'. *Review of Educational Research* 74 (3): 255–316.

Young, M. D., Crow, G. M., Murphy, J., and Ogawa, R. T. (eds) (2009). *Handbook of Research on the Education of School Leaders*. New York, NY: Routledge.

Young, M. F. D. (2008). *Bringing Knowledge Back In*. Abingdon: Routledge.

Yu, H., Leithwood, K., and Jantzi, D. (2002). 'The effects of transformational leadership on teachers' commitment to change in Hong Kong'. *Journal of Educational Administration* 40 (4): 368–89.

Zorn, D. and Boler, M. (2007). 'Rethinking emotions and educational leadership'. *International Journal of Leadership in Education* 10 (2): 137–51.

Index